OSCAR WILDE

IN AMERICA

OSCAR WILDE
• IN AMERICA •

The Interviews

EDITED BY

Matthew Hofer & Gary Scharnhorst

University of Illinois Press

URBANA, CHICAGO, AND SPRINGFIELD

First Illinois paperback, 2013
© 2010 by the Board of Trustees
of the University of Illinois
Manufactured in the United States of America

⊗ This book is printed on acid-free paper.

Frontispiece: Oscar Wilde in New York City.
Photo taken by Napoleon Sarony, January 1882.

The Library of Congress cataloged the cloth edition as follows:
Oscar Wilde in America : the interviews /
edited by Matthew Hofer and Gary Scharnhorst.
p.   cm.
Includes bibliographical references and index.
ISBN 978-0-252-03472-5 (cloth : alk. paper)
1. Wilde, Oscar, 1854–1900—Interviews.
2. Authors, Irish—19th century—Interviews.
3. Wilde, Oscar, 1854–1900—Travel—United States.
I. Wilde, Oscar, 1854–1900.
II. Hofer, Matthew.
III. Scharnhorst, Gary.
PR5823.O655   2009
828'.809—dc22   2009015053
[B]

PAPERBACK ISBN 978-0-252-07972-6

Printed and bound in Great Britain by
Marston Book Services Limited, Didcot

For Scarlett and Sandy

• CONTENTS •

• PREFACE •

To date, there has been no complete or reliable record of Wilde's interviews in the United States and Canada in 1882. In *Oscar Wilde Discovers America* (1936), a trade book with few pretensions to scholarly accuracy, Lloyd Lewis and Henry Justin Smith identify forty-four interviews with the author in 1882, but they rarely quote more than two or three sentences from any of them, and they provide only fragmentary information about their sources. E. H. Mikhail includes nineteen interviews conducted in 1882 in his edited collection *Oscar Wilde: Interviews and Recollections* (1979), all of them originally identified by Lewis and Smith. Mikhail also fails to indicate his omissions from the interviews he reproduces. Virtually none of the interviews in his edition is complete or accurate. Moreover, neither the Lewis-Smith volume nor the Mikhail collection contains any significant annotations.

Our book repairs the neglect of Wilde's interviews and supplies reliable, comprehensive, and annotated transcriptions. (Because these interviews are records of verbal conversations rather than written texts, we have standardized spelling and punctuation and silently corrected other obvious mistakes.) To be sure, not all Wilde's conversations with reporters merit reprinting, and we have made judicious selections for this volume. It contains the complete texts of forty-eight of the ninety-eight interviews known to have been published during his North American tour. We reprint in an appendix a transcript of the lecture about America that he delivered in England in 1883. We also append a chronological list of all 107 interviews with Wilde known to exist, fifty-eight of them new to scholarship.

• • •

Thanks to Susan Kayorie and Nicolas Witschi for their assistance in assembling this volume.

• INTRODUCTION •

"Interviewers are a product of American civilization, whose acquaintance I am making with tolerable speed," the twenty-seven-year-old Oscar Wilde told an interviewer for the *Boston Globe* on 28 January 1882. "You gentlemen have fairly monopolized me ever since I saw Sandy Hook. In New York there were about a hundred a day. . . . But then," he added, lest he seem unwilling to talk, "I am always glad to see you." As he later explained, "We have no interviewing in England."

Celebrity interviews began to appear in American newspapers in the early 1870s, and traveling lecturers were a convenient source of "copy" for reporters. Though Charles Dickens sat for no interviews during his final U.S. speaking tour in 1867–68, for example, Mark Twain satirized his own experiences on the hustings as early as 1874 in "An Encounter with an Interviewer." As the reporter in this sketch tells the author, "You know it is the custom, now, to interview any man who has become notorious."[1] Predictably, Twain declined most reporters' requests to meet him except while he was on tour and wanted the publicity. Henry James also burlesqued celebrity interviewers in the characters of Matthias Pardon in *The Bostonians* (1886) and Henrietta Stackpole in *The Portrait of a Lady* (1881). Henrietta even works for a gossip rag called the *New York Interviewer*, whose contents lead another character to remark that once "you had read the *Interviewer* you . . . lost all faith in culture."[2] Predictably, James studiously avoided reporters entirely. Moreover, unlike the Lyceum speakers before the Civil War, who spread a gospel of self-help, a lecturer of the new breed was expected not to edify but to entertain. He required a publicity mill, not a moral message, to attract an audience.

While James decried the new celebrity culture and Mark Twain held it at arm's length, Oscar Wilde eagerly embraced it. Like Walt Whitman, whom Wilde admired, the young poet promoted himself adeptly, carefully cultivating his public image. Shortly after his arrival in New York, he sat for a series of twenty portraits at the Broadway studio of Napoleon Sarony, the leading commercial photographer in the country, who had obtained exclusive rights to distribute them. When an interviewer asked him on 25 February for "some details of [his] private life," Wilde quipped, "I wished I had one." As far as the public was concerned, Wilde existed only in the persona he had created or the way he was perceived. For the most part, he charmed and even pandered to interviewers when he and they met face to face; after all, they were his collaborators in the creation of his public image. He told a reporter in Cincinnati on 20 February, "some of the brightest hours I have passed in this country have been with the gentlemen of the press who have interviewed me, and I have found them among the most intelligent men I have met here." A week later, speaking to an interviewer in St. Louis, he insisted, "My experiences with the press in the West have been very pleasant, and I have met gentlemen whose intelligent conversation I have enjoyed. They have talked with me of art and literature, and understood the subjects." But Wilde railed against interviewers in private. As he wrote the poet Joaquin Miller in late February,

> Who are these scribes who, passing from purposeless alacrity from the police news to the Parthenon, and from crime to criticism, sway with such serene incapacity the office which they so lately swept? "Narcissuses of imbecility," what should they see in the clear waters of Beauty and in the well undefiled of Truth but the shifting and shadowy image of their own substantial stupidity?[3]

Or as he wrote Mrs. George Lewis in late March, he was "weary of being asked by gloomy reporters 'which was the most beautiful colour' and what is the meaning of the word 'aesthetic.'"[4] In essence, he tired of the question—a feature of celebrity culture and the commodification of fame—"what are your thoughts on having your thoughts published so often?"

In all, Wilde sat for at least ninety-eight interviews while touring North America between January and November 1882. He was interrogated by local reporters in the predictable venues, including all the major cities from New York and Boston to San Francisco. But he was also questioned in towns of the American outback, such as Ogden, Utah; Leadville, Colorado; Topeka, Kansas; and Dubuque, Iowa.

• • •

Wilde was an international celebrity, born to privilege if not to the manor, when he arrived in New York aboard the steamer *Arizona* on 2 January. His father had been a successful Dublin surgeon and Irish patriot; his mother, a popular poet, a propagandist for the Young Irelanders, and an ardent proponent of Irish Home Rule. The second of their three children, young Wilde studied from 1871 to 1874 at Trinity College, Dublin, and from 1874 to 1878 at Magdalen College, Oxford, where he received the Newdigate prize for his poem "Ravenna" and graduated with a "double first" in modern and classical literatures. While at Oxford he also became a disciple of John Ruskin and Walter Pater, as well as a self-described "aesthete," or devotee to the religion of art and the cult of beauty. Wilde moved to London in 1879 and published his first volume of poetry in 1881. Still in his twenties, he was sufficiently controversial and (in)famous that he soon became an object of ridicule, repeatedly satirized in *Punch* and caricatured as the poet and poseur Reginald Bunthorne in Gilbert and Sullivan's comic opera *Patience, or Bunthorne's Bride* (1881).

The theatrical producer Richard D'Oyly (aka "Oily") Carte capitalized on controversy by booking simultaneous U.S. tours for both the operetta satirizing aestheticism and Wilde's lectures promoting it. Though he was originally scheduled to spend only a few weeks in America, Wilde remained nearly a year, lectured almost 150 times from coast to coast, expanded his repertoire to include four different talks ("The English Renaissance," "The Decorative Arts," "The House Beautiful," and "Irish Poets and Poetry of the Nineteenth Century"), and earned about $5,600, or a third of the total box-office receipts less expenses.[5] That is, he was able to turn Gilbert and Sullivan's satire to his advantage; in effect, the operetta helped to publicize Wilde, not vice versa. Still, while he addressed thousands of curious listeners in New York, Boston, and Chicago during the first weeks of his travels, his audiences dwindled thereafter; in April, speaking in Atchison, Kansas, he attracted a house of only about thirty people. Part of the problem was Wilde's topics, which emphasized practical or "lived" aesthetics, which hardly appealed to rural folks scratching out a living. Another part of the problem was Wilde's speaking style: it was, by most accounts, abysmal.

The following year, back in England, Wilde returned to the platform to deliver a comic exposition of his experiences in America. He also returned to New York briefly in August to oversee the Union Square Theatre's production of his first play, *Vera, or the Nihilist*, which closed after only a week. In 1884 he married Constance Lloyd, the daughter of the queen's counsel. Wilde's literary reputation soared over the next decade with the publication of *The Picture of Dorian Gray* (1890), his only novel, and productions of his plays *The Duchess of Padua* (1883), *Lady Windermere's Fan* (1892), *Salomé* (1893), *A Woman of No Importance* (1893), *An Ideal Husband* (1895), and *The Importance of Being Earnest* (1895). In May 1895, thirteen years after his North American lecture tour, he was convicted of "gross indecency," or homosexual behavior, at the Old Bailey in London and sentenced to two years of hard labor. His health broken by his imprisonment, Wilde fled to France upon his release and lived in Paris in poverty and under a pseudonym for three years, until his death at the age of forty-six.

• • •

Wilde often conducted an interview as if it were a performance. The interviewer would arrive to find him playing the part of the idle aesthete, lounging in a chair or on a sofa. Wilde would leap to his feet, shake the interviewer's hand, and offer him a seat. At the first prompt he would deliver a scripted line (e.g., "No art is better than bad art" and "Life without industry is barbarism, and industry without art is barren"). The conversation would end at a predetermined moment when his manager or valet would enter the room, interrupt the talk, and explain that the poet had another appointment. In his interviews Wilde touched on a wide range of topics, including American architecture, Chinese porcelain, the state of the American theater, Irish Home Rule and the Land League, the American expatriate painter James McNeill Whistler, and his plan to visit Japan and Australia. He freely expressed his opinion of such American writers as Whitman, Emerson, Hawthorne, Poe, and Howells and of such British authors as Milton, Shelley, Dante Gabriel Rossetti, William Morris, and Tennyson. Nonetheless, at least publicly, he rarely mentioned Henry James, who in conversation with Clover Adams, the wife of Henry Adams, once called Wilde a "tenth-rate cad" and an "unclean beast."[6] Few other subjects were off-limits, however. Wilde commented with equal facility on grain elevators, train station sandwiches, hog butchering, oil cars, boxing matches, the Chicago water tower, the mudflats of New Jersey, and the Mormon Tabernacle in Salt Lake City ("the most purely dreadful building I ever saw"). He preferred the West (for its topography and people) and the South (for its aristocratic history) to the northeastern United States and eastern Canada. He was never bereft of opinions, especially irreverent ones. Who would have guessed, for example, that he considered Nathaniel Hawthorne's novel *The Scarlet Letter* "the greatest work of fiction ever written in the English tongue" (interview 10)? Or that parts of Whitman's *Leaves of Grass* reminded him of Homeric epic (interview 23)?

Of course, Wilde spent much of his interview time defining and defending aestheticism and the aesthetic movement. During an interview with the *San*

Francisco Examiner on 27 March, for example, he insisted that "a poem is well written or badly written. In art there should be no reference to a standard of good or evil."

The idea that animates Wilde's aestheticism—that language colors and even shapes our world, that "life imitates art" and not the other way around—remains influential. For the contemporary U.S. avant-garde movement of L=A=N=G=U=A=G=E writing, for example, Charles Bernstein has championed the aesthetic and even the political value of a conscious use of artifice—and invoked Wilde's precedent to make the point. Wilde's early opposition to didacticism and his advocacy of formal standards in the evaluation of art anticipate the well-known assertion in his preface to *The Picture of Dorian Gray* that "there is no such thing as a moral or an immoral book. Books are well written, or badly written. That is all." They foreshadow, too, his testimony on the opening day of his first trial thirteen years later. He spoke virtually the same sentences in his failed self-defense: "I am concerned entirely with literature, that is with Art. The aim is not to do good or to do evil, but to try and make a thing that will have some quality of beauty."[7]

This volume of interviews with Wilde offers a series of lost snapshots of the so-called Apostle of Aestheticism in a variety of venues and at the height of the aesthetic movement in England. In both their range and their repetitiousness, these interviews exhibit a style that informs their substance.

During his lecture tour Wilde repeatedly challenged the gender norms of middle-class America. His performances, both on stage and in conversation with reporters, flouted convention. His interviewers described him with equal degrees of inconsistency and precision. They were extremely inaccurate in estimating Wilde's height—anywhere between five feet, three inches, and six feet, four inches. They generally agreed he was fundamentally androgynous, however, with his clean-shaven face; the "womanly air" of his "thick locks of brown hair" (interview 19); his "lisp" (interview 20); his "feminine way" (interview 21); his "sapphic speech" (interview 23) or "effeminate voice" (interview 24); "his overfull features, which are almost effeminate in apparent lack of vigor and force," and "the almost boyish fullness and effeminacy of his face" (interview 31); his lips, "full and as bright-colored as a girl's" (interview 34); and "his soft effeminate flesh" (interview 37). According to the *Denver Tribune,* he appeared to be made "half of man and half of woman," with a grace of movement that "gave an effeminate shade to his masculinity" (interview 35). While in Toronto he gazed admiringly on the muscular body of Rors Mackenzie, one of the most famous lacrosse players of his day (interview 41). While there is no evidence Wilde had any same-sex experiences before he toured the United States, his foppish attire, fondness for flowers, and self-aggrandizing poses certainly defied gender boundaries and invited public scrutiny. Invited to dine with Kate Field at the Women's Dress Association on 11 January, Wilde was ridiculed in the pages of the *New York Daily Graphic,* a working-class tabloid. He was ostensibly "measured for his petticoats" at the luncheon and was given "a pair of gilt-edged corsets" while "the shareholders of the Association" assumed "poses of aesthetic adoration."[8] The very term *aesthete,* as Richard Ellmann observes in his biography of Wilde, was sometimes a euphemism for "sexual invert,"[9] and in a letter to the sculptor William Wetmore Story in December 1882, after eleven months in the United States, Wilde allowed that he had sometimes heard "the word 'aesthetic'" pronounced "with the *soupçon* of a sneer."[10] The poet E. C. Stedman refused even to meet him, and Clover Adams described him privately as "a noodle," or limp penis, whose sexuality was "undecided."[11]

Wilde's gender-bending and coded performances were also scorned publicly, of course. He was mocked as a degenerate in satirical cartoons, a monkey with a flower, in such papers as *Harper's Weekly* and the *Washington Post.* He was mimicked by Harvard students when he appeared in Boston and by students at the University of Rochester when he spoke there. Even Wilde's defenders, including Julia Ward Howe, acknowledged that "the poison found in the ancient classics"—his ambiguous sexuality—may "linger too deeply in his veins."[12] George William Curtis, a former Brook Farmer and American man of letters, agreed that public criticism of the cheeky Wilde was "not undeserved":

> A man who wishes to show the worth of the modern renaissance is bound, first of all, not to make it or himself laughable. Mere eccentricities of dress or conduct are sure to prejudice any good cause. The cheapest distinction is that which the tailor or barber can furnish. The "mission" of Mr. Wilde to this country has been quite lost under the accidents and incidents of his career. What kind of a country did he suppose himself to be about to visit? If he had gone through England in knee-breeches and other oddities of apparel, he could hardly have hoped to win a more favorable audience for his views of the uses of beauty and the desirableness of the cultivation of the sentiment of beauty in every form and detail of life than if he had forborne all extravagance.[13]

Perhaps the most vicious *ad hominem* attack on Wilde was leveled by Thomas Wentworth Higginson, an old abolitionist warhorse best known today as Emily Dickinson's "preceptor," in the Boston-based *Woman's Journal.* In a piece entitled "Unmanly Manhood," Higginson vilified the poet. Wilde had become "something very like a buffoon for notoriety and money," he charged. His verse, according to Higginson, was not only "mediocre" but "prurient"; for

HARPER'S WEEKLY.

JOURNAL OF CIVILIZATION.

Vol. XXVI.—No. 1310.
Copyright, 1882, by Harper & Brothers.

NEW YORK, SATURDAY, JANUARY 28, 1882.

TEN CENTS A COPY.
$4.00 PER YEAR, IN ADVANCE.

THE ÆSTHETIC MONKEY.—Engraved, by Permission, from the Picture by W. H. Beard, in the Possession of Mr. Hugh Auchincloss.

"The Aesthetic Monkey," engraved from the picture by W. H. Beard, cover of *Harper's Weekly,* 28 January 1882.

example, "Charmides" titillated with its "forcible unveiling of some injured innocence." Instead of remaining in Ireland, where he might have worked to "right the wrongs" there, Wilde had crossed the Atlantic to "pose in ladies' boudoirs," eclipse "masculine ideals," and influence men by his example to "become effeminate dandies."[14] Wilde was not amused, to say the least. "Who . . . is this scribbling anonymuncule in grand old Massachusetts who scrawls and screams so glibly about what he cannot understand?" he groused to Joaquin Miller.[15]

For better or worse, Wilde was more inclined to transgress gender norms than racial or class boundaries. He treated his valet with undisguised condescension, for example. He explained to Norman Forbes-Robertson soon after his arrival in New York that he had been assigned "a black servant," whom he called "my slave," adding, "in a free country one cannot live without a slave—rather like a Christy minstrel, except that he knows no riddles."[16] Wilde never mentioned the name of the valet in either his private letters or his published statements, and while he appears in the margins of many of Wilde's interviews, his name (W. M. Traquair) was invariably omitted. Wilde also occasionally insisted that Traquair perform minstrelsy for visitors. Wilde not only exoticized African Americans when he toured the South but failed to register any thoughts on segregation or Jim Crow law—a startling omission for a tourist with ready opinions on less important topics. He acquiesced to local custom and law on at least one occasion, during a night trip from Atlanta to Jonesboro, when a rail conductor forbade Traquair from sleeping in a berth reserved for white passengers.[17] Similarly, while in the West he mostly ignored the presence of Native Americans, whom he had professed a desire to see (interview 10), except to deride their "unintelligible" conversation.[18] Yet he praised Jefferson Davis's monumental history of the Confederacy and famously visited Davis at his estate in Mississippi, a measure of his own aristocratic pretensions. Although Wilde often paid lip service to the salutary influence of art on the working class, it seems that aestheticism as social theory endorsed not egalitarianism but rather a democracy of snobs.

Notes

1. Mark Twain, *Uncollected Tales, Sketches, Speeches, and Essays 1852–1890*, ed. Louis J. Budd (New York: Library of America, 1992), 584.
2. Henry James, *The Portrait of a Lady* (1881; repr., Boston: Houghton Mifflin, 1963), 52.
3. Oscar Wilde, *The Complete Letters of Oscar Wilde*, ed. Merlin Holland and Rupert Hart-Davis (New York: Henry Holt, 2000), 143.
4. Ibid., 154.

5. Richard Ellmann, *Oscar Wilde* (New York: Knopf, 1988), 192.

6. Ibid., 179.

7. H. Montgomery Hyde, ed., *The Trials of Oscar Wilde* (London: William Hodge, 1948), 122–23.

8. *New York Daily Graphic*, 11 January 1882, 486.

9. Ellmann, *Oscar Wilde*, 84.

10. Wilde, *Letters*, 190.

11. Ellmann, *Oscar Wilde*, 178, 179.

12. Julia Ward Howe, "Colonel Higginson on Oscar Wilde," *Boston Globe*, 15 February 1882, 4.

13. George William Curtis, "Editor's Easy Chair," *Harper's Monthly* 64 (April 1882): 790.

14. T[homas] W[entworth] H[igginson], "Unmanly Manhood," *Woman's Journal*, 4 February 1882, 1.

15. Wilde, *Letters*, 143.

16. Ibid., 127.

17. "Oscar Wilde's Valet," *Atlanta Constitution*, 6 July 1882, 7.

18. Wilde, *Letters*, 153–54.

INTERVIEWS

1. "OSCAR WILDE'S ARRIVAL," *NEW YORK WORLD*, 3 JANUARY 1882, 1

Oscar Wilde, the great English exponent of aestheticism, reached this port last evening on board the Williams and Guion steamship *Arizona*. Shortly after the vessel came to anchor off the Quarantine Station on Staten Island a *World* reporter put off in a rowboat managed by two sturdy oarsmen, and although the steamship was not much over a quarter of a mile from the shore it was three-quarters of an hour before he stepped upon the deck of the *Arizona*. Prior to undertaking the mission he had consulted Worcester,[1] according to whom aesthetics (the good old man gives no such word as aestheticism) is set down as the science of the sensations, or that which explains the cause of mental pain or pleasure, as derived from a contemplation of the works of art or nature; the science which treats of the beautiful and its various modes of representation in nature and in art; the philosophy of the fine arts. Thus armed the reporter stepped upon the broad deck of the *Arizona* and was soon ushered into the presence of Mr. Wilde in a gangway about amidships.

Mr. Wilde is fully six feet three inches in height, straight as an arrow, and with broad shoulders and long arms, indicating considerable strength. His outer garment was a long ulster trimmed with two kinds of fur, which reached almost to his feet. He wore patent-leather shoes, a smoking-cap or turban, and his shirt might be termed ultra-Byronic, or perhaps—décolleté. A sky-blue cravat of the sailor style hung well down upon the chest. His hair flowed over his shoulders in dark-brown waves, curling slightly upwards at the ends. His eyes were of a deep blue, but without that faraway expression that is popularly attributed to poets. In fact they seemed rather everyday and commonplace eyes. His teeth were large and regular, disproving a pleasing story which has gone the rounds of the English press that he has three tusks or protuberants far from agreeable to look at. He is beardless, and his complexion is almost colorless. In manner, Mr. Wilde was easy and unconstrained, and his attitude as he conversed with the reporters and others was very graceful. A peculiarity of Mr. Wilde's face is the exaggerated oval of the Italian face carried into the English type of countenance and tipped with a long sharp chin. It does not, however, impress one as being a strong face. His manner of talking is somewhat affected—judging from an American standpoint—his great peculiarity being a rhythmic chant in which every fourth syllable is accentuated. Thus, when asked what was his mission in

America, he replied in a singsong tone: "I came from *Eng*-land because I *thought* America was the best *place* to see."

"I have come," said the reporter, "to ask you as to your intention in visiting this country. The American public have imbibed an opinion (possibly from *Punch*)[2] that you have visited this country in the interests of aestheticism. And, while we are about it, will you give me your definition of aestheticism?"

"Well," replied Mr. Wilde, "aestheticism is a search after the signs of the beautiful. It is the science through which men look after the correlation which exists in the arts. It is, to speak more exactly, the search after the secret of life."

"It has been said by some of our philosophers that aestheticism, instead of bringing forth principles, develops a certain marked line of individuality."

"It has been noticed in all great movements," replied Mr. Wilde, "that they bring out individuality. A movement that has not sufficient inherent force to develop individual characteristics would be of little or no worth to the world as a general movement of improvement."

"What are your intentions as to your American tour? Will you lecture?"

"That will depend considerably upon the encouragement with which my philosophy meets. I shall lecture in Chickering Hall, in New York, on 9th of January, but whether I shall continue my labors will depend, as I said, upon the results attained."

"It is said that you design to introduce a play in this city."

"My play, *Vera, the Nihilist*, was not produced in London for the reason that I could not get a cast fitted for its representation. It must be produced with able actors. If a satisfactory cast can be obtained here it may be produced."

"You spoke just now of aestheticism as philosophy. Is that your classification of the science?"

"Assuredly. It is a study of what may be found in art and in nature. It is a pursuit of the secret of life. Whatever in art represents eternal truth expresses the great underlying truth of aestheticism."

"Are you here to secure a copyright on your play? Some say that you are."

To this question Mr. Wilde made no reply, and being asked as to the duration of his stay in the United States, replied that he had not decided.

Mr. Wilde is the son of Lady Wilde, who wrote many patriotic poems during the Irish troubles of 1848,[3] under the *nom de plume* of "Speranza."[4] He is, as far as can be judged from his appearance, not over twenty-six years of age.

On the journey over Mr. Wilde did not attain, it appears, to very great popularity among the passengers. Before the ship had been five days out he said to a gentleman with whom he was promenading the deck (and this gentleman kindly retailed the conversation to the writer), "I am not exactly pleased with the Atlantic. It is not so majestic as I expected. I would like to see the ship's bridge carried away!"

1. Joseph Emerson Worcester (1784–1865), an innovative American lexicographer, published *A Dictionary of the English Language* (1860).
2. *Punch* (1841–2002) was a British humor magazine famous for its cartoons. As part of *Punch's* mockery of aestheticism, George du Maurier (1834–96) produced a series of cartoons caricaturing Wilde as the effete poet "Maudle." In interview 4 Wilde identifies himself as the source for Maudle but claims that "Jellaby Postlethwaite"—who also resembles the poet—is a "combination or a conglomeration of the peculiarities of a number of [his] friends."
3. The revolutionaries in the Young Ireland movement unsuccessfully agitated for Irish independence in 1848, soon spawning the Fenian movement.
4. "Speranza" (1826–96) was the pen name of Jane Francesca Agnes, Lady Wilde (née Elgee), an Irish poet and supporter of the nationalist movement and Oscar Wilde's mother.

---

2. "OSCAR WILDE," *NEW YORK EVENING POST,* 4 JANUARY 1882, 4; EXCERPTED IN "THE CHIEF YEARNER," *BOSTON GLOBE,* 4 JANUARY 1882, 4

Mr. Oscar Wilde stood on the pier of the Williams and Guion steamship line at 11 o'clock this morning when a reporter of the *Evening Post* pushed through the crowd of admirers who surrounded him and asked the poet of the aesthetes what he understood by aestheticism. "I have defined it about two hundred times since last night," answered Mr. Wilde, with a patient smile, "but I am here to diffuse beauty, and I have no objection to saying that—I say, porter, handle that box more carefully, will you?" This was said to a hotel porter who had seized Mr. Wilde's luggage and was tossing it, box after box, up to the roof of the hotel stage, unmindful that the boxes might contain frail objects such as lilies and the like.

While Mr. Wilde expostulated with the man, the reporter was able to get a good look at him: a tall, well-built, blue-eyed, beardless young man, six feet high at least with a large white, flat face surrounded by a sealskin cap many sizes too small for him; irregular and protruding teeth, light long hair flowing over the color of a sort of bottle-green dressing gown extending down to the feet; a manner in which ease and amusement contrasted strangely, with an embarrassed laugh used in lieu of punctuation. Such is Mr. Oscar Wilde at the first glance. Further study reveals the ends of a sky-blue necktie, a pair of patent-leather boots, and large hands. That Mr. Wilde had with very moderate success attempted something after the style of Raphael's famous portrait of himself[1] would occur to anyone who sees him with his sealskin cap on.

"Aestheticism," he continued, "is an attempt to color the commonplace, to make beauty stand out wherever it is. There is a subtle relation between beauty and everything—a correlation of one sensible beauty with another— that is not seen or felt, except by—by—well, by persons who have studied the matter."

"For instance," asked the reporter, "where is the beauty in that striking grain elevator which is the chief object in New Jersey's landscape across the river there?"

Wilde looked across the river but said that he was too near-sighted to see the object in question; he would examine it some other day and make a note of it.

"Beauty," went on the poet, puffing vigorously at a cigarette and plunging both hands deep into the pockets of his dressing gown, "is nearer to most of us than we are aware. The material is all around us, but we want a systematic way of bringing it out. It may be subjective, don't you know, or objective; but it is there, and the science of how to get at it is what I come to lecture about."

"Then you have found the key to pure beauty or such beauty as there may be in the lily or in Hoboken. Is that it?"

"Something of the kind. It's a wide field which has no limit, and all definitions are unsatisfactory. Some people might search and not find anything. But the search, if carried on according to right laws, would constitute aestheticism. They would find happiness in striving, even in despair of ever finding what they seek. The renaissance of beauty is not to be hoped for without strife internal and external."

"Where is this movement going to end?"

"There is no end to it; it will go on forever, just as it had no beginning. I have used the word *renaissance* to show that it is no new thing with me. It has always existed. As time goes on the men and the forms of expression may change, but the principles will remain the same. Man is hungry for beauty; therefore he must be filled. There is a void; nature will fill it. The ridicule which aesthetics have been subjected to is only the envy of blind, unhappy souls who cannot find the path to beauty."

"What will the last expression of aestheticism be? Has anyone yet succeeded in carrying the science to its highest degree?"

"Now, see here; don't you know I came here to lecture? You come next Monday night to the hall and I'll answer these questions. The last expression of aestheticism is one of the points of my lecture. I must get some breakfast now and see the town. Our voyage over was so monotonous that I am glad to get on land and see some people. Good-bye. You can define aestheticism for your paper as the science of finding the beautiful by looking for it in pursuance of fixed laws. As I said before, there is beauty all around us—even here," looking around upon the horde of hackmen shouting "Carriage, sir!" at the top of their lungs. "Where?" eagerly asked the reporter, following the direction of Mr. Wilde's gaze to an old lady selling apples.

"Everywhere," said the poet, relapsing into the indefinite.

Mr. Wilde's agent hurried him into a carriage, and the party drove off to the Brunswick Hotel. The most noticeable peculiarities about Mr. Wilde's talk were a singsong division of words into a species of blank verse of his own, and a vacant smile which seemed to be part and parcel of the spoken lines. When talking of aestheticism, the smile seemed to suggest that he looked upon the whole business as an absurd farce and his arrival in New York upon a lecturing tour as its most ridiculous incident.

   1.   The famous self-portrait of Raphael, or Raffaello Sanzio (1483–1520), variously
       dated between 1500 and 1504, bears a rather remarkable resemblance to the young
       Wilde's studied dishevelment.

---

3. "OUR NEW YORK LETTER," *PHILADELPHIA INQUIRER*, 4 JANUARY 1882, 7

Oscar Wilde, the young English poet and apostle of aestheticism, reached this city this morning. He came in the *Arizona,* which arrived last night but anchored off quarantine until this morning. Mr. Wilde is a smooth-faced young man, twenty-six years of age and six feet, four inches, in height. His hair is long, his face is large and flat, and he dresses in an aesthetic costume, of which the most conspicuous parts this morning were a long bottle-green overcoat trimmed with fur, a sky-blue necktie, yellow kid gloves, patent leather boots, and a sealskin cap several sizes too small for him. The most noticeable peculiarities about his talk were a singsong division of words into a species of blank verse of his own, and a vacant smile which seemed to suggest that he looked upon the whole business as an absurd farce, and his arrival upon a lecturing tour as its most ridiculous incident.[1] He talked freely, and said among other things:

"My philosophy, about which I have been so grossly ridiculed, is the appreciation of the beautiful, and coarse, indeed, must be the intelligence of the man who will knowingly sneer at that which makes the world about us so glorious. I have always loved nature in its wild, magnificent beauty. When I can meet her in the wilderness amid towering cliffs and hanging cataracts, then I love her and become her slave. I have since I can remember been impressed by the intensity of nature; but, alas, for the past few years I have been unable to gratify my longing. I have been a London man and have been surrounded by naught but smoke and fog. It is in the midst of the city life that I first saw all the follies of the present society and the grotesqueness of modern customs. I admire the Middle Ages, because their social life was natural and unharassed by petty rules. I approve of the mediæval costumes, because they are graceful, because they are beautiful. The surroundings of art, no one doubts, enhance one's existence and make life worth living. This talk about the sunflower and lily is nonsense, sir, especially as I am represented gazing fondly over it. I love flowers, sir, as every human being should love them. I enjoy their perfume and admire their beauty.

"I saw *Patience,* the comic opera, while it was played in London.[2] I fail to see its point, sir, but think it a very pretty opera with some charming music. As a satire on the philosophy of the beautiful, sir, I think it is the veriest twaddle. Before I had made my mind up to come to America I had been informed that the Americans were very impressionable. I find them so, sir, and am extremely gratified. Grand ideas, sir, are more likely to attain the fullness of their foliage in the soil of a new civilization than in the wasted energies of effete governments. The cultivation of aestheticism, sir, is a grand idea, and I am ready to sacrifice my 'life, enmity, and amity' in its successful development. Aestheticism has not an enervating influence on society; it redeems it from gross errors and cleanses it from the accumulation of the scraps of ages. I do not know, sir, whether or not I shall make an extended lecture tour. It will depend on circumstances. Good morning!"

1. Parts of interviews 2 and 3 are repeated verbatim because reporters sometimes copied from out-of-town newspapers, not because the reports were syndicated.
2. In Gilbert and Sullivan's *Patience,* the poet Reginald Bunthorne, based on Wilde, sings a piece entitled "I'm an Aesthetic Sham." The operetta premiered at London's Opera Comique in April 1881, and that October it was the inaugural production staged at the newly built Savoy Theatre. Wilde also attended a performance at the Standard Theater in New York on the evening of 7 January (Richard Ellmann, *Oscar Wilde* [New York: Knopf, 1988], 160).

4. "THE THEORIES OF A POET," *NEW YORK TRIBUNE,*
   8 JANUARY 1882, 7

Oscar Wilde, the poet and apostle of aestheticism, is at present living in a private house so that he may secure the quiet and freedom from interruption which his work demands. He occupies two rooms furnished in matter-of-fact style, and has his meals sent in from a neighboring restaurant. The center table of his parlor yesterday was covered with letters and invitations of all kinds and a few books. The poet himself had on a brown dressing gown with red cuffs and brown trousers with red silk cord along the sides. His shoes were patent leather, with red silk stockings. On the lounge was thrown carelessly a heavy ulster of olive green, with a fur collar and cuffs.

"The groundwork of aestheticism," said Mr. Wilde, in answer to the question of a *Tribune* reporter, "is that you cannot teach a knowledge of the beautiful; it must be revealed. A boy could become learned in any scientific subject by the study of books; the knowledge of the beautiful is personal and can only be acquired by one's own eyes and ears. This truth was the origin of the theory of beautiful surroundings. A child should have around him from his infancy beautiful things. Suppose you take up a volume of Keats.[1] If you are in a library furnished as most are, you have to take a spiritual jump, so to speak, before you are in the proper frame of mind to appreciate his poetry."

"Where were you first impressed with these ideas?"

"When I went to Oxford, which was the most beautiful city I had ever been in. I was given a wonderful set of old wainscoted rooms in Magdalen overlooking the river,[2] near that graceful bridge which they are now pulling down for the sake of a tramway. Ruskin was then delivering a series of lectures on 'Florentine Art' and I came under his influence.[3] I am rather luxurious in my nature, I think, but I used to assist Mr. Ruskin on dull November mornings in the prosaic occupation of breaking stones and making roads. In 1875 I went to Florence, and there the whole splendor of Italian art was revealed to me. When I returned to Oxford I sounded my companions (most of them have since become artists or literary men in London), and finding that their opinions coincided with mine we formed a little coterie for the purpose of carrying out our ideas and laid our plans for a great revolution in English life and art. In doing this, there is no doubt but that we all purposely went to the wildest extremes in dress and expressions.

"The first time that the absolute stupidity of the English people was ever revealed to me was one Sunday at the University Church, when the preacher opened his sermon in something this way: 'When a young man says, not in polished banter but in sober earnestness, that he finds it difficult to live up to the level of his blue china, there has crept into these cloistered shades a form of heathenism which it is our bounden duty to fight against and crush out, if possible.' I need hardly say that we were delighted and amused at the typical English way in which our ideas were misunderstood. They took our epigrams as earnest and our paradoxes as prose. In 1877 rumors of the movement began to reach London, and extravagant expressions which we had used were quoted in the public prints. Du Maurier finally began his illustrations, which have been kept up ever since. I had never met him when he did so. I have never felt pained at all by his caricatures or those of anyone else, and I think I have enjoyed them fully as much as anyone."

"Will you tell me something of your life in London?"

"In 1878 I went to London and took a home on the banks of the Thames, near Charing Cross Bridge. It was almost a counterpart of the one in which I lived in Oxford and embodied our ideas. Since then I have frequently met Du Maurier in society and have talked with him about his caricatures as if I were not interested in them at all. When I have thought they were clever I have told him so, as I did when I thought them stupid. A party of my friends and myself went to see *Patience* on the first night, and we laughed, or jeered, at it as it deserved. As to Du Maurier's characters, I suppose that I am the original of *Maudle,* the poet. *Postlethwaite,* the artist, has no original but is a combination or a conglomeration of the peculiarities of a number of my friends. As an artist, my attitude toward all this is that a true artist who believes in his art and his mission must necessarily be altogether insensible to praise or blame. If he is not a mere sham, he cannot be disturbed by any caricature or exaggeration. He has the truth on his side, and the opinion of the whole world should be of no consequence to him."

"How far has this theory of beautiful surroundings spread?"

"It has had the widest influence among the best classes of society. Its effect is plainly marked in their houses and their furniture. No one in the best society in England would think now of building a house without taking into consideration the ideas which are the basis of aestheticism. The rich middle-class it has not influenced, and nothing can influence them. The real strength of our movement lies in the great spread of beautiful designs among the handicraftsmen of the various cities."

"What influence has aestheticism had in regard to dress?"

"As far as men are concerned it is not so perceptible. But among women there is a distinct tendency toward the most radical change both in the form of the dress and in the introduction of novel and beautiful colors."

"But in America it has been understood that in the matter of color the tendency of the movement was toward neutral tints."

"There can be no beautiful color without tone. If any tone in an orchestra is intensified two or three times, it ceases to be music and is mere sound. The people who believe in aestheticism follow out this same theory in regard to color; but this doesn't shut out any ordinary ones. This is the only concession they make to neutral tints. So far as the form of the dress is concerned, there has been a tendency among ladies toward a suppression of tight waists and French millinery and a return to more natural drapery. I have seen many lovely dresses on ladies in society not unlike those in *Patience*. I mean, of course, without that exaggeration in embroidery which you see in the dresses in *Patience,* particularly that of *Lady Jane*. As far as the men are concerned I have a hope that they will find their dress so utterly incongruous and discordant with that of the ladies that they will be insensibly influenced, so that there will be a complete and radical reform in the matter."

"Have you carried out your ideas in your own dress?"

"Well," said Mr. Wilde, with a laugh, "I don't know. I have conformed it somewhat to my theories, but I intend after a right interval to follow them out entirely. The essence of good dressing is perfect congruity. One must be careful not to be too premature, but I feel that at present velvet is the most beautiful dress for a man. As a rule I wear gray or brown velvet myself."

"I believe myself," said Mr. Wilde, in conclusion, "in the correlation of the arts; that painting, poetry, and sculpture are only different forms of the same truth. I do not believe that poets and artists should live in solitude, but rather that they should associate with each other and mix freely in society. I have always done this myself, and I have preached my theories in every salon in London. I have not the slightest doubt of the complete success of the movement; the desire for beauty is merely a heightened form of the desire for life."

1.   John Keats (1795–1821) was a Romantic poet with whom Wilde identifies for his emphasis on the imagination and his short but intensely poetic life. In his 1881 volume of poems Wilde included a sonnet entitled "The Grave of Keats."

2.   Established in the fifteenth century, Oxford's Magdalen College initially stood outside the city walls, adjacent to the river Cherwell, and retains a rural flavor even today.

3.   John Ruskin (1819–1900) was, with Walter Pater (1839–94), one of Wilde's two most important influences at Oxford. Wilde attended Ruskin's 1874 lectures on Florentine art during the fall of his first year, and from November through the end of the term he also participated in his mentor's project to build a flower-bordered

road in Ferry Hinksey, outside Oxford. The influence of these mentors is evident in the American lectures, which do not always attribute their sources accurately and assiduously. For example, "The English Renaissance," Wilde's initial and most formal lecture, adapts material from Ruskin's essay "The Nature of Gothic" from *The Stones of Venice* (1851–53) and his book *The Two Paths* (1858–59), Morris's *Hopes and Fears for Art* (1878–81), and especially Pater's book *The Renaissance* (1873). For more on Wilde and plagiarism, see Paul K. Saint-Amour, "Oscar Wilde: Orality, Literary Property, and Crimes of Writing," *Nineteenth-Century Literature* 55 (June 2000): 59–91.

---

5. "THE SCIENCE OF THE BEAUTIFUL," *NEW YORK WORLD*, 8 JANUARY 1882, 2

Mr. Oscar Wilde was visited by a *World* reporter yesterday morning in his new home in Twenty-eighth Street. He was seated before a writing table which was covered with invitations. He was dressed in a simple black velvet jacket, below which he wore a pair of beautiful brown trousers, from the bottoms of which his patent-leather pumps were seen covering a very shapely pair of feet. His cravat was of a light olive green, brown and green being apparently his favorite colors. Being asked to explain his peculiar theory Mr. Wilde said: "My theory is that you cannot teach anybody what is really beautiful. The true spirit of a painting or a poem cannot by any method be taught—it must be gradually revealed. A schoolboy, for instance, can arrive at an understanding of a scientific truth under a competent teacher, but the only way in which anybody can come to a knowledge of the beautiful is by being thrown among beautiful surroundings. I think if you desire a cultured society, you must put the youth of the land into beautiful homes and let them gradually come to feel a necessity for such surroundings. A young man reared among such surroundings has not got to make a distinct effort to appreciate the beautiful. He will, if reading, come at once into sympathy with his author in his description of the true and the beautiful."

"When did you go to Oxford, Mr. Wilde?"

"In 1873, and entered Magdalen College. It was at this time that this theory of the effect of beautiful associations began to manifest itself to my mind. This town was by far the most beautiful one that I had ever been in and I experienced its effect on myself. Ruskin was there and I became a disciple of his, and his teachings gave impetus to this thought. Every one of my theories are, if I may say so, Ruskin's theories developed. He was at that time giving a course of lectures upon Florentine art and had all the youth of the colleges after him. After we had listened to a lecture we would go out with him on the road. They were the most charming rambles imaginable. In 1876 I visited Italy and went through all the churches there, drinking in everything of the beautiful in art, and its whole splendor was revealed to me by association as it never could have been from any mere description. I came back to Oxford more confirmed than ever in the correctness of my theories, and it was then that I began to write my poetry and gradually gathered around me a group of young men; an aesthetic clique, if you will.[1] I had a beautiful house by the riverside, which I fitted up in consonance with my peculiar ideas. We were very enthusiastic young men, and insensibly, as it were, we became extravagant in our expressions as compared with the common manner of converse. Meanwhile, rumors began to reach us that this movement of ours, for such it might now be called, had reached London, but we did not realize how far it had gone until one Sunday in the University Church the preacher—we used to have the most distinguished men of the day to preach to us in town—opened his sermon by saying in effect that when young men in the university, not in polished banter but in sober earnest, declared that they were striving to live up to the level of their blue china, it must become very apparent that a form of heathenism had crept into these cloistered shades which it was their bounden duty to fight with all their power. Well, all this was great sport for us. We were not martyrs, nor were we disposed to be. Just on top of this came Du Maurier's first caricature, and we found very much to our astonishment that we were becoming famous."

"Then you went to London?"

"Yes. In 1878. I had then fully developed in my own mind what I may call my social idea of art; that is that in past times the artist was isolated to a wonderful degree—was cut off from his fellow-workers in all branches and also cut off from immediate contact with the public, the only medium of communication with whom being their books, their paintings, or their sculptures. My idea was to sweep away these barriers and bring them more in unison as far as possible, and to establish what may properly be called a correlation of art, so that the artists in different lines should receive distinct assistance from each other. They are all striving to express essentially the same thing, only in different ways. So in the case of society my idea was the same, to sweep away all barriers and bring the artist in direct communication with his patrons."

"How were you received at first in London?"

"I found on arrival there that I was already known, and I was well received, and I took every possible opportunity to preach the doctrines I had evolved and crystallized during my college career. Du Maurier had not seen me when he made his first caricature, but he continued them after he did meet me in society, and I took especial pains to greet him cordially, praising his pictures when they were clever and pointing out defects if I discovered them."

"And you found converts to your theory in London, did you not?"

"Oh, yes. I found myself surrounded by a clique there, just as I had in Oxford. I was somewhat surprised at this at first. I had not thought it strange that this should have been the case at Oxford, but I did not expect it at London. The movement, if you choose to call it that, grew from week to week and began to affect the drama. *The Colonel* was written by Burnand[2] and *Patience* by Gilbert and Sullivan. We attended at the opening night and had all manner of fun. I was not to be laughed out of my theory. I had arrived at what I sincerely believed to be the truth in these matters, and the praise or blame of the public was to me a matter of no consequence whatever. I regard it only as a help or a hindrance to the development of what I regard as an important social theory."

"What was its effect on society?"

"Through all the upper circles its effect was very general and marked, and no English gentleman would now think of building or furnishing his house without taking into consideration the ideas that have been developed during the progress of this aesthetic movement."

"Does it add to the expense of furnishing?"

"Not at all. On the contrary, it tends to lessen the cost and so far as dress was concerned this introduction of a true art in women's attire cost much less than the former productions of French milliners or dresses from Worth."[3]

"Has the dress of men been at all affected?"

"Not much, as yet, but I hope that as the women's dresses have been so much improved, after a while men will bring themselves unconsciously into harmony with their surroundings."

"Are the dresses in *Patience* exaggerated?"

"Not much. I have seen among the advocates of my theory in society some that nearly equaled them, allowing, of course, for the necessity of larger decorations for stage effect. As to myself," continued Mr. Wilde, "I have gone somewhat in the true direction, conceding, of course, something to custom."

Mr. Wilde expressed himself as delighted with his reception in this country. "Nothing could have been more cordial," he remarked. He said he thought he should have to stay the winter out. "I shall go from here to Philadelphia," he said, "and from there to Boston."

1. The very loose association of artists Wilde refers to as an "aesthetic clique" may be said to have formed around the influence of Wilde's mentor Pater, who espoused "art for art's sake." The London clique, an equally loose construction, included in the popular mind such figures as Dante Gabriel Rossetti (1828–82), William Morris (1834–96), James McNeill Whistler (1834–1903), and Algernon Charles Swinburne (1837–1909).

2. Sir Francis Cowley Burnand (1836–1917) wrote *The Colonel,* a play about the putative dangers of aesthetic infiltration to conservative family structures; it began its long run in February 1881.

3. Charles Frederick Worth (1826–95) was an important Parisian haute-couture designer of the later nineteenth century whose signature designs showcased luxurious fabrics and trimmings.

---

6. "A TALK WITH WILDE," *PHILADELPHIA PRESS,* 17 JANUARY 1882, 2

As a Pennsylvania ferryboat swung into her slip at Jersey City at a few minutes before one o'clock yesterday afternoon, the crowd scattered about the dock explained in subdued tones: "There he is; see him, that's Oscar Wilde." The tall figure of the apostle of Aestheticism, clad in his olive-green overcoat with its otter trimmings, and with his large face brightened by a smile and framed in long brown locks, blown about by the wind, was a conspicuous figure as he stood in the very front of the crowd of passengers pressing against the gunwales of the boat. He had evidently been enjoying a breezy trip across the tawny Hudson, for his eye sparkled and his face was flushed with pleasure as, with a long stride which kept him far in advance even of the eager rush in which a New York crowd escapes from a ferry, and which left his valet struggling hopelessly in the rear with a burden of baggage,[1] he entered the Pennsylvania station and passed to the waiting Philadelphia express. His sole companions were W. F. Morse,[2] business manager for D'Oyly Carte, and a *Press* reporter. The party took seats in the smoking compartment of the Pullman car "Jupiter," and shrinking from curious eyes into a corner, Mr. Wilde alternately read *Fors Clavigera* and *The Poetry of Architecture*[3] until the train had fairly started. Then, as he saw through express marshes which skirt Jersey City, his eye became melancholy, and he contemplatively puffed a cigarette. As the train sped on its way through New Jersey, he scanned the flitting landscape closely, sometimes smiling like a child at a glistening stream or a stretch of yet green meadow, and again seeming to find the sorrow of old age in the frequent expanses of brown country and dripping black undergrowths made more dreary by the overcast sky.

The truth is, the poet had not had his breakfast; and thus unfortified against the horrors of a New Jersey landscape on a rainy day, it was no wonder that he finally relapsed into a state of hopeless dejection. Incredible as it may seem, the most nonaesthetic object on earth, a way-station sandwich, restored his spirits enough for him to enter into an animated conversation with the *Press* reporter.

"I am very tired," he said. "I have been so kindly received in New York, and so cordially welcomed by so many lovely people that of course I wanted to see many of them before I went away. Was up late last night dining at Mrs. Paran Stevens's[4] and afterward going to a reception at Mr. S. L. M. Barlow's,[5] and I was so late today that I had no time to breakfast. Then I have been kept so busy answering letters. Why, it is strange how people seem to think I have nothing to do but answer letters!"

"This is your first railway ride in America, is it not?"

"Yes, this is the first time I have ever been in an American railway car. We go so swift—much faster than in England. There are but a few fast trains there—the Edinburgh and Liverpool trains. And then there isn't any such comfort as this. There are but two or three cars like this," indicating the sumptuous Pullman with a sweep of the arm, "in the country. I hate to fly through a country at this rate. The only true way, you know, to see a country is to ride on horseback. I long to ride through New Mexico and Colorado and California. There are such beautiful flowers there, such quantities of lilies and, I am told, whole fields of sunflowers. Your climate is so much finer than that of England, so bright, so sunny, that your flowers are luxuriant," said Mr. Wilde, with a polite disregard of the clouds, and with a delightful ignorance of how hothouses are robbed of their treasures to let him breathe an atmosphere of fragrance.

"You have reason to be pleased with your reception in the United States?"

"Oh, yes, indeed. Do you know, the night before I landed I was wondering how it would be—thinking of the cloud of misrepresentation that must have preceded me and wondering whether the people would wait to know me for what I am. But a poet must be indifferent to blame, as he must be to praise. He deserves neither till long after he is dead. Not till then can he be judged. While one is living, one can only work for what is to be. Do you know"—his face lighting up with a sudden smile while his eyes roamed reflectively—"our people in England took the greatest interest in my coming to America?— No"—in reply to a suggestion by the reporter—"no, they did not regard it at all as an aesthetic mission to a barbarous clime, but our artists wish very much to have their ideas planted and growing in America."

"What are your plans for the development of aestheticism in America?"

"It is impossible to define them yet. In this, my first lecture, which I am now delivering, I am endeavoring to explain the *spirit* of our art theories. As for the particular form it may take, I must wait to tell that in a second lecture after I have become acquainted with the country and have come to know something of its artistic materials and possibilities and have learned to appreciate its national spirit. I must know something of your woods for ceilings, for example, and numberless things of that kind. Art must differ with place and people. What would be quite right in England might be quite wrong here. It is only the general principles that I can teach now; their definite application must come later."

Here the poet gazed thoughtfully out of the window, and the reporter suggested that his impressions of American scenery must be as yet very limited. "Yes," was the reply, "but I enjoy very much what I have seen. But one cannot expect color in winter, when everything is so drear and brown. How dreadful those marshes are this side of New York. What a pity! And how unnecessary. They might plant them with something; so many beautiful things will grow in a marsh. Why, they might have great fields of callas growing there! Do you understand my love for lilies, and roses, and sunflowers? No? Oh, don't you know, there is no flower so purely decorative as the sunflower. In the house it is perhaps too large and glaring. But how lovely a line of them are in a garden, against a wall, or massed in groups! Its form is perfect. See how it lends itself to design; how suggestive it is! So many beautiful, very beautiful wallpapers have been designed from the sunflower. It is purely decorative," and the sunflower worshipper became lost in reverie. Then, opening his eyes wide, his whole face radiant, he resumed: "And the lily. There's no flower I love so much as the lily. That, too, is perfect in form, and purely decorative. How graceful, how pure, how altogether lovely its shape, its tender poise upon the stem. And you have such beautiful lilies in America. I've seen a new one that we do not have in England, that star-shaped lily. I always loved lilies. At Oxford I kept my room filled with them, and I had a garden of them, where I used to work very often. As for roses, they are so full of color, so rich, so passionate. They suggest the feeling where the others suggest the form. They richly fill what the others outline. Why do not people grow them everywhere? I was pleased with the Raritan back there, with its brown current and brown banks; but still, those banks ought not to be bare and bleak—cover them with hardy lilies. Did you ever see those wonderfully beautiful books William Blake published so magnificently illuminated? In one of those books, enclosed in a charmingly appropriate border, are three lively poems—one on the sunflower, one on the lily, and one on the rose.[6] It is a page altogether exquisite."

"Do you hope to teach the 'common people,' even the abjectly poor, to find these beauties, and by them to elevate their lives?"

"The two classes we must directly work upon are the handicraftsmen and the artists. As for the class between, the idle people, rich or poor, it is useless to go to them and tell them, 'You must do this, and you ought to do that.' There must be a great mass of handicraft produced before you can hope to affect the masses. And the handicraftsmen must be directed by the artists; and the artists must be inspired with true designs. It is only through those classes we can work."

"Do you not hope to bring back picturesque dressing as one of the forms in which the spirit of your art will work itself out?"

"All that must take time. We have to move very carefully, you know. Prejudice cannot be carried by storm. And, by the way, one of the most delightful things I find in America is meeting a people without prejudice—everywhere open to the truth. We have nothing like it in England. But to return—we must get the women to dress beautifully first; the men will follow. Velvet is such a beautiful material—why do not men wear it? Gray or brown or black velvet is always beautiful."

"You have been quoted as saying that the women's dresses in *Patience* are not exaggerated."

"Oh, the embroidery and painting on the dresses are made for stage effect and are larger than are worn in which is called good society. But in design they are correct. *Patience,* by the way, has done our cause no harm. Ridicule may be a serious weapon, but there should be that in a true poet or a genuine cause which is indestructible; and there is indestructibility in our cause. Oh, no; people understand that *Patience* is merely a burlesque. I enjoyed it very much. The music is delightful, and that is certainly on our side, even if the words are not."

"Speaking of dresses—how do you like the beauty of their American wearers?"

"I am charmed with American beauty. They possess a certain delicacy of outline surpassing English women. And there is a charm about this curve, here," said Wilde, drawing his finger from cheek to chin, "that is peculiarly fascinating. But the color of English women is richer and warmer, I think. I saw Clara Morris on the stage in New York one evening,[7] and I was as delighted with her as with Sarah Bernhardt,[8] who had told me very much about her charm; and I have met many surpassingly beautiful young ladies since my arrival. Mrs. Langtry,[9] I may tell you, is quite with me in all this movement. She has an artistic house, deserves all her reputation for beauty, and sympathizes thoroughly with the aesthetic school."

"What are your politics, Liberal or Conservative, Mr. Wilde?"

"Oh, do you know, those matters are of no interest to me. I know only two terms—civilization and barbarism; and I am on the side of civilization. It is very strange, that in the House of Commons you never hear the word 'civilization.' They spend night after night squabbling over petty things, when they ought to be working against barbarism. Then, in our country there is seldom a piece of legislation that does not benefit one class more than another; and that perhaps makes the wretched party spirit more bitter. But Gladstone is the greatest prime minister England ever had.[10] A short time before I came to America, he said to me that from the United States would come at once the greatest danger and the greatest good to civilization. The greatest danger in the vast accumulation of capital, and the greatest good in the perfect simplicity of American politics, and in the fact that the only reason for the passage of a great law over here is that it is for the good of the whole people. The personal control of capital, with the power it gives over labor and life, has only appeared in modern American life. We have as yet nothing like it in England. We call a man rich over there when he owns a share of Scotland, or a county or so. But he doesn't have such a control of ready money as does an American capitalist. He is often pressed even for a matter of fifty or sixty thousand pounds," said Mr. Wilde, carelessly.

"What poet do you most admire in American literature?"

"I think that Walt Whitman and Emerson[11] have given the world more than anyone else. I do so hope to meet Mr. Whitman.[12] Perhaps he is not widely read in England, but England never appreciates a poet until he is dead," said Mr. Wilde with a trace of bitterness. "I admire him intensely—Dante Rossetti, Swinburne, William Morris, and I often discuss him. There is something so Greek and sane about his poetry; it is so universal, so comprehensive. It has all the pantheism of Goethe and Schiller.[13] Poets, you know, are always ahead of science; all the great discoveries of science have been stated before in poetry. So far as science comes in contact with our school, we love its practical side; but we think it absurd to seek to make the material include the spiritual, to make the body mean the soul, to say that one emotion is only a secretion of sugar and another nothing but a contraction of the spine. Why does not science, instead of troubling itself about sunspots, which nobody ever saw, or, if they did, ought not to speak about—why does not science busy itself with drainage and sanitary engineering? Why does it not clean the streets and free the rivers from pollution? Why, in England there is scarcely a river at some point is not polluted; and the flowers are all withering on the banks!" And Mr. Wilde again lapsed into melancholy.

"Do you think Mallock's *Romance of the Nineteenth Century* a correct picture of a section of English society?"[14]

"No novel can include England," was the quick reply. "I enjoyed reading that book, though it has its many faults. But I have repeatedly upheld it against attack, because it is the first attempt by an English novel-writer to grapple with English society as it actually is. I mean by that, it is the first attempt to picture lives that are themselves interesting. George Eliot has made perfect pictures of lives in the provinces, and so have others; but Dickens and Thackeray[15] are our only novel-writers who have touched London life realistically. We have nobody in English literature, for example, like Balzac,[16] who has lived through so many changes of government and upheavals of society, and who mirrors all so exactly. A novel-writer must himself live what he portrays."

At this point, the train reached Trenton, where Robert E. Winner joined the party, and the conversation became general. During the approach to Philadelphia, Mr. Wilde showed an eager interest in the many novel things he saw. He listened with wide-open eyes to an explanation of a long train of oil cars, but did not say whether he found any beauty in them. A glimpse of Fairmount Park brought back his happy smile, and he was greatly pleased with the ride over the elevated tracks and with the Broad Street station. As his conspicuous figure walked through the waiting room, many a whispered comment flew about; but the Aesthete dived into a cab and was whirled quickly away to his quarters at the Aldine Hotel.

1. See Oscar Wilde, *The Complete Letters of Oscar Wilde,* ed. Merlin Holland and Rupert Hart-Davis (New York: Henry Holt, 2000), 127, and Nicholas Mirzoeff, "Disorientalism: Minority and Visuality in Imperial London," *Drama Review* 50 (Summer 2006): 56.

2. Colonel W. F. Morse was a New York–based agent for D'Oyly Carte. Morse arranged the details of Wilde's speaking engagements and was connected to the poet primarily as a business manager. See Morse's "American Lectures," in *The Works of Oscar Wilde,* vol. 15, *His Life with a Critical Estimate of His Writings* (New York and Boston: Brainard, 1909), 73–137.

3. Both titles are by John Ruskin: *The Poetry of Architecture* (1837), an early work, and *Fors Clavigera* (1871–84).

4. The socialite Mrs. Paran Stevens (d. 1895), formerly Marietta Reed, gave a dinner in New York City in Wilde's honor.

5. Samuel L. M. Barlow (1826–89), a prominent New York lawyer.

6. This is a reference to the plate from William Blake's *Songs of Experience* that includes the three short poems "My Pretty Rose Tree," "Ah! Sun-Flower," and "The Lily."

7. Clara Morris (1849–1925), one of the great emotional actresses of her age, opened in the play *The New Magdalen* on 5 January 1882 at New York's Union Square

Theatre; this production of the play, based on a Wilkie Collins story, featured James O'Neill, the father of Eugene O'Neill, in a supporting role. See also "New York Gossip: Meeting of the Aesthetic Poet and Clara Morris," *Boston Herald,* 22 January 1882, 4.

8. Sarah Bernhardt (1844–1923), a theater diva and sometime courtesan known as the "Divine Sarah," made her first appearance in New York City in 1880.

9. Lily Langtry (1853–1929) married Edward Langtry of Belfast and entered London high society before embarking on her theatrical career, during which she was popularly known as the "Jersey Lily." She made her American debut on Broadway in September 1882 as Hester Grazebook in Tom Taylor's *An Unequal Match.* See also Wilde's comments in "Mrs. Langtry on the Hudson," *New York Herald,* 30 October 1882, 5.

10. William Gladstone (1809–98) was a Liberal reformer who championed Irish Home Rule and ethical foreign policy and served as prime minister of England during 1868–74, 1880–85, and 1892–94.

11. Ralph Waldo Emerson (1803–82), American transcendentalist poet and essayist.

12. Walt Whitman (1819–92), American poet and patriot.

13. Johann Wolfgang von Goethe (1749–1832) and Friedrich von Schiller (1759–1805), German Romantic poets and playwrights.

14. *A Romance of the Nineteenth Century* (1881), a novel by the controversial novelist, poet, religious thinker, and economist William Hurrell Mallock (1849–1923).

15. George Eliot (1819–80), Charles Dickens (1812–70), and William Makepeace Thackeray (1811–63) were Victorian authors and journalists famous for their literary realism—scientific, psychological, and satirical, respectively—and social critique.

16. Honoré de Balzac (1799–1850), French novelist whose prodigious fiction engages literature and philosophy as well as politics, science, and visual culture.

---

7. "THE AESTHETIC BARD," *PHILADELPHIA INQUIRER,* 17 JANUARY 1882, 2

Mr. Oscar Wilde, the English aesthetic poet, arrived at the Aldine Hotel yesterday afternoon about four o'clock and proceeded at once to his rooms, where he passed the afternoon in seclusion. He had been very busy during the morning in New York and, with that and his journey to this city and the trying two hours of lionization before him in the evening, felt the need of rest.

Toward six o'clock, however, he consented to receive a representative of the *Inquirer,* to whom he extended a welcome with the graceful courtesy which is always characteristic of true breeding. Whatever may be said of Mr. Wilde's costume and manner in society, in the privacy of his own apartments he was distressingly like any other gentleman.

The only peculiarity in his appearance was his very long brown hair, fine and glossy as silk, parted in the middle, and hanging below his collar and round a face essentially English—or Irish—but thoroughly refined, and endowed with a liberal share of the beauty of expression. His head has something of the Gothic arched poetical outline; the forehead is rather low, but broad and fair, though seemingly narrowed by the flowing locks; the nose is aquiline, the eyes bright blue, and clear, as if you could see down into the lowest depths of thought within, and the mouth and chin are Hibernian, but of the highest Celtic type, and there is an air of refinement and gentle breeding pervading not only the face, but the entire man, and idealized in the full, flexible, delicately finished lips. He has the low cultured voice of refined society, and his personal magnetism sufficiently accounts for the extent to which society both in London and New York has taken him up.

Any man in the same independent position, with the same charm of manner, and the same pleasant genial face and nature, would be a general favorite had he never written a line of poetry or anything else but letters, or put forth to the world any even quasi-original ideas.

In reply to his visitor, who plunged at once into business, and asked for some concise information on his views, Mr. Wilde replied:

"There is more in the movement, as you say, than appears upon the surface. Our aim is to unite all artists in a brotherhood of art, and to draw closer together those who cultivate the beautiful."

"Let me give you," he continued, "an illustration. Take, for example, Keats. When Keats was alive, how lonely he was. He had the fellowship of no brother artists. This movement is designed in part to remove that isolation, to bring all artists, whether in painting, sculpture, music, or poetry, together, that they may aid each other in every way, and that each art may profit by the advance of its sister arts."

"And especially," he went on with increasing animation, "especially does the movement aim to reach the handicraftsman, and to raise him by familiarity with the truly artistic and by the sympathy of his brothers."

"The movement, then, is democratic in its tendency?"

"It is the most democratic impulse in the history of the world," said Mr. Wilde, earnestly. "I don't know, of course, how it is in this country; but we in England believe that the people, the artisan class, have toiled long enough in unloved labor and amid unlovely, hard, repulsive surroundings. A man's work should be a joy to him. Make him an artist, make him a designer, and you render it so. What a man designs he delights in bringing to completion."

"Hence," said he, "you see the politico-economic importance of aestheticism. The toiling thousands of Great Britain are growing more and more dissatisfied every year with their dreary lives, filled only with incessant, unattractive toil. The time when they could be kept down with the strong hand has departed, and," with the evident allusion to Kingsley's "Yeast,"[1] "the problem of controlling them is only to be solved by making them happy in their labor, and brightening their lives with such material surroundings as it is in the power of art to bestow."

As this seemed feasible only for such artisans as were also designers—though obviously of value to them—Mr. Wilde was asked by his visitor whether he deemed it possible to extend the benefits of aestheticism to the people most in need of his own theory of their blessings, and, on his replying in the affirmative, it was suggested, after a word of explanation, to the effect that the questioner was not arguing but only seeking a clear conception of the inner light; that while designers and artists were no doubt in demand to a certain extent, yet that there was also a demand for operatives to carry out their ideas and designs, and that, however happy it might make the loomhand to go into the fields and study the flowers for his patterns, or the stonecutter to imagine his groups of statuary, the tyranny of trade would prefer that the one should be in the stoneyard chipping at the marble for somebody else's designs, and the other hard at work in the factory keeping his loom in good running order.

To this Mr. Wilde replied that it was the tendency of aestheticism to raise all to a higher level, and to bring about among artisans a greater independence and a condition of things approaching in some respects to the better features of life among handicraftsmen in India.

In reply to the inquiry whether Tennyson[2] sympathized with the movement, Mr. Wilde replied that within certain limits there could be no question of the laureate's sympathy with it, but added that ever since the severe criticism which had assailed his earlier poems, "an ordeal which," said he with a good natured smile, "every English poet has had to go through," the laureate had held himself in a great measure isolated from the world of art. That his poems had endured was due to the intrinsic beauty, "for," said the aesthetic bard, "what is really beautiful has within itself an inextinguishable principle of life."

He would not say, however, he added, that Tennyson had absolutely held aloof from the movement; but, as one of its chiefest apostles, he might mention William Morris, whose rooms were a perfect museum of beautiful things, on every one of which he had bestowed somewhat of his own thought or he had handiwork in its organization.

1. *Yeast* (1848), the first novel by Charles Kingsley (1819–75), endeavors to address some of the key social and religious issues of Victorian England.
2. Alfred Lord Tennyson (1809–92) succeeded William Wordsworth as poet laureate of England in 1850.

8. "WHAT OSCAR HAS TO SAY," *BALTIMORE AMERICAN*, 20 JANUARY 1882, 4

Washington, January 20.—It having been rumored that the reason why Mr. Oscar Wilde passed through Baltimore today en route to Washington, without stopping in that city, was owing to some disagreement with Mr. Archibald Forbes,[1] the English war correspondent, who is at present in Baltimore. The correspondent of *The American* called upon Mr. Wilde at the Arlington Hotel this evening. He at first refused to be seen, and had denied admittance to several newspaper men, but a note from your correspondent proved effective. Before reaching the door a number of young ladies were seen hurrying in the direction of the room, anxious to catch a glimpse of its inmate. As the door was opened to admit *The American* man, Mr. Wilde was found reclining on a sofa immediately opposite, attired in a tight-fitting dressing gown, trimmed with red, his long hair brushed carelessly back from his forehead. The waiter, in order to afford the ladies an opportunity to behold Mr. Wilde, held the door open until sternly told to shut it. Mr. Wilde advanced cordially and shook hands with your correspondent.

"I beg pardon for the intrusion, Mr. Wilde, but your passing through Baltimore without stopping has given rise to the unpleasant rumor that you and Mr. Forbes are not on amiable terms."

"Well, really, this is most extraordinary. Mr. Forbes and myself are on terms of the greatest intimacy, and I cannot imagine the cause for any such rumor. Besides, why should I stop in Baltimore, as my engagement to lecture in Washington is prior to my Baltimore engagement? Lecturing here on Monday evening next, I shall go to Baltimore on the following Tuesday morning. So I left Philadelphia at noon today and came through to Washington, arriving here at 5 o'clock, and came right to my room, where I propose spending a quiet, uninterrupted evening, which will be the first since my visit to your wonderful country."

"I regret having disturbed your quiet," remarked the correspondent.

"Not at all; I am only too happy to have had an opportunity to positively deny that any unfriendliness exists between Mr. Forbes and myself, which you will do me the kindness to state emphatically."

"You will no doubt see much to interest you in Washington."

"Yes; I have many letters of introduction to distinguished people in this city, and I have a great desire to see the politicians of your wonderful country, whom I shall no doubt find assembled here now; and I regret that my limited stay will prevent my making that earnest, careful study of your leading men that I earnestly desire."

"Yes," suggested the correspondent; "you will find at this season, during the assembling of our National Congress, a great many of the politicians of both the great parties."

"I expect so; and, by the way, tell me what city do you consider the most purely American city? I do not fancy that either New York or Philadelphia are true types of that American idea which we are impressed with on the other side."

"Well, I think you will find Baltimore about as near an approach to an American city as any we have."

"Yes, I have been told so; and as I propose visiting there, I shall, no doubt, satisfy myself."

Mr. Wilde, in addition, stated that he had passed a charming time in Philadelphia, and one of his most delightful evenings was the one spent last night at the residence of Mr. George W. Childs,[2] in that city; that he desired very much to travel over this country, and store up knowledge which he proposed using in his books and poetry. He asked a great many questions regarding America, and dwelt in ecstasy over Walt Whitman, two pictures of whom were lying amid a mass of papers on the table in the room, and one of which he was to mail to Swinburne. He expressed himself as worn out and tired, and stated that it was a positive luxury to have one night to himself. Your correspondent bade Mr. Wilde good-night. "And pray contradict that report with reference to myself and Mr. Forbes," were his last utterances as the door closed.

1. Archibald Forbes (1838–1900), British war correspondent and lecturer.
2. George W. Childs (1829–94), founder and editor of the *Philadelphia Public Ledger.*

9. "WILDE AND FORBES," *NEW YORK HERALD,* 21 JANUARY 1882, 3

Some of the Baltimore papers today charge Mr. Oscar Wilde with having broken faith with the Baltimore public in not appearing according to advertisement on the stage when Mr. Archibald Forbes lectured in that city last evening. A graver charge is that he had snubbed Baltimore society by rudely neglecting to appear at a reception arranged for his entertainment last evening at the residence of Mrs. Charles Carroll, of that city,[1] a disappointment which it is asserted caused the hostess much embarrassment. Another count in the Baltimore indictment against Mr. Wilde is that the Wednesday Club of Baltimore invited him to an entertainment and were politely informed that he charged $300 for his appearance at receptions not held at private houses. It was represented that Mr. Wilde came from Philadelphia to Baltimore with Mr. Forbes and had a miff with Forbes on the train, so instead of stopping he came on to Washington.[2] Mr. Wilde and Mr. Forbes are both lecturing under the management of Mr. D'Oyly Carte. A *Herald* reporter found Mr. Oscar Wilde in all the glory of dressing gown, knee breeches and slippers in his parlor at the Arlington this evening. He was just sitting down to a repast of oysters, to what is known as "half a dozen raw" in this unaesthetic capital. Three colored waiters stood about his little table to hand him his wine and attend to his other wants.

"Pray be seated," he said, rising from his seat when the *Herald* reporter was ushered in. Mr. Wilde then resumed his own chair and proceeded to the disposition of the oysters before him, pausing occasionally to press a dainty napkin to his lips. The reporter called his attention to the publication in a Baltimore paper charging him with having broken faith with the Baltimore people.

"This is an invention," he said, "an invention of someone in that city. It is shameful, disgraceful. I heard much about the character of American journalism in England. If you expect English gentlemen to come to your country, especially gentlemen of letters and art, you must improve the character of your journalism. I do not intend to come to this city again until this sort of thing is changed. I received a letter from Mr. Forbes," said Mr. Wilde, rising and getting a letter from his writing table. He ran over the contents of the letter hastily and continued:—"It is a private letter and, of course, it would not be proper for me to give it for publication. You can say that I have received a letter from Mr. Forbes saying that he regrets that such insinuations have been made against me, and he assures me that he was not the author of them. I have only a slight acquaintance with Mr. Forbes."

"Was it true," asked the reporter, "that you were to attend the lecture at Baltimore?"

"The other day Mr. Carte asked me if I would not like to hear Mr. Forbes lecture. I told him that I had read some of his books; I was not particularly interested in the subject but I would go. It was arranged then that Mr. Carte or Mr. Morse would meet me in Philadelphia. Neither of these gentlemen could come with me, however, and Mr. Carte sent his clerk to the depot to tell me to go right on to Washington, as I am to lecture here Monday. Mr. Forbes took the train at Philadelphia too and we rode in the same car. He introduced me to two ladies whom he had with him. There was no difference between us at all. I came right on to Washington. Of course I could not think of stopping in Baltimore alone. I am a perfect stranger and could not go to any place like that unless someone was with me."

"It is said," pursued the reporter, "that the Baltimoreans are particularly incensed against you on account of your not attending a social entertainment to which you were invited."

"After I arrived here," replied Mr. Wilde, "I received a dispatch from Mr. Morse asking me if I could not return to Baltimore and attend this reception. I replied that it was impossible. I had traveled all day, was worn out, and it was utterly absurd to think of returning to Baltimore then. I presume Mr. Morse received some urgent telegrams of this reception, but [I] was told by Mr. Carte to come right through to Washington. Another thing in that publication is that some artistic club had tendered me a reception, and that I replied that I did not appear at evening entertainments unless I was paid for it. I never heard of this club before. As to the rest it is too gross to think of. When there are so many interesting truths, why is it that these untruths should be published?

"I am glad this thing did not come from New York. I was quite charmed with New York and with its men and beautiful women. The city has a cosmopolitan air, quite like Paris or Vienna. In England the papers would never publish such things. Since the publication of my poems few personalities appear against me. When a man has achieved a work they attack his work. There may be some satire, some announcement that Mr. Oscar Wilde wore a blue necktie or a red necktie or something else that will revolutionize the world, but that is all. I have heard before I came here," continued Mr. Wilde, "how low journals here ridiculed the art movement in England. I did not expect such vile things. It is quite too disgraceful. If you expect to have art in this country you must first have good morals to back it. There are so many things worth thinking of and worth talking of that one hasn't time for such things. If I could live 10,000 years—and my poems may get me something like immortality—if I could live 10,000 years I might find time to write letters to editors and correct this thing. I will go to Baltimore to lecture next Tuesday, and I will tell them about art if they choose to listen to me, but I will say nothing about this."[3]

1. Mrs. Charles Carroll, née Caroline Thompson of Virginia, married Charles Carroll VI (1828–95) in Maryland on 24 June 1857.

2. See "No Oscar for Us," *Baltimore American,* 20 January 1882, 4.

3. See also "A Card from Oscar Wilde," *Baltimore American,* 24 January 1882, 3.

Washington, D.C., January 23, 1882.

Editor American: Dear Sir—America should be a country without prejudice; so I will pray you to permit me to say that my failing to visit your city was due entirely and absolutely to some misunderstanding on the part of a messenger from my manager's office, who met me at Philadelphia with instructions to proceed direct to Washington, and not stop at Baltimore, as I had hoped to do. Since my arrival in America I have received in each city that courtesy for which your country is famous, and I would not wish it to be thought that I could willingly be capable of any such unpardonable rudeness as your papers would seem seriously to charge me with.

I remain, sir, your obedient servant,
Oscar Wilde.

---

10. "AN INTERVIEW WITH THE POET," *ALBANY ARGUS*, 28 JANUARY 1882, 8

An *Argus* reporter met Mr. Wilde after the lecture and found him to be a bright and sprightly young man, showing no signs of the languid demeanor so noticeable upon the stage. He was seated at a desk writing autographs for a number of young ladies.

"I hope," said he, "that I am obliging beautiful young ladies, for I make it a point to grant my autographs to no others."

In answer to an inquiry as to how he liked America, the poet said, "I really have seen almost nothing of your country. As I came up from New York this afternoon, I caught occasional glimpses of the river and I was charmed with its beauties. The blue hills in the distance, the forest still green in place, and the strange, regular outlines of the Palisades formed a most pleasing picture. I am always delighted to study human nature, and I felt much richer by my contact with so many new phases of character. I think that the theories I have propounded in my lecture will be adopted to some extent in America, for your countrymen are not opposed to revolutionary ideas, and I believe truth will force its way to conviction."

Mr. Wilde complained that he could obtain no cigarettes to suit him in this country. "I smoke only Turkish tobacco, and that you do not have here. I have used up all I brought with me and am now quite lost for a further supply."[1]

> 1. In chapter 6 of *The Picture of Dorian Gray* (New York: Penguin Classics, 1985), Lord Henry Wotton proclaims that "[a] cigarette is the perfect type of a perfect pleasure. It is exquisite, and it leaves one unsatisfied. What more could one want?" (90).

---

11. "OSCAR WILDE," *BOSTON HERALD,* 29 JANUARY 1882, 7

Mr. Oscar Wilde arrived in Boston Saturday morning, after an all-night railroad journey from Albany, and went straightway to the Hotel Vendome,[1] and was assigned to pleasant rooms, which, however, had not been specially decorated in his honor, as announced by some imaginative writer. In fact, good friends of Mr. Wilde assert that at least three-quarters of what has been written about him since his arrival in this country is purely imaginative. Mr. Wilde's arrival in Boston was made particularly pleasant by the fact that his old friend, Mr. Boucicault,[2] is here in the midst of his engagement at the Museum, and is also stopping at the Vendome. Mr. Wilde's visit in Boston promises to be an enjoyable feature of his American journey, for, while he is not to be ostentatiously lionized, he will quietly meet with many of the most congenial people here and be received with cordial hospitality. At 2 o'clock yesterday afternoon he lunched with the Literary Club, as the guest of Dr. Oliver Wendell Holmes;[3] in the evening he dined with his friend, Mr. J. Boyle O'Reilly,[4] who afterward presented him at the St. Botolph Club,[5] where he met many of the leading literary and artistic men of the city.

At noon Mr. Wilde received a caller from the *Herald* in Mr. Boucicault's parlor, where he had been breakfasting with Mr. Boucicault and Mr. Charles H. Thayer, the manager for Mr. Boucicault's coming American tour, and also the business representative of Mr. Wilde for his Boston lecture engagement. It was seen at once that the eccentricities of Mr. Wilde had been much exaggerated, for his dress was no more of a departure from the ordinary than that of a dozen musicians and painters in Boston who might be mentioned. He wore a breakfast jacket of black velvet, and the rest of his costume was of the usual cut. Indeed, if his personal peculiarities had not been repeatedly heralded from England, it is hardly likely that they would have attracted unusual remark in this country. Mr. Wilde received his visitor with amiable courtesy, as he was presented by Mr. Boucicault, and the hope was expressed that his journey to Boston had been a pleasant one.

"I came in a late train from Albany last night," said Mr. Wilde; "I lectured in Albany last night, you know."

"I suppose you have had all sorts of experiences with newspaper men?" remarked the caller, feeling that he might be apprehensive regarding the results of the present visit.

"Yes, some of them have been very tedious, while some others have succeeded in being very amusing. I was dressing one night when I received the card of a person; on the card was printed his name and also that he was a correspondent for a lot of western papers. 'This must be an immense newspaper man,' I said; I cannot dream of keeping him waiting. So I put on my dressing gown and he was shown right up. A very young gentleman, or rather a boy, came into the room, and as I saw him I judged that he was nearly 16. I asked him if he had been to school. He said he had left school some time since. He asked my advice as to his course in journalism. I asked him if he knew French. He said no. I advised him to learn French and counseled him a little as to what books to read, and, in fact, I interviewed him. At last I gave him an orange and then sent him away. That experience was really amusing to me, and the meekness with which he took it all was very charming."

"It is a pity that you could not see America in a more pleasant season."

"I have been able to see nothing but newspapers so far. I have a great desire to see the beauties of America. Yesterday was the first day I have really seen anything of your beautiful country. Going up the Hudson to Albany—the beautiful, clear, bright day, the dark hills encircled with blue. I imagine in summer time it must be extremely beautiful."

"It is a pity you cannot be here in the summer, especially in Boston, where the suburbs are the most beautiful in America."

"Boston has the most beautiful surroundings?"

"It is more like England—exquisitely cultivated, but very natural," remarked Mr. Boucicault.

"I am hoping to see in New England many fine old houses like the 'Seven Gables,'"[6] said Mr. Wilde.

"Oh, yes, we have some old houses left; the Seven Gables is still standing in Salem, but, unfortunately, the most of the old-time houses are destroyed. Being of wood, they have not lasted as long as they would in England. But you should take a drive out through the country while in Boston."

"Oh, yes, that I certainly shall have to do."

"Shall you be here in the summer?"

"I never have any plans in seeing a country; when it pleases me I stay, and go away when it ceases to please me. I should like to be here in the time of flowers."

"They are very beautiful."

"What are your trees here?"

"The American elm, maple, beech; also the hornbeam and the birch. These are among the principal deciduous trees."

"I wonder if we have the hornbeam in England; perhaps we call it by a different name. What is it like?"

"It is a very graceful tree. It rises up about 30 or 40 feet, and then droops over, something like drooping willows, or a fountain."

"I remember reading in William Morris's poems of the hornbeam,[7] when I was a boy, and I was much puzzled to know whether it was a tree or an animal."

"You spoke of Hawthorne—then you have read Hawthorne's stories?"

"Oh yes. I admire Hawthorne greatly. I think his *Scarlet Letter* has the grandest passion and is the greatest work of fiction ever written in the English tongue."[8]

Mr. Wilde was asked if he took any interest in politics, and he replied that he took an interest in everything in which humanity was active in thought and deed. "In Washington," said he, "I saw much of your leaders in politics, and visited in their houses, among them Mr. Blaine.[9] Your American politics are a little difficult for us to understand, on account of the names of the two parties, Republican and Democratic. In Europe we have a greater difference in names. There they are the Conservative and Liberal."

"The origin of America was in democracy and in Europe it was centralization," said Mr. Boucicault; "and the tendency in America is from democracy to centralization, while in Europe it is the other way, from centralization to democracy."

"In England it is a class interest that subdivides a party," said Mr. Wilde. "In England no measure is brought forward that does not touch the right of some particular class. You have no such distinction here."

"They have one class here, the moneyed class," said Mr. Boucicault.

"They never have in England such enormous capitalists as you have," said Mr. Wilde. "We call a man rich who has got a large amount of land but who probably has not so much as your magnates—that is, so much cash."

"Like our Jay Gould,[10] for instance, who buys half a dozen railroads or so about every day, or sells them."

"The moneyed interests are more solid in England, because the wealth is in the land, which has a fixed value; and not in stocks, which are constantly fluctuating. If, as I understand, the speculation is so great here, the commercial community must be always in that condition. The stocks and other securities are constantly changing in value, whereas the great values in England are in land, which has a fixed value."

"And not in Ireland," remarked Mr. Boucicault, "that has a very unfixed value."

Mr. Wilde was asked if he had thoughts about art, visited any of the art schools in this country.

"I went to a school of design in Philadelphia," said he. "I saw a young lady occupied in painting a moonlight landscape on a large plaque. Now a landscape, and above all, a moonlight scene, should never be painted on a plaque, or any round surface, but on canvas or paper. The surroundings of a school of design ought to be very beautiful. It is quite impossible to expect the designer to create beautiful designs in a whitewashed room with bare windows."

"Have you ever noticed one peculiarity of the studios of different artists? While the portrait painter or figure painter will generally have his studio decorated most delightfully, the landscape painter will have his studio perfectly bare, as if he were not dependent upon his surroundings?"

"Yes, but I think the true way for all artists to work is with the most beautiful surroundings. But I think in America the great future of yours lies with sculpture. You see, your clear, transparent atmosphere is best adapted to the grandest sculpturesque effects. It is so in Greece and Italy, where the greatest schools of sculpture in the world have existed, and I believe it will be so in America. In England, in our damp, dripping atmosphere, sculpture has a dreary look. It is absurd to attempt to revive Greek architecture without sculpture. That is the life of it, and the architecture is the life of it. So many public buildings in Washington in the Greek style, with most of their pediments empty, are lifeless. Sculpture gives animation to Greek forms in building pediments full of figures, and a grand frieze around the side, with reliefs—that is the beauty of it all. Without sculpture it is expressionless and purposeless as an empty picture frame."

"One of the foremost sculptors here, whom I was talking with the other day, spoke of our lack of feeling for form in this country as yet, except among the very few."

"I suppose you mean by the lack of form the want of proportion," said Mr. Boucicault. "You can take the purest Greek form, and by elongating or shortening it, you can turn it into anything that is most repulsive."

"That is an immense difficulty in art," said Mr. Wilde. "It is so absolutely dependent upon delicate proportions. The Parthenon in Athens is most beautiful, and the Madeleine,[11] which is a copy of the Parthenon, is most abominable."

"One is aesthetic proportion and the other is not," said Mr. Boucicault.

"No people went into the question of proportion as fully as the Greeks. There was a time in England, and always has been in Greece, when everything was beautiful. There was a time like that in England, and whatever we find built or made in that time, even for the most ordinary purposes, is beautiful. Then came the Puritan movement and destroyed all the artistic impulse. We are just beginning to recover from Puritanism in England."

"And we are also beginning to recover from the same in New England."

"I am also a great admirer of the Japanese, of eastern art especially, in which there is a most delicate sense of the beautiful, but I object to the predominance of the grotesque. A people which has such an exaggerated sense of the grotesque is generally found not to have a love for the wonderful beauty in the human face and form."

"Does not Mr. Ruskin ignore too much beauty of the human form? Mr. Poynter,[12] one of your leading British painters, makes that charge against him."

"Yes, I know all sorts of things are said against Mr. Ruskin, but it is better to read what men have to say for themselves rather than what is said against them. Mr. Ruskin has an exquisite sense of the physical beauty of man. In the opening part of *Modern Painters* there is a fine passage on this very subject. In England there is now a passionate love of physical beauty, so that if a woman there is very beautiful, she becomes, just on that account, as celebrated as a great poet or a great artist."

"Where, on the whole, do you think you have seen the most beautiful women?"

"In London, I think. You know all things naturally come to London, and thus the finest examples of beautiful women may be found in London. Here in America I find a vast amount of pretty women, and the greatest number I have ever seen together in my life thus far I have seen in Baltimore; it was at the Wednesday Club, where I was entertained last week."

"Irish!" laughed Mr. Boucicault; "there is a deal of fine Irish blood in the old Baltimore stock! That accounts for the mass of feminine beauty there."

"Do you know," said Mr. Wilde, "that the greatest fault I have to find with you Americans is that you are not American enough? You are all too cosmopolitan. What I am wishing to meet is a true American. I mean a man of whom it can be said, He is entirely the product of American conditions."

"You will find that in Walt Whitman," was suggested; "have you met Walt Whitman?"

"Indeed I have," said Mr. Wilde, his face kindling with enthusiasm. "I spent the most charming day I have spent in America with him. He is the grandest man I have ever seen. The simplest, most natural, and strongest character I have ever met in my life. I regard him as one of those wonderful, large, entire men who might have lived in any age and is not peculiar to any one people. Strong, true, and perfectly sane: the closest approach to the Greek we have yet had in modern times. Probably he is dreadfully misunderstood. If people would only know that no artist lives for praise; he only wants one thing, to be understood. I hope that America will not treat its great poets as England too often has. Now, in France, it is different; they are proud that they have poets and artists there, but in England they not only expect them to look to posterity for their fame, but also for their bread and butter."

"Have you visited any of the universities in America yet?"

"I have visited the Johns Hopkins University in Baltimore and certainly will not leave Boston without visiting Harvard."

Mr. Boucicault here spoke, with earnest feeling, of the efforts that had been made in New York to make Mr. Wilde an object of ridicule, no slanders and malicious lies being too atrocious for certain people to invent. He compared the abuse heaped upon Mr. Wilde to that poured upon Mr. Millais,[13] Holman Hunt,[14] and other artists of the Pre-Raphaelite school in London 25 years ago. There is no one better entitled to a respectful hearing than Mr. Wilde, who comes to this country with a friendly interest for it, and therefore, a desire to become acquainted with the American people.

"All America naturally takes a great interest in what is done in England, as is natural," said Mr. Wilde, "for England is the mother of this country. I came here with a desire to tell you what the artists of England have been trying to do, for, of late, they have been doing some things which, I think, are worthy of telling about. It is on this account that I have prepared my lecture."

"It is to be hoped that you will have no fault to find with Boston's reception of what you have to tell us. At any rate, an entire community cannot be held to account for the disagreeable conduct of certain of its individuals."

"That is very true," said Mr. Wilde, "and I have not yet met any American gentleman who has not discountenanced and deplored all this ridicule and abuse. Whom are they harming? Not me, not the artist—for the artist, if he is an artist, must know what he is going to say, what he is going to do. He goes his way and produces his work. Keats wrote his poems and nobody read them at the time, but now you would think that that youth must have been loved, when he lived, by every man in England. Now to decry an artist thus is harm done to the public more than to the artist. There was only one artist in England who took any notice of what was said of him. That was Byron.[15] Byron began by being a great lyric poet and should always have been one. But he read the newspapers and it soured his nature, and at last he became a satirist, which is a low order of a poet. People in England condemn 'Don Juan,' but thereby they condemn themselves, for England is responsible for everything in 'Don Juan.' An artist should not listen to, nor heed, ridicule and abuse, but he wants to be understood. Shelley[16] was abused, but he did not heed it, and it had not the least effect upon him."

Mr. Wilde was asked if his play was to be produced in this country.

"I cannot tell yet. I brought it with me, and Miss Clara Morris has it. She is one of the greatest actresses I have ever seen anywhere, here or in Europe."

"Have you seen any of our leading tragedians?"

"I saw Mr. Booth in London,[17] and Mr. McCullough,[18] and I went to see Mr. Lawrence Barrett in New York.[19] I thought Mr. Barrett had a thorough knowledge of his art, remarkable facial expressions, and a striking quickness in adapting himself to his situations."

"Do you not intend to go to the Pacific coast?"

"Well, I should like very much to go through to California when the snow on the mountains is melting and the flowers come out. I am told it is wonderfully beautiful then. And I want to see Mexico particularly, and to examine the wonderful remains of its ancient art. But one never sees a country by passing through it by railway. By racing through the country as we all do no one sees anything of it. The true way to see a country is to ride through it. I should like to ride through Mexico. I rode through Greece once, rode through the Peloponnesus;[20] saw every little hill and tree, and knew it all. I want very much to see some of your Indians, to see men who spend all their life in the open air. I want to see how they carry themselves."

"Have you noticed particularly our domestic architecture?"

"I have not had a chance to see much of it yet, but I saw in Washington some very beautiful new houses of red brick, with a great deal of charming woodwork about them and balconies to sit out on in pleasant weather. They were altogether very beautiful, and were full of flowers. I consider the most abominable style what they call Greek in New York, like Fifth Avenue in New York, so depressing and monotonous, and entirely unadapted to the building material and the climate. In Philadelphia their old red brick houses, with white doors and window shutters, were quaint and charming, so simple and unpretending. You could see that they were well built, and they were warm and clean-looking."

"You will find many brick buildings here in Boston. It is the prevailing building material here."

"That is right. The cheerful red, especially in the sunshine, combines so finely with the clear blue sky."

Here a visitor was announced and the conversation ended.

1. The luxurious and palatial Vendome in Back Bay would become Wilde's favorite hotel in Boston.
2. Dion Boucicault (1859–1929) was an influential Irish playwright, a theatrical producer, and a popular actor. Wilde hoped to persuade him to produce his play *Vera* in America.
3. Oliver Wendell Holmes (1809–94) was a physician by profession and a poet by

avocation. Wilde carried a letter of introduction from James Russell Lowell to Holmes and dined at the Saturday Club at the Parker House at Holmes's invitation. See also "Saying and Doings" in Boston's *Home Journal*, 4 February 1882, 2.

4. John Boyle O'Reilly (1844–90), Irish-born poet, novelist, and editor.

5. The St. Botolph Club was just two years old when Wilde visited Boston. The name pays homage to the seventh-century abbot whose monastery had sprung up in the fens of East Anglia's Botolph Town, later corrupted to Boston.

6. Wilde alludes to Nathaniel Hawthorne's *House of the Seven Gables* (1851).

7. Wilde alludes to William Morris's "Shameful Death," a poem about the unheroic death of a knight, narrated by the knight's detached brother, that turns on an ambush in a place thought to be safe.

8. Hawthorne's novel *The Scarlet Letter* (1850) addresses moral and spiritual issues from a distinctly American perspective.

9. James G. Blaine (1830–93) had served two Republican residents as secretary of state and was also a former Speaker of the House of Representatives. He was the 1884 Republican nominee for president but lost the election to Grover Cleveland.

10. Jay Gould (1836–92), a major financier of British colonial and Scottish parentage, became one of America's premier railroad developers and "robber barons."

11. The Madeleine (L'Eglise-Sainte-Marie-Madeleine), or Church of Saint Mary Magdalene, a Parisian temple of glory in gigantic proportions, was indeed modeled on the Greek Parthenon.

12. Edward John Poynter (1836–1919) was a leading British painter, draughtsman, designer, and art administrator.

13. John Everett Millais (1829–96), a British painter and illustrator, was one of the cofounders of the Pre-Raphaelite Brotherhood.

14. William Holman Hunt (1827–1910), British painter and founding member of the Pre-Raphaelite Brotherhood.

15. George Gordon, Lord Byron (1788–1824), the British Romantic poet, is famous for his innovative writing but equally so for his extravagant and controversial lifestyle.

16. Percy Bysshe Shelley (1792–1822) was a British Romantic poet whose resistance to convention stemmed from his uncompromising idealism. While he was certainly a fine lyric poet, his skepticism, atheism, and political radicalism gave rise to his notoriety and made him susceptible to denigration.

17. The American actor Edwin Booth (1833–93) was arguably the greatest Hamlet of the nineteenth century. His father, the Englishman Junius Brutus Booth, was a well-known actor, and his younger brother, John Wilkes Booth (also an actor), was Abraham Lincoln's assassin.

18. John McCullough (1837–85) was an Irish-born American actor perhaps best known for his secondary Shakespearean roles, which he played in support of both Edwin Forrest and Edwin Booth. McCullough was less well received in London than he was in American cities. Of Wilde, McCullough reports, "I have met him socially and have found him to be a delightful man, one who has brains, and no mistake, very charming in his manner and in social society, with very little of this lah-da-da style that, from the broadcast accounts of him, one would be led to expect was habitual" ("John McCullough," *Boston Daily Star*, 14 January 1882, 2).

19.	Born Lawrence Brannigan to Irish emigrant parents in Paterson, New Jersey, Lawrence Barrett (1838–91) was an American stage actor known for Shakespearean roles. He most famously played Othello to Edwin Booth's Iago.

20.	The Peloponnesus is a large peninsula forming the southern part of Greece, south of the Gulf of Corinth. This area, which Wilde had observed via train after the manner of the Pre-Raphaelite Brotherhood, figures in an 1879 essay he wrote for the Chancellor's English Essay Prize at Oxford (which was not awarded that year) entitled "The Rise of Historical Criticism."

## 12.	"THE AESTHETIC APOSTLE," *BOSTON GLOBE,* 29 JANUARY 1882, 5

"Will Mr. Oscar Wilde favor the *Globe* representative with a few moments of his presence and attention, with a view to rectify some of the numerous misrepresentations that have preceded him to this city?"

Such was the card borne on a silver platter to the apostle of aestheticism, as he sat in his elegantly furnished parlors at the Vendome last evening shortly after his return from dining with Oliver Wendell Holmes, James Freeman Clarke, Phillips Brooks, and others at the Saturday Club.[1] A gracious affirmative being received in reply, a newspaper man, with his heart full of indignation at America's lack of appreciation of the truly beautiful and languid, soon found himself seated in a pensive chair by Oscar's drooping fireside—the fire, by the way, had drooped so much that it had gone out altogether, but what is the heat of vulgar coals when one is burning with a passion for sunflowers, crockery, poetry and all that sort of thing? The leader of the great English renaissance of the beautiful did not appear immediately, but through the half-open door to an adjoining apartment came a few impatient words in undertone, which might have been occasioned by the total depravity of a necktie in refusing to be adjusted according to the standard of high art. On the lounge was carelessly thrown the heavy fur-lined ulster of olive green, with which the country has become so familiar. On the center table was a litter of letters, invitations of all kinds, a fine caricature, and *A Thing of Beauty,* one of Ruskin's books.[2] There was not a sunflower nor even a lily about the room. They had evidently not been unpacked. Without doors a disagreeable drizzle made Commonwealth Avenue look particularly unpicturesque; in fact, the conduct of the weather was disgraceful in its supreme disregard of aesthetics.

The entrance of Mr. Oscar Wilde put an end to all such observations. As the poet posed for a moment on the threshold, it was evident how atrociously he has been misrepresented. Only the fertile fancy of the veteran interviewer would have described his luxuriant hair as falling upon his shoulders and flowing down his back. It seemed instead to be brushed forward over the ears and corners of the eyes, and indeed might have been tied under the chin and done excellent service as a muffler. To such extremes went the heated imaginations of the New York reporters that they impressed the public with the idea that his nether garments extended only to the knees; the writer can aver from careful observation they modestly reached an inch and a half below. The innumerable implications of this nature that have been spread before the public cast an indelible stigma upon American journalism.

Oscar has large, mobile, and passably good-looking features, with full eyes that appear to languish but are really very shrewd and all-observing. He wears no beard and has only slight hirsute indications on the superior lip.

"Ah, yes," said he, lolling on the mantle and crossing his shapely calves; "interviewers are a product of American civilization, whose acquaintance I am making with tolerable speed. You gentlemen have fairly monopolized me ever since I saw Sandy Hook. In New York there were about a hundred a day. I had to leave my hotel and go to a private house when I wanted to push along my work, don't you know? But then, I am always glad to see you," with a benignant smile, "when you don't misrepresent the movement, you know."

"It is understood, Mr. Wilde, that you are very much dissatisfied with the manner in which you have been treated by the press."

"Well, I don't care much. I don't read the papers a great deal. But if they were rather better strangers to fiction, and on somewhat more intimate terms with truth, there would be nothing lost."

"Will you kindly explain the true state of that Baltimore affair, Mr. Wilde, about which so many contradictory things have been said and written?"[3]

"That was scandalous treatment," said the pioneer of the era of beauty, a trifle bitterly. "Those lies were invented by a Baltimore sheet, a rag of a newspaper, and every other paper in the country copied them like so many sheep. It was through a pure misunderstanding that I did not attend the lady's reception. I saw her when I returned from Washington, and we are now on charming terms. She is one of the most gracious ladies I have ever met. The idea that I made any amount of dollars a condition of my favoring a company with my presence is another malicious canard, but too absurd to do me any harm. The clout of a sheet that started these lies has never had the moderate amount of decency to retract them. The American papers are often a screed of falsehoods. Now, in England, you know," and the innumerable shining writers of English luminaries were here contrasted with the unfathomable frivolity and depravity of the American press. But through all this harangue a mysterious winkle in the great aesthete's orbs seemed to intimate that he very well understood the advantage of free advertising, and didn't so much care whether he was represented or misrepresented, as long as he was as far from a failure as at present. As a matter of fact, had the American papers ignored him as the English have done, his venture in this country would possibly have fallen short of its present measure of success.

"What were your impressions of New York society?" was queried.

"Charming—very charming—quite cosmopolitan. In fact you are all cosmopolitan here. I have yet to discover the true American. I searched diligently for him in New York and he was not there. All in vain was I on the qui vive for him in Philadelphia, Baltimore, and Washington. I am getting skeptical now and begin to doubt his existence. But possibly, as some of your people have told me, I shall find him further west."

"You have met many of our literary men, I believe, Mr. Wilde?"

"Well, yes, and for a young country your literary class, though very small, is highly developed and evinces an acute appreciation of the more exalted ideals of thought and art. Longfellow is very pleasant,[4] Dr. Holmes is extremely clever, James Russell Lowell, Aldrich,[5] and others rank high. But, of course in the childhood of your nation, so to speak, you could hardly expect to produce a glorious trio as burst upon England with the advent of Keats, Shelley, and Byron. Of all your authors, I consider Walt Whitman far the grandest and noblest. Many of his lines are like a blast fresh from Olympus. I have met him and enjoyed his society more than words can express."

"In regard to your own poetry, it has been stated that you are at work on a new volume."

"Yes; I have been engaged for a long time in that direction, and devote all my leisure to its preparation. I intend that it shall be a great advance upon my first venture and entirely distinct in tone and style—more soulful, more throbbing, more exalted, I trust."

"Do you propose to publish it during your sojourn in this country?"

"Well, I have thought of so doing. It was at one time announced that I should do so. But on mature consideration I have come to the opinion that the American atmosphere is not conducive in the best development of poetic thought. I shall defer publication until my return to England. After my travels here are consummated I shall continue my work at home. To write true verse is the primary object of my life. Thus shall I best promulgate the principles of this great modern movement in the direction of the beautiful."

At this point the apostle, in a somewhat singsong and parrot-like way, gave an account of the great eternal and inevitable underlying principles of the "movement," what had been done, what was doing at present, and what it was hoped to accomplish in the near future. This, however, is already familiar to the *Globe* readers.

Mr. Oscar Wilde dined last evening with John Boyle O'Reilly, dropped in at the St. Botolph Club, and later attended the Greek play at the Globe Theater.[6] There is little doubt about his being received in what is known as "our best society," in case he cares to enter it. He lectures at Music Hall Tuesday night, and is already assured a full house, with three score of Harvard students in the front seats.[7]

1. James Freeman Clarke (1810–88) was an American Unitarian minister, author, and abolitionist. Phillips Brooks (1835–93) was a clergyman and author who later served briefly as bishop of Massachusetts in the Episcopal church. The Saturday Club, founded in 1855, comprised a coterie of high-profile Boston-area writers and intellectuals who met the fourth Saturday of every month at the Parker House, on Tremont Street.

2. John Ruskin did not write a book called *A Thing of Beauty*. It seems that the interviewer conflated titles in the five-volume work *Modern Painters* (1843–60): volume 3, part 4, is entitled "Of Many Things"; volume 4, part 5, is "Of Mountain Beauty"; and volume 5 includes part 6, "Of Leaf Beauty," and part 7, "Of Cloud Beauty."

3. For more on the Baltimore "affair," see interview 9.

4. Henry Wadsworth Longfellow (1807–82) was an American poet, educator, and linguist. Wilde's praise of Longfellow here is tellingly faint, especially in relation to Whitman, Hawthorne, and even some lesser-known American writers.

5. James Russell Lowell (1819–91) was an American poet, critic, diplomat, and abolitionist. Thomas Bailey Aldrich (1836–1907) was an American poet, novelist, and editor.

6. The Greek play Wilde attended was *Oedipus Tyrannus,* with George Riddle (1853–1910) in the title role. See also "Oscar Wilde on Greek Drama," *Philadelphia Inquirer,* 20 January 1882, 8: "Mr. Oscar Wilde was interviewed on the production of *Oedipus Tyrannus* of Aeschylus yesterday and said: 'I regret much to learn that the *Oedipus,* when performed here, is to have only one actor who will speak the lines in Greek, while the other actors will make use of English. The effect of this will be to destroy the unity of the performance, and it will be rendered only curious, whereas it should be beautiful. The play is the best acting play of the Greek literature, and is mentioned by Aristotle as an absolute type of perfection in the dramatic art. I saw it performed in the Comedie Francaise in Paris last summer.'"

7. Some sixty Harvard students dressed in swallow-tail coats, knee-breeches, and green ties, with lilies in their lapels and sunflowers in their hands, entered the Music Hall and took their reserved seats in the front rows at the beginning of Wilde's Boston lecture on 31 January. Warned in advance, Wilde had dressed in a standard dinner jacket and prepared an opening statement that lampooned his

imitators. See Ellmann, *Oscar Wilde,* 182. See also "Oscar Wilde in Brooklyn," *New York Sun,* 4 February 1882, 1: "Referring to the sixty Bunthornes, [Wilde] said laughingly: 'Oh, I could sympathize with them, because I thought to my-self that when I was in my first year at Oxford I would have been apt to do the same; but as they put their head in the lion's mouth, I thought they deserved a little bite.'"

---

13.   LILIAN WHITING, "THEY WILL SHOW HIM," *CHICAGO INTER-OCEAN,* 10 FEBRUARY 1882, 2

Jan. 29.—The poet of the aesthetes arrived at the Hotel Vendome yesterday. I did not see the lily-laden lyrist make his entrée in the portals, but I have the assurance of one of our Sunday morning papers of today that "Mr. Wilde arrived about noon and entered the Vendome like any ordinary person"—a statement that one must credit, considering the high local authority I quote, although I regret the fact, as I am sure something extraordinary was expected of Oscar in this important moment. The local historian neglects to chronicle whether or not his manner was intense, and whether he appeared in good spirits thus separated from his "mamma." (For the full force of this last allu-sion vide a Mrs. Gustafson's glowing eulogy on Miss Genevieve Ward.)[1] One would fancy, by the by, that Miss Ward's prayer to the gods would have been "Save me from my friends," on the appearance of this amazing chronicle.

But to return to the aesthete: I chanced to meet Mr. Wilde for an hour or two before dinner last night, and I found little of that eccentricity which has seemed so pronounced to his numerous interviewers. From some supremely poetical perception of the eternal fitness of things, I suppose, he proceeded to entertain me with tales of the atrocity of the American press. In the evening I was laughingly relating Mr. Wilde's power of natural selection, conversation-ally considered, to a musical artist—a prima donna, in fact—who assured me in return that half the people whom she met would regale her with unflatter-ing allusions to her profession. However, I listened with equanimity to Mr. Wilde's tale of "the dangers he had passed" less moved than Desdemona, yet not without a sympathetic perception of truth in his strictures.

The fact is he has been greatly misrepresented, his individualities carica-tured, his tastes exaggerated, his appearance burlesqued. He is not great enough to merit so much attention, and he is not necessarily an object of ridicule.

Mr. Wilde has more than the average intelligence, is a scholarly and suf-ficiently well-appearing young man, whose intellectual method is strongly flavored with the ideas of Ruskin, Swinburne, Morris, Rossetti, and who, without being at all an original genius, is yet remarkably assimilative of genius. He is one of the people who produce the right atmosphere for art. He is not an artist, but he is artistic; not creative, but intensely appreciative. The truly poetic mind is reverent. "Poets become such through scorning nothing." Mr. Wilde is perceptively egotistic, and, in so far, is not a poet.

"My object in coming to America," remarked Mr. Wilde to me last night, "is to tell the American people what is the most important movement of thought in England, wishing that all should exactly understand what we artists intend to do. Our object is to produce more concentration, more definite artistic movements of value than ever before."

"Do you limit this movement to what are termed, distinctively, the 'fine arts,' or do you also include the decorative, Mr. Wilde?" I asked.

"No one art is finer than any other," he replied. "All true art is decorative."

Now the avowed object of Mr. Wilde's visit here indicates his ignorance of current life. The American people need no missionary to proclaim to them the latest thought in England. It is very probable that Mr. Wilde might learn rather than teach, while here. We all take our Pre-Raphaelitism—our Ruskin, Shelley, Keats, Swinburne, and Burne-Jones[2]—at first hand, and need no apostle to translate or dilute it for us. However, we have contributed so largely to the growth of Mr. Wilde's conceit that [it] is merely a bit of poetic justice that we should suffer from it. His goings-out and his comings-in have been chronicled, his dressing gown, slippers, and neckties have figured in our newspapers, and he is quite justified in fancying himself to be an utterly utter young man.[3]

If you care to take a microscopic view of an unimportant subject, O, cosmopolitan *Inter-Ocean,* you will see that Boston will take the conceit out of Oscar. He will meet all the gentle courtesy of well-bred life, but he will not be regarded as an object-d'art, to be placed under glass and gazed upon. He will neither be considered vaguely wonderful for some inexpressible reason, as he was in New York, nor will his really pleasant qualities be ignored.

Mr. Wilde's greatest need is to be taught how to talk. He will make some commonplace statement with the air of an oracle, and ten chances to one his listener has known this same fact all his life and is probably far more familiar with it than is this aesthetic young man.

I heard him expounding the ethics of Schools of Design last night to a lady who had visited them, studied them, and who had probably written more in the newspapers about them than Mr. Wilde had ever dreamed of.

Yet, withal, he says some good things. For instance, he remarked that "the desire for beauty is the desire for life; for that enduring element in existence which is life. It is the essential part of all civilization," he continued. "Without beauty civilization has no meaning, because industry without beauty becomes barbarism."

The thought is derived from Ruskin, of course, yet it was well put, and many epigrammatic turns of thought expressed by Mr. Wilde are entertaining to the listener. I asked about Burne-Jones, and he told me he considered him an artist "of the loftiest spiritual imagination, of a fervid type, of splendid range of vision, of a joyous color, and a wonderful fertility of design."

Mr. Wilde is to give his lecture on "The English Renaissance" in Music Hall on Thursday evening. No one expects to hear anything original or striking, yet it is anticipated that it will be a rather pleasant intellectual entertainment.

> The interviewer, Lilian Whiting (1847–1942), was an American poet, critic, memoirist, and journalist.
>
> 1. Genevieve Ward (1837–1922), born Lucy Genevieve Theresa Ward, was an American-born British soprano and actress. As the dates just given show, Mrs. Gustafson's review, or "eulogy," only metaphorically killed the performer.
> 2. Edward Coley Burne-Jones (1833–98) was a British painter and designer closely associated with the Pre-Raphaelite Brotherhood.
> 3. The phrase "an utterly utter young man" echoes Robert Coote's popular song, "for voice or piano parodying or inspired by Oscar Wilde," entitled "Quite Too Utterly Utter: an Aesthetical Roundelay" (1881).

14. "A MAN OF CULTURE RARE," *ROCHESTER DEMOCRAT AND CHRONICLE,* 8 FEBRUARY 1882, 4

Oscar Wilde, his knee breeches, his business manager and his colored body servant arrived in the city late yesterday afternoon and were at once driven to the Osburn house, where rooms had been assigned them. The great leader in modern aestheticism at once retired to his apartment and did not again make his appearance until half past 7 o'clock, when he rode to the Grand Opera house, where a blushing reporter of this paper was presented to him in the dressing room. There was certainly nothing limp nor languid in the hearty English grip with which he clasped the proffered hand, and had it not been for the singularity of his attire there would have been nothing in particular to distinguish him from an ordinary English gentleman. In appearance he was the typical Bunthorne of *Patience.* He was dressed in knee breeches, black silk stockings marvelously fitted, low patent leather pumps, regulation dress coat, low cut double-breasted white vest, shirt collar turned low with a voluminous white tie, and a broad expanse of shirt bosom, ornamented with a single stud, in which were set two pearls and a diamond. A fob with double seals jingled below his vest, and the only other article of jewelry visible was a large seal ring upon the third finger of his left hand. The effect was curious if not picturesque, and it was heightened by the remarkable face and head. Thick and heavy hair, parted in the middle, fell nearly to his shoulders on either side, enclosing a long, narrow, and oddly marked face. The forehead is low, the cheek bones high, the eyes bright and full of expression, the mouth large and mobile, the lips full, and the chin giving the impression of unusual length. It is not a handsome face; it is not a strong face; but it is an exceedingly interesting face, made doubly so, perhaps, by a knowledge of the man's life and position. It is emphatically the face of a dreamer, intelligent and refined, but not the face that would inspire confidence in earnestness of purpose and vigor of execution. This is the first strong impression, but the judgment of the mind is wonderfully shaken by a brief experience with his conversational powers.

As the reporter perched gingerly upon the edge of a chair, Oscar Wilde inquired if art had gained any foothold in Rochester, which enabled the visitor with pardonable pride to refer to Powers's art gallery[1] and the art exchange, never failing sources of inspiration. He admitted that the art exchange was good so far as it went, but that in reality nothing could be done until there was founded a school of design. "You must teach the people to do artistic work," he said, "and then the movement will begin to assume form. It is not to the rich who can afford to be patrons but the workers in art to whom we must look for development."

"How about the treatment you have received from the newspapers in this country?"

"I have no complaints to make. They have certainly treated me outrageously, but I am not the one who is injured. It is the public. By such ridiculous attacks the people are taught to mock where they should reverence, to scoff at things to which they will not even listen. Had I been treated differently by the newspapers in England and in this country, had I been commended and endorsed, for the first time in my life I should have doubted myself and my mission. What possible difference can it make to me what the *New York Herald* says? You go and look at the statue of Venus De Medici[2] and you know that it is an exquisitely beautiful creation. Would it change your opinion in the least if all the newspapers in the land should pronounce it a wretched caricature! Not at all. I know that I am right, that I have a mission to perform. I am indestructible! Shelley was driven out of England, but he wrote equally well in Italy. It was not he who was injured. It was the people. I cannot expect—I do not wish better treatment than Keats and Shelley received, and yet I must confess that I am surprised. You have sent many Americans to us in England, and at least we have received them courteously. You have sent us a good many actors, some of them good, some of them very bad; but I do not think they can justly complain of rudeness on our part. How would it have appeared had we accused Booth of blackmail, as I was accused in Baltimore?"

The listener gave expression to his vagueness and Mr. Wilde continued: "We have many eminent men in our country, men eminent in art and letters, but they would not think for a moment of venturing here in a public capacity. They know well enough the treatment they would receive, the questionable courtesy I have experienced."

"How were you pleased with the demonstrations of the Harvard students?"

"There was nothing offensive in that. I understood well enough that it was meant as a good natured joke, and I entered into the spirit of it fully. It recalled to my mind many incidents of my life at Oxford."

"As you do not read what the newspapers say about you, I suppose you know nothing of the thousands of paragraphs that are flying about the country about you. Most of them, I presume, originated in the newspaper offices. For instance I read the other day that you were presented to a prominent society lady in Washington, and she exclaimed, 'And so this is Oscar Wilde: but where is your lily?' The quick reply was, 'At home, madame, where you left your good manners.' I suppose, of course, that had no foundation in fact?"

"On the contrary, it is absolutely true, with the exception that it happened in London and that the lady was a duchess."

"What did she do then?"

"She did what any duchess would do under the circumstances, I suppose—blushed and remained quiet."

"Well, then there is another story in which the boot is on the other foot. It is said that you complained that there were no quaint ruins in this country, no curiosities, and a lady replied, 'Time will remedy the one, and as for curiosities, we import them.'"

"Yes, that is an excellent story. It was first told of Charles Dickens when he visited this country. I find every community has its lady who is remarkably bright in her repartee and she is always credited with the latest *bon mot* going the rounds. Those two stories are following me all over the country, localized in almost every city."

"Pardon the digression, but I would like to know your opinion, from a thoroughly artistic standpoint, upon the prize fight which took place today?"[3]

Mr. Wilde laughed and said, "Even that has its artistic side. You know the ancient Greeks—"

At this point, Mr. Vale,[4] the manager, made his appearance at the door and announced that it was 8 o'clock and time to go on. The lecturer at once sprang to his feet, excused himself, walked quickly to the back entrance, walked to the front of the stage, and without preface, commenced at once to deliver his lecture on "The English Renaissance." There was a slight ripple of applause as he made his appearance. The lecture has been extensively printed, so that it is hardly necessary to reproduce even a sketch of it here. It was delivered in rather a tiresome monotone, but the small audience present was apparently interested and listened attentively until the close. At the beginning of the lecture, two or three young rowdies in the gallery attempted to make a disturbance by "Oh's" and "Ah's," and turning down the gas, but they were quickly suppressed by Ed Moore, the officer in charge, and compelled to leave the house. It was said that the young men were students at the university, but it is sincerely to be hoped that none of the students are boorish enough to be guilty of such a stupid insult. Among those to arrive before the lecture commenced was Peter Craig, arrayed gorgeously in dress coat, white vest and knee breeches, a take off which some one must have considered the essence of wit.

> The interview's title, "A Man of Culture Rare," refers to Bunthorne's song from the first act of *Patience*, "I'm an Aesthetic Sham": "If you're anxious for to shine / in the high aesthetic line / as a man of culture rare, / You must get up all the germs / of the transcendental terms, / and plant them ev'rywhere."

1. Powers's art gallery in Rochester was founded in 1875 when Daniel W. Powers (1818–97) filled four rooms with pictures, art objects, and curios that he brought back from a trip abroad. By 1884 it consisted of more than thirty rooms.
2. The Venus de' Medici, or Medici Venus, is a Hellenistic marble sculpture, a first-century B.C.E. copy of a Greek bronze original depicting the goddess Aphrodite.
3. This is an exemplary instance of an American interviewer baiting Wilde on multiple levels, aesthetic and nationalistic. On 7 February John L. Sullivan beat the Irishman Paddy Ryan for the heavyweight boxing title with a ninth-round knockout. Wilde's recourse to Greek aesthetics in his truncated response deftly avoids the interviewer's least attractive implication.
4. J. S. Vale was Wilde's American business manager.

15. "WILDE SEES THE FALLS," *BUFFALO EXPRESS,* CA. 9 FEBRUARY 1882; REPR. *WHEELING REGISTER,* 27 FEBRUARY 1882, 3

Niagara Falls, Ont., Feb. 9.—The day was all that could be desired for sight-seeing. Oscar Wilde, who made his headquarters at the Prospect House, breakfasted early, and wrapping himself in his long fur coat, stood out on the veranda of the hotel for nearly an hour steadily gazing at the scene before him. A carriage was ordered at 9 o'clock, and in company with his agent, Mr. Vale, they started for the different points of interest. They returned at 2 o'clock. The change of scenery and fresh air seemed to please Mr. Wilde.

After dinner Wilde conversed on his morning's adventure. To use his own words, he said: "When I first saw Niagara Falls I was disappointed in the outline. The design, it seemed to me, was wanting in grandeur and variety of line, but was beautiful. The dull gray waters flecked with green are lit with silver, being full of changing loveliness; for of all, the most lovely colors are colors in motion. It was not till I stood underneath the falls at Table Rock that I realized the majestic splendor and strength of the physical forces of nature here. The sight was far beyond what I had ever seen in Europe. It seems to me a sort of embodiment of pantheism. I thought of what Leonardo da Vinci said once, that 'the two most beautiful things in the world are a woman's smile and the motion of mighty water.'"

Mr. Wilde wrote in the Prospect House private album:

"The roar of these waters is like the roar when the mighty wave democracy breaks on the shore where kings lie couched at ease. Oscar Wilde."

16. "THE APOSTLE OF ART," *CHICAGO INTER-OCEAN,* 11 FEBRUARY 1882, 4

Oscar Wilde, the apostle of aestheticism, the lover of all sweet, beautiful, and darling things in nature, the John the Baptist of the religion of art, the much-talked-of English lecturer, arrived in Chicago last night and took rooms at the Grand Pacific. A reporter for the *Inter-Ocean* called upon him and was kindly received. The aesthetic young man had been reclining in a very utter and languid attitude upon a sofa which was drawn up before the blazing grate, and the sofa was covered with a fine wolf-skin robe and a tiger skin, while where his head had lain was a silk shawl of the color of old gold and soft as the sigh of a maiden. He was found to be a tall and strongly-built young man, not too strong, not enough to be gross in flesh or muscle. His long hair, which curls up on the ends, was parted in the middle and fell to his shoulders. His face is smooth, oval, with no feature very strongly marked except the mouth. The lips are red, rather thicker than with most people, and have a little nervous trick of compression. The whole expression of the face is pleasant, especially when lighted up with a smile, which, when it happens, makes him very beautiful. The ears are entirely concealed by the thick locks, which he ever and anon brushes back carelessly, yet with a lingering and caressing motion. Mr. Wilde was dressed in a coat of black velvet, scarlet necktie, and handkerchief of the same color protruding from the pocket, light pantaloons, slippers and red socks. He was smoking a cigar, and handled it with the grace which only comes from long practice. His greeting was kind, and the grasp of his hand cordial and soulful. The pressure was not intense, but the firm clap of the white, nervous fingers was like the clinging of a vine.

"It has been a fine day for traveling, Mr. Wilde," said the reporter.

Mr. Wilde had thrown himself back upon the skins in a very picturesque attitude, and was gazing at the fire. He paused a moment, and then the sweet tones of his voice, full and round, and with a suggestion of a sea-shell held to the ear, made reply: "I have been traveling so long, you know. But," with a sigh, "it seems a bright and clear day." Then he relapsed into an utterly utter attitude and caressed his cigar thoughtfully.

"You have been often interviewed, I believe," said the reporter.

"Yes, but never with ordinary accuracy. All have relied upon their imaginations, and the result has been a libel upon that novel quality."

"Meaning—"

"The imagination."

"How do you like the West?"

"I should imagine it is far more free of prejudice. The East seems to catch too much of the little floating follies of Europe. For that kind of thing you in the West have no time. In the East I found many cities pervaded by some folly of misinterpretation which they are already tired of in England."

"What did you think of Niagara? I understand you paid the falls a visit?"

"When I saw the falls for the first time, the thought came over me that they were not so noble in design and action as I had expected, perhaps; but the colors were full of change."

"Did you change your mind?"

"Not till I had stood underneath the cataract did I realize how enormous was the physical force of nature in the midst of which I was standing."

"What are your general impressions of America?"

"That is a difficult question. I have only as yet seen your towns, not the country at all. I have not yet seen anything in the least that seemed definitely and absolutely American."

"How do you like the cities?"

"The best cities have a very high cosmopolitanism; in the lesser cities, a curious provincialism. What strikes me most here in the West is really the type of civilization definitely American, created by yourselves and for yourselves."

"What is the nature of your mission?"

"The whole essence of this artistic movement in England is that we had a desire to discover in every city those men and women who have the power of artistic design; to give them the best models and expression possible to train them in the noblest surroundings to produce the noblest work."

"Is that its whole object?"

"In regard to people who are not handicraftsmen, who have not this power of design nor the capacity for artistic vocation, we wish to produce in them that artistic temperament without which there is no individuality in art, no real joy of life; in a word, no civilization."

"How can that be done?"

"There is only one way of producing this artistic temperament, and that is by accustoming them from childhood to the abiding presence in their own houses of beautiful and joyous color and noble and rational design. We want to make art not a luxury for the rich but, as it should be, the most splendid of all the chords through which the spirit of any nation manifests its power, [and] to make it part of the daily atmosphere in which people live."

"What is art?"

This question seemed to arouse Mr. Wilde. He flashed a scornful glance at the reporter, but it was followed immediately by a sunny smile. He arose and stood with his back to the fire and his hands clasped under his coattails.

"An artistic thing," he said, "is anything which, independent of its practical use, pleases one by the beauty and delicacy of its form, the wonder of its design, or the nobility of its color. A man who creates an artistic thing is a man who works not with his hands only, but with his heart and with his head."

"But what of industry?"

"Life without industry is barren, and industry without art is barbarism."

"Do you think more of the works of Michael Angelo than of Edison?"

"One production of Michael Angelo is worth an hundred of Edison. It is a sign of a nobler, fresher civilization among the people. Modern civilizations are not good or bad in themselves at all. They certainly increase one's wonder at the mysteries of nature and one's admiration for the genius of man. But their use for civilization depends entirely upon the spirit in which they are used."

"Modern inventions are useful?"

"A tramway is an exceedingly useful and economical means of conveyance, but in Oxford today they are pulling down one of the most beautiful old bridges of England in order to substitute in its place what they call in England a light and elegant cast-iron structure."

The last few words were spoken with undisguised contempt.

"This," he continued, "is in order to facilitate the running of a tramway. In this there is no gain to England at all, only the irreparable loss of stately and noble architecture."

"We are not troubled that way here," said the reporter, "for we have no old buildings or bridges to pull down."

"That is good fortune for you," he said. "There is hardly a beautiful thing left us. The history of a country should live not in books but in its architecture. That is the most solemnly beautiful record of the past that man can create. There is hardly a single beautiful thing left in London," said Mr. Wilde with a sigh.

"But are not useful things more important to civilization than beautiful ones?"

"Useful is a dangerous word. Useful for what? I deny that between the noblest usefulness and the noblest beauty there is anything but the most complete accord and sympathy. Westminster Abbey is useful, and it's also beautiful—the most useful because it is the most beautiful."

"What is civilization?"

"That condition under which man most completely realizes the perfection of his own nature. Civilization without beauty or art is an impossibility. The best bookcase is the one which will best hold your books. Then add to it whatever you love best in the world as decoration."

"What do you think of our architecture?"

"Mr. Wilde looked at his questioner pityingly. "You have none," he said. "You want in this country, to begin with, the primary element of beautiful cities, that is, noble architecture. The old, red-brick houses your Puritan fathers built you are much more beautiful, much more simple, much more natural than the sham Greek porticos, the Doric chimneys, and Corinthian upper stories of Fifth Avenue. In domestic architecture, there is nothing more suitable or beautiful than red brick."

"But it is not necessary for a building to be old to be beautiful?"

"Very true. A Gothic cathedral with half the side clipped away by a storm is not beautified by the operation. Age will add a certain charm, or what people call picturesqueness, to a building, but age will never make an ugly building beautiful."

"But is not modern civilization the greatest?"

"The greatest civilization of the world existed ages ago, and existed without steam engines. Of what use is it to a man to travel sixty miles an hour? Is he any better for it? A fool can buy a railway ticket and travel sixty miles an hour. Is he any the less a fool?"

---

17. "TRULY AESTHETIC," *CHICAGO INTER-OCEAN*, 13 FEBRUARY 1882, 2

Oscar Wilde sat in his room in the Grand Pacific last night, a room made bright and artistic with beautiful things. A large center-table was heaped with choice old books, some of them rare old curios, with precious broken binding and soulful mediaeval dogs' ears. In the window's embrasure was a beautifully intense writing desk, all inlaid with pearl, quite Japanese and early English, heaped with letters answered and unanswered. The bright coal blazed in the grate. The sofa, with its covering of skins of wild beasts and its further curtain of the old-gold silk shawl, with netted fringe, was drawn up to a comfortable angle with the fire, and upon the couch thus made reclined the aesthetic young man, this time smoking a cigarette. He was dressed in a quilted black silk smoking jacket with scarlet collar, lapels, and waistbands. He wore the same scarlet necktie, handkerchief, and socks, or at least they were of the same color as upon the previous visit of the *Inter-Ocean* reporter. His pantaloons were black, with a scarlet cord down the seams to match the trimming of the jacket. He greeted his visitor with languid eyes.

"As my former interview with you was necessarily brief,"[1] said the reporter, "there were a few questions I should like to ask you."

Mr. Wilde made a gesture of assent, and the reporter asked him what he thought of Chicago.

"That is a difficult question to answer," he said. "I don't pretend to have seen the city yet. I have been here too short a time; but from what I have seen I like it much better than New York. The streets are wider, cleaner, and there are not all the railways overhead and in the middle of the street, and that dreadful noise is not here. It is wonderful to think how you have built such a large city in so short a time, especially after such a great calamity as your great fire.[2] But of course it is a little sad to think of all the millions of money spent on buildings and so little architecture."

This he said with a sigh, and glance out of the window upon the twinkling lights of the city.

"But that will come in time, no doubt."

"Have you seen any art in Chicago?"

"I have seen one Chicago artist, whose work is of the highest artistic quality, whose work is beautiful—more beautiful than the work of any sculptor I have seen yet, and of whom you should all be proud. I refer to Mr. Donoghue."[3]

"Is Donoghue a sculptor?" asked the reporter.

"Do you tell me you don't know him? He is a native of Chicago, studied in Paris, has come back to his own city, having done beautiful work already, and prepared to do beautiful work for you if any of you care for it," said Mr. Wilde, with ill-concealed sarcasm.

"Here is a plaque he designed for one of my poems—a figure of a girl—so simple, so powerful, so pretty. It is perfect."

The reporter took his word for it.

"What do you think of the people of America?"

"In the Eastern cities the people are very cosmopolitan. I think this is strongly characteristic as regards the men and women. It was in the West of America that I expected to find real American life—life made by yourselves and for yourselves."

"How have you liked your audiences?"

"At all important large cities I find the audiences intelligent, courteous, and sympathetic. In some of the small provincial towns which I have visited on my journey there have been attempts at disturbances. However, in all these cases the good sense and good feeling of the majority of the audiences entirely stopped any attempts of the kind."

"You refer more particularly to Rochester?"[4]

"Yes."

"How was it in Boston with the Harvard students?"

"What the young men did there was a mere piece of undergraduate high spirits. I received it in the same spirit, and my lecture at Boston passed off most brilliantly. It was not intended as an attempt to disturb my lecture, but merely a bit of schoolboy fun. You don't suppose for a moment that a movement of any importance can be affected by sixty young men?"

"What do you think of athletic sports?"

"When I lectured in Boston I told these young men of Harvard that so far from their athletics being opposed to art, the best motives for the noblest sculptures would most probably be found on their running ground, on the river, in the gymnasium. I reminded them that Greek sculpture never looked for any nobler motive than a young man starting for a race, trying his sandals before leaping, hurling the weight, and the like, and advised them to put up in the beautiful gymnasium a few casts of the best Greek statues of young athletes, so as to remind them that all their own physical perfection and strength and fleetness of foot and the like might give to the artist beautiful subjects for his art."

"Where does your lecture tour extend?"

"I lecture next week in Detroit, Fort Wayne, and Cleveland; after that in St. Louis, Cincinnati, and other cities."

"Will you go south?"

"I do not know yet whether I can go to Canada or your own southern states."

"Will you go to the far West?"

"I don't think I shall have time to go to the far West. So many lectures to give, so much traveling to do. I am afraid I shall have to give up what I had looked forward to meet in America—California in the spring, Colorado and a ride in Mexico. I want to see Leadville immensely."[5]

"Those mining towns are quite a curiosity."

"Yes; those new forms of life—new attempts at civilization that have sprung up in your mining cities—are objects of the keenest intellectual interest to us in Europe."

"In speaking of Rochester," said Mr. Wilde, rising and helping himself to a fresh cigarette, "I must say that I am trying to keep as good an opinion of your country as I can. Your great cities confirm me in my best opinion, while the pretty provincial villages are what such always are, entirely unimportant. Let a young man go to England and lecture on any subject he chooses, he will at least be treated with respect."

"Are you satisfied with the results of your tour financially?"

Mr. Wilde mildly stared with surprise at such an outrageous question, but evidently thinking that this was a type of civilization "created by ourselves and for ourselves," he confessed that he had done pretty well.

"I have had large audiences," he said. "By the way, how much easier it is to speak to a thousand people than a few dozen. Wendell Phillips[6] told me that it was a test of a true orator for him to interest an audience of twenty."

"How much do you get a night?"

This was too much for Mr. Wilde. He pushed back his hair and threw his cigarette away. Finally he said:

"How much do your best lecturers get?"

"Some of them get $500 a night."

"Well, I got $1,000 a night in Boston, and shall get the same here. Of course, in little cities I don't expect so much. But it is merely filling in the time."

"I am extremely impressed by the entire disregard of Americans for money-making—"

Here the reporter was so surprised that he dropped his pencil.

"—as shown by the remarks made by many of the western journals. They think it a strange and awful thing that I should want to make a few dollars by lecturing. Why, money-making is necessary for art. Money builds cities and makes them healthful. Money buys art and furnishes it an incentive. Is it strange that I should want to make money? And yet these newspapers cry out that I am making money!"

1. Interview 16, published on 11 February 1882.
2. The Great Chicago Fire occurred in October 1871; the city was rebuilt by 1873.
3. John T. Donoghue (1853–1903), an Irish-American sculptor, was discovered by Wilde during his 1882 tour, and the attention he gained as a result of Wilde's interest enabled him to continue his studies abroad. See also Wilde, *Complete Letters*, 177n1.
4. While speaking in Rochester, New York, on 7 February, Wilde was interrupted by a group of students who tried to embarrass him by hiring a laborer to parody him as a blackface minstrel with a flower. The students seemed to find in Wilde's aestheticism an "inverted" effeminacy that was analogous in their minds to degeneration, in which his whiteness as well as his masculinity were compromised. This allusion to pseudo-Darwinian "reverse evolution" feeds on many of the same anxieties about race, class, gender, and sexuality that had been registered recently in cartoons in the *Washington Post* and *Harper's Weekly*, which published a representation of a monkey admiring a sunflower.
5. Leadville, a mining boomtown on Pike's Peak in Colorado, made its fortune in silver and once boasted a population of 30,000.
6. Wendell Phillips (1811–84) was an American abolitionist, advocate for Native American rights, women's rights, universal suffrage, temperance, and the labor movement.

18. "WILDE," *CLEVELAND LEADER*, 20 FEBRUARY 1882, 6

He came yesterday on the afternoon train over the Lake Shore Road. By "he" is meant the great apostle of aestheticism; the man who proposed, so far as lies within the power of one person, to revolutionize modern English and American art and bring us to a true conception of the beautiful and a perfect understanding of the graceful. If he fail in this attempt, as fail he may, it is evident that Mr. Wilde has another object in view, and this latter purpose is more apt to result in full fruition than the former. He has an advance agent and a business manager, the same as any other attraction, and is fully prepared in other respects to increase the size of his bank roll. As his preparations for producing a regeneration in art are much less elaborate than his arrangements for swelling his own exchequer, and extend beyond nothing but suggestions without any practical place, it is fair to presume that Mr. Wilde's creed was adopted merely as a means to an end, and is not the moving cause in his present tour. To the energy and enterprise of Mr. Will J. Cotton the Cleveland public is indebted for a sight of the much-advertised one. The terms, $500 per night, made the prospect look misty for a time, but Mr. Cotton perfected an arrangement, and brought the gentleman here.

Mr. Wilde was met at the N.Y.P. & O. depot by Mr. Cotton and by him escorted to the Forest City House. At 5 o'clock, as per previous arrangement, the aesthetic young man of the *Leader* called at the hotel and was presently shown into the presence of Mr. Oscar Wilde. The gentleman received his visitor with cordiality—not too cordial, but just the exact degree—and requested him to be seated. Having done so, the reporter took in the surroundings.

Mr. Wilde had caused his colored servant to cover the tete-d'-tete with a silk shawl of an old gold tint, and over this a bear skin. A small table had been brought out into the center of the room, and on this rested a small teapot, one of the impossible blue kind, in which the ladies of two centuries ago delighted. A pair of cups and saucers to correspond and a box of cigarettes were the only other articles on the table.

Mr. Wilde is a splendidly formed man of six feet or more in height. His head is large, almost ponderous, and well set on powerful shoulders. It is an undeniable fact that Mr. Wilde is almost too fleshy.[1] He wore a tightly fitting sack coat of brown velvet, vest of the same material, and loose trousers of subdued tint but of very self-assertive cut. His throat was encircled by a pale green tie, and the corner of a handkerchief to match stood out in relief against the brown of the coat. A large seal ring made gesturing with the left hand somewhat wearisome.

Having satisfied his yearnings by a careful inventory of property and person, the reporter, by way of beginning, asked:

"What shall we do to be saved,[2] with reference to art only?"

"What you need in America are good art schools, academies of design. They are the absolute essentials of aesthetic development and progression. The great popular mistake is that art should be of a national character. People forget that the great schools of art have been purely local. There never was a national Italian school of painting. Every city in Italy had a different school. From Venice to Naples they were unlike, but all beautiful. The same is also true of the styles of embroidery and metalworking."

"Will you explain to me your conception of true poetry?"

"The essence of all art," said Mr. Wilde, "is a combination of perfect freedom with perfect beauty. If you ask me what attitude our school adopts toward poetry, I will tell you. A great deal of careless and bad work has been strutting about the world, sheltering itself under the name of inspiration. We don't care to discuss what inspiration may be, but we feel that it possibly belongs to a man's private life, and as a rule never appears in his work. We think that poetry is an art like the other arts, with rules and laws. A thing not to be kept as many young poets have for moments of deep depression, but an art dependent primarily on beautiful workmanship. A young poet, like a young painter, must study the great masters of style, and must be able to use language as a musical instrument. He should be a master of perfect technical excellence. Romantic sentiments and moral maxims are not the essence of poetry."

"May I ask why people generally associate you with sunflowers and lilies," asked the reporter.

"I will tell you why we have so loved and valued the flowers mentioned. It is because they are the two flowers of England which are the most perfect in design, and which lend themselves most materially to decorative art, giving the handicraftsman the most beautiful motives. But you must remember that there are no flowers in the valleys and gardens of England which we have not and will not use in the service of art. The flowers to be used in America are your own, not ours. You do not need to borrow our flowers any more than our money. Then, as regards satire and caricature. Rebellions in politics are shot down; rebellions in art are slandered. It is the surest sign of the strength of any movement that it should be assailed by the impertinent insolence of ignorance and folly."

"Do the doctrines of your school extend any further than decorative art and poetry?"

"We embrace all the arts, and in this the real strength of the movement lies. Art must no longer be the individualized expression, but must be democratic. It must be an art that can appeal to the enormous masses of the people; an art that will not be a luxury for the rich, but the atmosphere in which men and women are to grow up."

"How do you like America as far as you have become acquainted?" asked the reporter, preparing to leave.

"To begin with, America is not a country; it is a world. Every city has different types and there is no permanent type at all as regards her men and women. I think the society delightful. I find New York brilliant and cosmopolitan; Philadelphia, literary; Baltimore, pleasant; Washington, intellectual;

Boston, more like Oxford than any city you have. The people in Chicago I found simple and strong, and without any foolish prejudices that have influenced East America. I found the audiences in Chicago very sympathetic, and it gives me a sense of power to sway such large multitudes. It is grand. In fact, the side of your American civilization those of us in Europe who are watching your young republic are most interested in is not the East but the West. We want to see what civilization you are making for yourself and by yourselves."

During the conversation Mr. Wilde refreshed himself by frequent cups of the potent oolong fusion[3] and blew out vast volumes of smoke inhaled from the fragrant "Old Judge" cigarette.[4]

1. A reference to an essay by Robert Buchanan entitled "The Fleshy School of Poetry," originally published in the *Contemporary Review* (Aug.–Nov. 1871) and later reprinted as a pamphlet, which accuses Rossetti and his Pre-Raphaelite Brothers of obscenity. Rossetti's reply, "The Stealthy School of Criticism," appeared in the *Athenaeum* in 1872. In 1895, during Wilde's trials, Buchanan was among the few public figures who offered him public, if limited and qualified, support.
2. In Acts 2:37 the apostle Peter is asked "What must we do to be saved?"
3. The comment about a potent oolong fusion refers to Wilde's tea.
4. "Old Judge" cigarettes were produced by Goodwin and Company in New York.

19. "WITH MR. OSCAR WILDE," *CINCINNATI GAZETTE*, 21 FEBRUARY 1882, 10

Mr. Oscar Wilde arrived in this city yesterday morning from Cleveland, en route to Louisville, where he is to lecture this evening. He remained over a day, wishing to have a preliminary glance at certain objects of interest here before his return on Thursday for his lecture on "The English Renaissance" at the Grand Opera House on the afternoon of that day.

A *Gazette* representative having early information of the arrival of the great apostle of aestheticism, called upon him at the Burnet and was duly requested to follow his card to parlor No. 62, where Mr. Wilde was bestowed. The poet and aesthete was found rather languidly reclining upon a couch, over which was thrown, in careless grace, a rich fur-lined railway traveling rug, smoking a cigarette in a thoughtful mood. There was a litter of letters upon the table, in the midst of which was a magnificent basket of roses, pink and red, which Mr. Wilde explained were a rest and comfort to his soul after the horrors of a railway journey. Against the side of the room stands a battered, but substantial English leather "box," which the *Gazette* representative gazed at reverently in the pauses of the conversation, knowing that it was the casket which contained the silken raiment which has excited the rage of the heathen[1] in two continents.

Mr. Wilde is curiously like, but yet utterly unlike the Maudle of the organ of the Philistines, *Punch,* and the fact reminds one of the proverb that a lie is never so dangerous as when it has in it a modicum of truth. The large, long face, framed in thick locks of brown hair, parted in the center and falling on either side of the cheeks almost to the shoulders, which gives to it a certain womanly air, is Du Maurier's, but in place of the vacant stare is a bright smile, and a perpetually changing expression, clear gray eyes, a tall and manly figure, a carriage the perfection of good form, and a bearing that bespeaks him a thorough man of the world. He wore a morning suit of light mastic colored tweed; the coat of velvet, a little pronounced in the matter of braid; a pale red silk handkerchief drooped from the breast pocket, and matched in color the ample neckerchief knotted in sailor fashion beneath his low-turned shirt collar. He was faultlessly shod in patent leather, with gray gaiters, and wore no jewelry but a very large seal ring—a fine antique intaglio of Mercury cut in amethyst. With this he seals his *billets-doux* and those other "winged messengers" which have roused the dull British Philistine from his vulgar lethargy—or anyhow have showed him the true path out of the mire.

Mr. Wilde was most cordial. Would the *Gazette* act as cicerone and show the stranger Rookwood, the School of Design, the Art Museum?

Why, certainly; if the *Gazette* desires one good thing more than another, it is to stimulate the zeal and devotion of the people, and make room for what is purely true and precious in art. Meanwhile, what does Mr. Wilde think of America?

"I am pleased with it. It has great possibilities; each city in the years to come will be the center of a school of art, as is Venice, Florence, Rome. It is folly to talk of a national art; there is no such thing. Each city has its center of inspiration. In Florence the inspiration was of a religious type, God and the angels; in Venice it was the noble men and woman of the republic; in Rome, traditions and noble deeds.

"I am especially delighted with the West, it is so new and fresh, and the people are so generous and free from prejudice. The older cities in the East," Mr. Wilde said, musingly blowing little rings of smoke from his lips—"the people are enveloped in a perfect mist of prejudice, quite unlimited; they have imported so many old world ideas, absurdities, and affectations that they have lost all sincerity and naturalness." (The Boston Philistines made the aesthete have a thoroughly "bad time" evidently.) "You have no architecture, no scenery, but individuals are doing beautiful work, and you have great art possibilities."

"In what direction?"

"America is the country for a great school of sculpture, because it is dependent upon the sunlight, which you have, and is an art which depends absolutely upon present and active conditions of life, and not upon remembrance or tradition. I met in Chicago," Mr. Wilde said reflectively, "a young sculptor whom we would love and be so proud of if he were in Europe—a Mr. Donoghue. He reminded me of the old Italian stories of the struggle of genius. Born of poor people, he felt a desire to create beauty. Seeing some workmen modeling a cornice one day, he begged some clay of them, and went home and began to model. A man who saw what was in him gave him money for a year in Paris. He went and has come back. The way I found him was, he sent to me a little bas relief of a seated girl, illustrating a verse of my poem 'Requiescat.'[2] I went and saw him; found him in a bare little room at the top of a great building, and in the center was a statuette of the young Sophocles leading the dance and the song after the battle of Seramis, a piece of the highest artistic beauty and perfect workmanship, waiting there in the clay, to be cast into bronze. It was by far the best piece of sculpture I have seen in America.

"Meanwhile, the artist starves upon a radish and a crust, the stoic's fare. Perhaps, but he will win in the end, and trouble is light if one is an artist. A man is not successful," said Mr. Wilde, sententiously, but truly, "because the world praises him, but because his work is good."

"What have you seen commendable in a decorative way in your visit?"

"Many good houses in Philadelphia, Boston, and Washington, and I have seen a Daisy Miller.[3] I can not tell you where [this in response to eager questionings] because I am to go back there, and I should never be forgiven, but the sight of her has increased my respect for Henry James a thousandfold.

"Col. John Hay,[4] of Cleveland, with whom I lunched yesterday, has a charming house. But the room which has most impressed me was a little bare whitewashed room in Camden town, where I met Walt Whitman, whom I admire intensely. There was a big chair for him and a little stool for me, a pine table on which was a copy of Shakespeare, a translation of Dante, and a cruse of water. Sunlight filled the room, and over the roofs of the houses opposite were the masts of the ships that lay in the river. But then the poet needs no rose to blossom on his walls for him, because he carries nature always in his heart. This room contains all the simple conditions for art—sunlight, good air, pure water, a sight of ships, and the poet's works.

"I saw another of your great poets in his beautiful home." Mr. Wilde looked out of the window into the smoke and mist and sighed. It was a day to make the children of light to sigh and the heathen to mock and rage.

"This kind of weather," he continued, consoling himself with a fresh cigarette, "always gives me a sense of failure. I am always on the side of extremes—

in winter I would be always sleighing, in summer always in a summer garden of flowers. I went to see Longfellow in a snow storm and returned in a
hurricane, quite the right conditions for a visit to a poet. When I remember
Boston, I think only of this lovely old man, who is himself a poem, and the
bright party of men I met at Dr. Holmes's."

At 1 o'clock Mr. Wilde donned his green overcoat, trimmed with otter,
adjusted a bon silene rosebud in his coat lapel, drew on a pair of pale tan
colored gloves, and with an ivory stick in his hand and a brown stiff felt hat
on his head, was driven first to Robert Clarke & Co.'s, where he selected various books, among them the works of Howells, James, Miss McLaughlin, and
others, and thence to Rookwood, the School of Design, the Art Museum,
whose doors were inhospitably closed, and a half hour was delightfully spent
at the delightful home of Mrs. Col. Nichols, on the Grandin Road. By request
of Mr. Wilde, his impressions of the art industries of the city are not made
public. He will embody them in his lecture on Thursday afternoon. Mr. Wilde
has a keen and quiet wit that enlivens his conversation upon worldly subjects
delightfully.

When shown the School of Design, with its forlorn corridors and dark
rooms, his eye lighted on the legend "No Smoking," painted in the window.
"Great heaven, they speak of smoking as if it were a crime. I wonder they do
not caution the students not to murder each other on the landings. Such a
place is enough to incite a man to the commission of any crime," and then,
"most unkindest cut of all,"[5] "I wonder no criminal has ever pleaded the
ugliness of your city as an excuse for his crimes!"

The suburbs Mr. Wilde kindly approved. Seen through the rain and mist,
the stately villas of Grandin Road were quite English with their green sweep
of turf and crowding chimneys.

Of all men Mr. Wilde least loves a critic. "Let the poet sing," he cries, "and
let the artist paint, and let the people look and listen—and so they would,
and learn, too—but the critic, a kind of middleman, comes between them,
and, like the bird in Shelley's song,[6] shuts his eyes and declares it is night.
Sometimes the critic himself, lured on by a hope of fame, paints, or writes,
or sings, and then a great and sacred joy fills the soul of all artists, and his
fate overtakes him." The real critic should be a poet, Mr. Wilde thinks, and in
proof cites Coleridge,[7] Keats, Goethe, Matthew Arnold,[8] the greatest of living
English critics, all poets, and quotes with glee Theophile Gautier's[9] reproof of
a critic who lectured him on the iniquity of his ways. "It is of great advantage
to a man never to have done anything, but he must not abuse it."

"I forgive everything, the critics' ignorance, even. I applaud Bunthorne
languidly from my opera box. I greet Du Maurier blandly at the club, but

the unpardonable sin is to say I am impractical. That is to stick a dagger in me. This aesthetic movement is the first of any practical value in art in England. It has changed the whole character of English decorative art. It has given to every handicraftsman in England beautiful designs, which are at the foundation of all good art. We have relieved the whole English people from the incubus of the upholsterer. He now exists only in the museums as a warning."

Mr. Wilde looked in at the opera last night to see the diva and the audience, and was in the manager's box for half an hour. He leaves this morning for Louisville, and returns, as before stated, for a matinee on Thursday at the Grand.

1. An allusion to Psalms 2:1: "Why do the heathen rage, and the people imagine a vain thing?"
2. "Resquiescat": an early poem commemorating the death of Wilde's young sister and composed of five heroic couplets broken at the caesura into five quatrains rhyming ABAB.
3. A "Daisy Miller" was a type of young American woman, impulsive and frank, so-called after Henry James's heroine in his 1878 novella.
4. John Hay (1838–1905), an American diplomat and author, was Abraham Lincoln's private secretary during the Civil War. He later wrote poetry, most notably *Pike County Ballads and Other Pieces* (1871), and coauthored the ten-volume *Abraham Lincoln: A History* (1886–90).
5. The reporter quotes Shakespeare's *Julius Caesar,* act 3, scene 2, line 183.
6. Probably the most famous Shelleyan bird is the eponymous one in "To a Sky-lark," though that particular bird never acts in the way that Wilde relates here. If, however, Wilde is instead paraphrasing "Archy's Song" from the fragmentary drama *Charles I,* his criticism of the critic seems imprecise: the failure of this nightingale in relation to the lark and the owl is not in blindly declaring day to be night but rather in making no distinction between "darkness and light."

   > Heigho! The lark and the owl!
   > One flies the morning, and one lulls the night:
   > Only the nightingale, poor fond soul,
   > Sings like the fool through darkness and light. [ll. 1–4]

7. Samuel Taylor Coleridge (1772–1834), British Romantic poet and literary critic.
8. Matthew Arnold (1822–88), a British critic, poet, and inspector of schools, was an important force in shaping contemporary literary critical practice.
9. Pierre Jules Théophile Gautier (1811–72), a French poet, playwright, novelist, journalist, and critic, was an ardent defender of Romanticism and an important figure for modernism. It was not Gautier, however, but Antoine de Rivarol (1753–1801) in *Le Petit Almanach de nos grands-hommes* (1788) who wrote "C'est sans doute un terrible avantage que de n'avoir rien fait, mais il ne faut pas en abuser."

20. "OSCAR WILDE" *CINCINNATI ENQUIRER,*
21 FEBRUARY 1882, 4

Oscar Wilde, the aesthete, arrived in the city yesterday, and took up his quarters in Burnet House, where a representative of the *Enquirer* met him late yesterday afternoon. The original of "Bunthorne" was reclining on a fauteuil when our ambassador entered his apartments. He arose rather more quickly than poetic grace demanded, and with a pleasant smile extended his right hand and gave him a cordial greeting. In person he is very tall, with broad shoulders and a plethora of arms and legs—that is, he has the usual complements of limbs, but they appear longer and more loosely jointed than perfect accord with manly beauty requires. His face is long and narrow, and appears narrower than it really is on account of the length of his hair, which is light brown in color, is parted in the middle, and touches the shoulders like a dark flaxen mane. His eyes are large and light blue in color. Their outside corners are lower than the inside like a Chinaman's, though they are far from being almond-shaped. His nose is long, large, and aquiline, and his mouth betrays his Hibernian origin, his lips being thick and the upper one so shut that his speech partakes somewhat of the character of a lisp. His teeth, especially, the upper ones, are long, large, and irregular. His chin is protuberant, and he has very high cheekbones. His sack coat and natty vest were of cobwebby grey velvet hue, with a cold gravy bloom; his trousers were light in color and loose and limp in make. His shoes were of patent leather, with buff gaiters, and his low-cut Byronic collar was encircled by a silk cravat that was tied in a sailor knot, and was between a Dunducketty grey and a dull pink in color. In the left lapel of his coat was a beautiful rosebud, and he held another in his left hand, whose delicate exhalations he ever and anon inhaled with evident rapture. Within easy reach stood a marble-topped table, on which was a vase containing four splendid calla lilies, whose faint perfume almost drowned the senses with olfactory delight. As soon as the greetings were over, and our guileless youth took the chair which was proffered him by Mr. Wilde, he began operations by remarking: "Mr. Wilde, I presume by this time you are sufficiently acquainted with the customs of this country to know that you are face to face with the ubiquitous interviewer?"

"Oh, yes," smilingly replied the aesthetic apostle, "and I am glad of it, for some of the brightest hours I have passed in this country have been with the gentlemen of the press who have interviewed me, and I have found them among the most intelligent men I have met here."

"Taffy,"[1] mentally ejaculated our reporter, and then said: "How long will you remain in the city?"

"Only until morning. I am on my way to Louisville, where I will lecture tomorrow evening; then I go to Indianapolis, and on Thursday I return to this city and lecture here. Today I drove to the Rookwood pottery, with Mrs. George Ward Nichols,[2] and inspected its work very closely."

"How did you like it?"

"Some of it was very good, and much of it indifferent. On the whole I was very much pleased, as it showed what can be done for art even by one person, as in the case of Mrs. Nichols. There is one young man named Bowen[3] at Rookwood who I am sure has true poetic art and fervor. His productions are wonderful, and he should be encouraged."

"I am going to tell you something that I fear will shock you," said our scribe.

"Shock me?" interrupted Oscar.

"Yes," was the reply. "Several years ago one of our most promising young artists was employed by a number of our merchants to make a series of pictures for the Vienna Exposition.[4] He executed the commission, his pictures attracted great attention, and, I believe, received a medal. What do you think was their theme?"

"Indeed, I can't tell."

"Hog killing!"

"Well, I don't know but even that could be treated in an artistic manner. You see, there is no such thing as a poetic subject no more than that there is a natural school of painting. You hear people speak of the Italian school of painting, when no such thing exists. The Venetian style differs from the Florentine as it differs from that of other Italian cities. Each locality has its own school as distinct and separate as the towns themselves. The so-called Dutch school is remarkable for its warmth of color, and yet its subjects are mostly commonplace. All through Holland you will see pictures mostly of brawls and quarrels in drinking rooms. Yet every once in a while you will see in one of them a gleam of light streaming through a window and tinting the glasses on the table with all the glories of the prism. Another will display a bit of coloring as warm and as sweet as the kiss of love. The men who painted these pictures poetized the subjects until the ordinariness of their character is forgotten. This shows that they were earnest and sincere, and that their heart was in their work. I have little faith in a young man who chooses what are called heroic subjects for his early efforts. It looks as though he was depending on his subject, and not on his own powers, for success. The lowliest subject, treated with loving earnestness and sincerity, will, if the artist is competent, give the best results, just as the plainest words are the most effective in the mouth of an actor."

"I understand that you will give us a new lecture here," inquired our representative. "What will be its subject?"

"Decorative art," was the answer.

"Will it contain any local allusions?"[5]

"Yes, I think it will. I think I will speak of what I have seen at Rookwood. Wherever I go I try to see what there is of decorative art in it, and I speak of what I see in my lectures. I think it will be judicious to do so here."

As Mr. Wilde's taste in decorative art is unquestioned, it will be seen that his lecture bids fair to be very interesting to our citizens. In the evening Mr. Wilde attended the opera concert at Music Hall, and was the central figure in the Director's box. He was dressed in black knee breeches and black silk stockings, white vest and black dress coat, with white tie and gloves. His presence speedily became known to those on the O. P. side, and many were the opera glasses that were leveled at him as he stood up in the box listening to Patti[6] and her supports. During the performance he was taken behind the scenes and introduced to the diva.

1. Around 1878 the term *taffy* entered the American vernacular as a way of referring to a "crude or vulgar compliment or flattery" (*OED*).

2. The Rookwood pottery company (1880–1941) was founded by Maria Longworth Nichols (1849–1932) as a place where women could indulge a then casual interest in ceramics and a hobby in decorating pottery.

3. Arthur Bowen Davies (1862–1928), an American symbolist painter, printmaker, and tapestry designer, was president of the American Organization of Painters and Sculptors and a principal organizer of the 1913 Armory Show in New York City, which introduced modernism to the American public.

4. Although the Vienna World Exposition of 1873 housed its key themes in the main exposition halls, there were already signs of the trend toward national exhibition concepts that would dominate later expositions. Here the local cast of the interviewer's anecdote corroborates this trend toward local, though not necessarily objective, self-representation.

5. For this nearly four-page addition to the Cincinnati lecture, see Kevin H. F. O'Brien, "An Edition of Oscar Wilde's American Lectures," Ph.D. diss., University of Notre Dame, 1973, appendix B. O'Brien's dissertation contains the most authoritative reconstructions of Wilde's lectures.

6. Adelina Maria Patti (1843–1919), a highly regarded international opera soprano, was also famous for her charm, tempestuous love life, and fiery temperament.

21. "UTTERLY UTTER," *ST. LOUIS POST-DISPATCH*, 25 FEBRUARY 1882, 4

An unusual bustle was visible about the corridors of the Southern this morning, which puzzled the guests as they entered. Knots of young men generally known in society stood around the pillars in attempted attitudes and seemed to be waiting intently. The clerks were more chipper than usual, and appeared to be expecting something. Many of the ladies who were down town shopping extended their promenade to Walnut Street, a thing very unusual, as they passed the hotel, craned their pretty necks in an attempt to gaze inside. Each carriage that stopped was watched curiously, and the appearances all indicated that something was going to happen. Every time a tall, slender young man with hair longer than usual advanced towards the register, the aforesaid young men would form ranks and follow him. As he registered "Fritz Hoffszieuttle, Omaha," or something equally astounding, the followers would turn, somebody would say, "Pshaw, that's not he," and back they went to the waiting place. The cause of the commotion was the coming of Oscar Wilde. He was expected on the morning train and the loiterers were on hand to see what he looked like. At 10 o'clock he had not come, and the watch was nearly given up. A half hour later Oscar alighted from a hack at the ladies' entrance, accompanied by his agent, stepped into the elevator and went to his room. He was clad in a large, heavy all-fur overcoat, with a slouched hat, such as Texans affect. His arrival soon became noised about, and the great questions as what did he look like. A *Post-Dispatch* reporter sent his card to parlor 70, where the aesthetic apostle had been domiciled, and was immediately invited to walk up. The tap at the door was answered by a musical "Come in," and the entrance was followed by disappointment. Anybody who imagines Wilde to be long, lank and angular is badly deceived. At the side of the room a sofa was placed, over one corner of which had been thrown a large and heavy drapery of old gold with tassels. The back was covered with a robe of long fur which hung down from the seat to the floor. Carelessly seated in the middle of the robe, and leaning back in a graceful pose, sat Oscar, with a tiny cigarette between his fingers.

As he rose to greet the visitor he looked as unlike the usual description of him as could well be imagined. He is a stout, rather heavily built young man, possibly 5 feet, 10 inches, in height. His hair, which is of dark brown, is his distinguishing feature. It reaches to his shoulders, is thick and heavy, not parted at all, but combed straight back in front, and he has a feminine way of tossing back stray locks which occasionally attempt to hang over the sides of his face. He wore a sack coat and high-buttoned vest of gray velvet, trimmed with wide braid of a like shade. His pantaloons were of a rough gray material, cut loose, and he wore shoes of patent leather and yellow morocco. His smooth face is large and pronounced and suggests at once the features of Henry Ward Beecher.[1] The eyes are big, brown and almond shaped, the nose slightly aquiline, the lips rather thick, and the chin pronounced and heavy. Oscar's worst features are his teeth, the under ones being large, projecting and uneven.[2] He wore a dark pea-green scarf, under a turn-down collar, which concealed the shirt front. A handkerchief of the same shade appeared from his side pocket. He wore no jewelry save a large seal ring on his left hand, a pair of wide flapped cuffs at his wrist being fastened with plain pearl buttons. He looks like a stout, well-fed, active young Englishman, and his long hair gives him a poetical aspect. The reporter gazed anxiously over the room, but Wilde understood the glances and with a smile seemed to say: "No there are no sunflowers and lilies, no flowers of any kind. I suppose you thought I could not travel without them. Well, I can. You see, I did."

"You must be fatigued after your journey?" ventured the reporter, not knowing how to begin an aesthetic interview, and, therefore, dropping to everyday subjects.

"Oh, no," said Wilde with a smile, in which the English accent was very noticeable. "I do not think I would have been able to endure it, however, but for one of your delightful novelists, W. D. Howells.[3] I have read all his books since I came here, and he is a most charming writer." A pause occurred here while Oscar hunted under his yellow dogskin gloves on the table. A little box was found, out of which a small cigarette was fished out and lit, and the aesthete was himself again.

"I was much disappointed in this way," continued he. "We in England have no idea of the distances in your country. The impression seems to be that all of the large cities are located in the suburbs of New York, then come the Rocky Mountains, next the Indians, then San Francisco and the ocean. We do not half understand that large cities like Chicago and Cincinnati are located in the heart of the country."

"How are you pleased with your visit so far?"

"Oh, your country is so large. It is a world. But it looks so barren and rugged in wintertime. To one accustomed to a little place like England, which has been tilled for centuries, this change is remarkable."

"What do you think of your treatment by the newspapers?"

"I do not mind that," said Wilde, with a smile. "It does not cause me any annoyance."

"Do you read what is said about you?"

"Oh, yes, every line. When I come in at night, tired and weary, the reading of a good vigorous attack acts like a dish of caviar. Of course, some of it is not what I have been used to, as the English papers still have a sort of old-fashioned regard for truth. They are not so much given to imagination as the journals here. Then the attacks come from such curious sources. I remember I was dressing at Washington for a dinner party when a card was brought to me. The name was a curious one, and the card detailed for how many western papers the owner was correspondent. I think there were eleven in all. I was slightly flurried, you may suppose. I said, 'Now here is the man who moulds the thoughts of the West; I must be in my best behavior.' I requested the gentleman to come up, when in walked a boy, positively not more than sixteen. 'Is this your card?' I asked. 'Oh, yes,' said he. The scene was too ridiculous.

"'Have you been to school much?' I asked.

"The juvenile interviewer said he had.

"'Have you learned French?'

"No, he had not. I told him that if he wished to be a journalist he ought to study French, gave him a big orange and dismissed him. What he did with the orange afterwards I don't know, but he seemed very much pleased to get it. Now I have had this experience several times. Boys have been my critics. What do I care about the expressions of a man who does not know anything in regard to my writings? It does not affect me any more than if the writers should say I had written a good sonnet or a bad sonnet. He does not know and I do not care."

"But there have been more bitter attacks?"

"Oh, yes. Before I came to Baltimore the *American* there published a most uncalled for attack upon me. It stated that I had accepted an invitation to attend a club reception there and at the last moment had sent word that my terms were $500 for such services, that the club had very properly declined the offer, and that I would therefore not be present. I had never heard of the club at that time, had never received any invitation, and the fact is that when I came to Baltimore they tendered me a reception. But the story was printed and was believed. There is no use denying such things, and I did not do so. When I went to Baltimore, however, I found out the man who wrote the article and sent for him. He came. He was a young man about my own age. I simply asked him what he was paid for writing the article. He said, 'Six dollars.' 'Well,' said I, 'the rate for lying is not very high in America. That is all I wanted to ascertain. Good day.'"

"It must have annoyed you considerably?"

"No. I mind nothing about their attacks but the effect they have on the public. I am not injured at all, but the public is deceived. After all, there is so much to do in life that there is not time to be troubled about such matters. Our duty is to admire and worship the beautiful and the good. Everything else, including the annoyances, is mere failures, simply shadows."

"What are your impressions of the people as you have met them?"

"Ah, there is a wide difference between your papers and your men and women. From the latter I have always met with the kindest treatment. You have a great country, and the things that are said about me I am willing to bear. Of course the treatment is not fair. Some of our best lecturers would not come here, Ruskin, for instance, on account of the newspapers. When I declared I was coming they all wondered. 'Why,' said Mr. Ruskin, 'everything will be said about you. They will spare nothing.' But I said I would come, and I came. The feeling there is almost fear of your papers, but I do not mind it. The ludicrous things are said in good part, and as for the rest I let it pass me by."

1. Henry Ward Beecher (1813–87), a clergyman, liberal social reformer, and advocate of woman suffrage, abolition, temperance, and the theory of evolution, was after 1875 a controversial figure as a result of his alleged affair with a married woman, Elizabeth Tilton.

2. In Richard Ellmann's estimation, Wilde contracted syphilis while at Oxford and underwent a course of mercury treatment. Although mercury does not cure venereal disease, it did have the effect of discoloring Wilde's already uneven, prominent, and slightly protrusive teeth (*Wilde*, 92).

3. W. D. Howells (1837–1920), American realist author, critic, and first president of the American Academy of Arts and Letters.

---

22. "SPERANZA'S GIFTED SON," *ST. LOUIS GLOBE-DEMOCRAT*, 26 FEBRUARY 1882, 3

A *Globe-Democrat* reporter awaited an hour when the Prince of Languor had presumably suspended the delights of deglutition, and then sent up a lily-white card, decorated with the legend by which he is known to his creditors. "He will see you in ten minutes," said "Front" on his return.

Mr. Wilde evidently desired time in which to run through the authorities on aesthetics in order to meet the reporter on equal terms. It must be remembered that he had entered the city at the Union Depot, had obtained a rear view of the Jail and the Four Courts, and had been whirled through the delightful boulevards known as Clark Avenue and Myrtle Street, and, having seen so much of the utterly utter in that brief ride, he was prepared to find in a St. Louisan a poet, and in one who assists to mold the opinions of St. Louisans he naturally anticipated a poem. When at last the reportorial aesthete entered the apartment where the lord of the lah-de-dah sat enthroned upon a sofa, over which had been carelessly thrown a dressed bearskin rug, it was to meet a boyish-faced young man, long-haired, smooth-faced, long nosed, thick lipped, uncertain-mouthed, of the general appearance of an overtasked medical student. His hair brushed back from his forehead and hanging about his shoulders gave him the romantic appearance of the tenor-lover in an opera, as he rose from the couch on which he half reclined in an attitude that somehow suggested the backline of a ballet, for studied as it palpably was, graceful it positively was not. He extended in a very languid manner a large, soft, rather fat hand, which half closed upon the aristocratic duke of the inquisitor, then relaxed, and fell slowly to position, where it dangled at the end of an angular arm. As if exhausted by the effort, he sank back on to the sofa, and assumed another position suggestive of cramp colic. Our Berry[1] could have done this much better. In a few moments he summoned strength enough to light a cigarette, which he puffed contentedly for a while, and seemed to await the first twitch of the reportorial rack. He said nothing, and the reporter hesitated to begin, for it is not often that a genuine worshipper of the sunflower happens along. Oscar sat, continuing to look intently at the reporter in the dim light. Oscar always affects Rembrandt shadows; he looks better in the dark, perhaps. The reporter, feeling that he was the object of the poet's attention and evidently filled his thoughts, at length ventured: "Talking about the beautiful, what do you think of St. Louis?"

"I have seen so little of your city, of which I have heard so much. Tell me, have you old families here? Old French families, that speak the delightful tongue, as handed down to them from generation to generation? I have heard that your city is so blessed. Am I wrong?"

"Not exactly. There are some old families here. Came here many years ago. Set up as cobblers, tailors, etc., and took land in payment for their work. Couldn't sell the land; left it to their children. The 'boom' set in, prices went up, they held on to their property and left it to their children. Prices still booming, they in turn left it to their children. Prices are still booming, and the children have still got the property. Some of them talk French a little. Most of them talk German. It is very useful in trade."

"But your city has schools of design and art academies?"

"That is where you are wrong. There are no schools of design or art academies."

"Have you no art, then?"

"Yes, some. Mr. Dousman,[2] a rich man, buys a great many pictures; and then there is the Sketch Club,[3] and every year we have a picture show in connection with the Cattle Fair, and there is the *Hornet,* an illustrated paper."[4]

"The Sketch Club; that must be artistic."

"It is; it is aesthetic."

"Pray tell me all about it."

"The Sketch Club is an organization of all our leading artists."

"Good."

"And once a month they meet and each artist brings a sketch, illustrating some subject selected at the previous meeting by one of their number."

"How truly Bohemian!"

"Yes, the man who picks out the subject sets up a lunch of beer and sandwiches, and things like that, and he gets all the pictures to keep for his own."

Oscar looked disappointed and braced up on another cigarette. Then he said, "But you have certainly some art institutions?"

"Yes, there is one art institution. It is called the Crow Art Museum,[5] and was built by a very wealthy gentleman who had a son that longed to be an artist. The father disapproved of the son's ambition, and discouraged it. The son died, they say partially of grief because he could not become a great artist, and the repentant father, recognizing the error of his judgment when too late, built this beautiful museum as a monument to his memory."

"How utterly pathetic, poor boy. I must visit that place this afternoon.

"St. Louis cannot be utterly without a love for the beautiful?"

"It is not, for you will find in St. Louis more beautiful homes than in any other large city. The artistic taste crops out also in the architecture of public buildings. The City Hall, the Grand Tower block, at Fourth and Market, the Lucas Market buildings, and the church at the corner of Eighth and Washington Avenue, are specimens that you should view before you leave the city."

"I shall endeavor to do so; but I have so many engagements. I shall at least view the church you speak of."

"Do; and you will never forget it. You have not seen our streets at their best."

"There are no avenues like the boulevards of Paris."

"You will certainly agree with most travelers that there are no such streets as our own in the known world. If fortunately it should rain tonight, you will see them as we know them best tomorrow."

"I shall await the morrow with supreme interest."

"I had forgotten to ask you—how do you like our country?"

"I am lost in wonder and amazement. It is not a country but a world. Englishmen know little of its extent, and but half believe when told of the existence of such cities as St. Louis, Chicago, and Cincinnati thousands of miles from the seaboard. I confess that I myself was greatly deceived in your magnificent distances. Looking at the map while at home, I planned for myself a trip through Colorado, California, Mexico, the southern states and

Canada. I now realize how foolish were such dreams. I shall barely have time to fulfill my engagements and return to Paris, where I expect to be by May 1. The West I like best. The people are stronger, fresher, saner than the rest. They are ready to be taught. The surroundings of nature have instilled in them a love of the beautiful, which but needs development and direction. The East I found a feeble reflex of Europe; in fact, I may say that I was in America for a month before I saw an American. My audiences in New York and Boston were cold, critical; in Chicago and Cincinnati they were so warm, cheerful, and enthusiastic. I shall return to both of those cities, and lecture, before I go East. On Monday I go to Springfield.[6] Is that near the center of the state?"

"Yes, most of our capital cities are. The hardy pioneers located them in the days when the members of the legislature traveled by horseback and canoe, and the geographical center was chosen instead of the center of wealth, population, or art. You would find a visit to the capital of this state of interest. It is most picturesquely located on bluffs, and would be considered a poem were it not for the boarding houses and the penitentiary."

"Penitentiaries are not artistic."

"How do you stand travel by rail?"

"The long trips are more than wearisome, and I hardly think that I would be able to survive them were it not for the charming companionship of Howells's novels. He is America's greatest author."

"You have visited Mr. Tennyson?"

"Grand old man. I spent a delightful afternoon with him. He is not only a poet, but a poem. And there is your Walt Whitman, dear old fellow, a poet that indeed writes poetry. America, match him if you can."

"Have you found time to read the newspapers?"

"I read all that is written about me."

"Do you like it all?"

"I expected ill-treatment at the hands of the American press. I was warned of it by my friends before I left for America. It is the certainty of this unfair treatment that keeps our great men at home."

"Dickens, Hughes,[7] Forbes,[8] and others were received with open arms, and treated with distinguished consideration on the occasion of their visit here, and lectured to large and delighted audiences until the press everywhere gave vent to nothing but encomiums."

Without noticing the interruption, Oscar continued: "At first I was greatly annoyed, and with difficulty restrained my feelings, but latterly I have schooled myself not to notice them. When made the object of absolute falsehood, as in the case of the Baltimore paper, which stated that I had refused to attend the reception of a social club in that city unless I was paid $500, I endeavor to set myself right, as I did in that instance. My critics have for the most part been mere boys, who knew nothing of the subjects which I treat, and why should I annoy myself by paying attention to their utterances? I must say that my experiences with the press in the West have been very pleasant, and I have met gentlemen whose intelligent conversation I have enjoyed. They have talked with me of art and literature, and understood the subjects. Such persons I like to meet."

Returning thanks upon behalf of the western press, the *Globe-Democrat* reporter ventured a little way into the field of literature. Mr. Wilde is under the impression that England has no great storywriter today. B. L. Farjeon[9] may be looked upon as the successor of Dickens in the field of Christmas stories. William Black[10] is a delightful novelist. He deals with the beauties of nature and is a true poet. Walter Besant[11] and James Rice[12] he considers great writers. The purely English performance of writing a novel to accomplish a reform, while ably carried out by Charles Reade[13] and Wilkie Collins, savors of the mechanical and is perforce not beautiful. Justin McCarthy is a writer of brilliancy, and in the *History of Our Times* has given a most enchanting resume of the dry and repellent mass of information found in the files of the London *Times,* and McCarthy has a son of great promise who may excel his father in brilliancy.[14]

"What has he done?" asked the reporter.

"He has written a volume of poems and several very clever sketches," replied Oscar, with a smile. He resumed his essay on literature, and had just remarked that the greatest writer since Shakespeare was Balzac, when a card was brought in. Oscar twirled the pasteboard in his fingers for a minute, arose and held out his hand for a farewell shake, remarking, "Another gentleman desires to see me now," and the *Globe-Democrat* reporter left, as another newspaper reporter entered the room to subject the by-this-time justly languid aesthete to what an Arkansas aesthete would call "a course of sprouts." Oscar wore a look of calm resignation when last seen.

1. This is perhaps Thomas B. MacDonough (b. 1835), an actor, theater manager, and stage manager who performed under the stage name T. B. Berry.
2. Hercules Louis Dousman II (1848–86), the son of a Wisconsin millionaire, became a prominent midwestern socialite and nationally known art collector.
3. In 1886 members of the St. Louis Sketch Club formed the more professional and ambitious St. Louis Artists' Guild.
4. An illustrated paper printed in St. Louis from 1880 to 1882.
5. Wayman Crow (1808–85), a cofounder of Washington University, donated a new museum to the university after his son's death in 1878. The St. Louis Museum of Fine Arts was dedicated in May 1881, and with the new building the university agreed to create its independent school of fine arts.

6. Springfield, Illinois, not Missouri.

7. Thomas Hughes (1822–96), author of *Tom Brown's School Days* (1857) and founder of a utopian community in Tennessee in 1880.

8. See interview 8n1.

9. Benjamin Leopold Farjeon (1838–1903), English playwright, printer, journalist, and author.

10. William Black (1841–98) was a Scottish novelist educated with a view toward becoming a landscape painter.

11. Walter Besant (1836–1901) was an English novelist, critic, and historian.

12. James Rice (1843–82) was an English writer best known for his collaboration with Walter Besant.

13. Charles Reade (1814–84) was a popular English novelist. Wilkie Collins (1824–89), another English novelist, is best known for the sensation novel *The Woman in White* (1860).

14. Justin McCarthy (1830–1912), an Irish writer, journalist, and politician, finally achieved the large sales he had long craved with the publication of *History of Our Times* (1877). The son to whom Wilde refers is Justin Huntley McCarthy (1859–1936), a writer and politician, who wrote biographies of Sir Robert Peel, Pope Leo XIII, and Prime Minister William Gladstone and also finished his father's *History of the Four Georges*.

---

23. "OSCAR AS HE IS," *ST. LOUIS REPUBLICAN,* 26 FEBRUARY 1882, 13

The pen pictures which have been drawn of Oscar Wilde universally by American newspapers are like the reflection of the convex mirror, faithful and yet distorted. No one seeing the true Oscar Wilde could fail to recognize him from them, and no one of any perception could fail to recognize just as clearly that the man is not what has been described. The pictures have at once been true and untrue, with the untruth predominating. A *Republican* reporter who called on him at the Southern yesterday afternoon and was shown up to his room was forcibly impressed with this.

Mr. Wilde met him at the door with a pleasant "good afternoon" and an invitation to be seated, speaking with the broad English accent which still obtains in portions of America, especially in Virginia, an accent which is rhythmic always, and which appeared to be perfectly natural with him. His appearance was much as it has been described so repeatedly in the different newspapers of the country, barring the exaggerations. His dress, which would have seemed *outre* enough on the stage, did not seem out of place as a chamber *negligee*. He wore a short drab jacket, hanging open and showing a waistcoat of the same material, loose pantaloons, and a collar turned negligently over a neckcloth tied in the loose sailor fashion, and there was something suggestive of the sea in his whole "makeup." The writer, who went altogether undecided as to the light in which the apostle was to be considered, found, after only a few words had been spoken, that there was a serious side to him which was altogether undeveloped for newspaper purposes, and which could be utilized to advantage. Perhaps no one has seen a man who has not been disappointed in some way. The disappointment here was that he was not the grotesque being that has been described, but a thoroughly well bred and well educated young gentleman, with a large share of good humor; disposed apparently to carry out the maxim from his own beloved Greek of "especially thinking well of himself above all things"; apparently too with much theoretical and little practical knowledge of men. This was the impression, but in his conversation there were keen flashes of wit which made it doubtful after all if he were not more a man of the world than he seemed.

Taking a seat and motioning the reporter to another, he lighted a cigarette and waited to be questioned, while his servant, who evidently from frequent experience knew that his master required something to sustain him through the ordeal, placed a small glass of what appeared to be sherry punch, very weak, on the table before him. Leaning his head against the easy chair, with his long hair flowing over his shoulders, Oscar waited with an air which was at once resigned and quizzical, but without a suspicion of embarrassment.

"Shall I put the question which was put to your countryman, Mr. Chuzzlewit, and ask you 'What do you think of our kentry, sir?'"[1] asked the reporter.

"You may if you like," was the reply, "although I might find some difficulty in answering it. It has changed greatly since Dickens's visit, no doubt. Every city in America is different from every other city—quite different. The West interests me more than the East, because the people of the West have created a civilization by themselves and for themselves. The East is a duplex of Europe, and therefore Chicago was more interesting to me than Boston, even though there I met Oliver Wendell Holmes, with whom I dined, and Longfellow, with whom I spent the afternoon. Eastern cities are imitations; Chicago is entirely American."

"I have read an account of your meeting with Joaquin Miller,"[2] said the reporter.

"That was true—one of the few true things that have been written about me. Yes, Joaquin is a very fine fellow, full of color; one of the great American poets, who is really from and of the New World. There is in his writing a resonance and an odor of not seen flowers; a wrath of the sea; he is quite swift and strong like the sea, full of new imagery."

"And Whitman?"

"By the way, what do you think of Whitman yourself?" was the parry which met the thrust.

"There are lines in his 'Blades of Grass'[3] which, insane as he is generally counted, remind one of Homer. But my opinion is valueless, and my question unanswered."

He smiled as he took a fresh cigarette from a box on the table and lighted it with the air of one who was weighing his words before answering. When he did answer he said:

"Whitman is a great writer. You are right, it seems to me. There is more of the Greek residing in him than in any modern poet. His poetry is Homeric in its large pure delight of men and woman, and in the joy the writer has and shows through it all in the sunshine and breeze of outdoor life."

"And since we speak of living poets, what of your own Swinburne?"

"We look on Swinburne as one of the great poets of the day in England. In America, you seem to judge him entirely by his first volume, *Laus Veneris,* which had in it many of the extravagances natural and proper enough, too, in the first attempt of genius. You judge him solely by this and not by his later writing, such as the *Songs of Democracy* and *Songs before Sunrise.*[4] Swinburne, Shelley, and Milton are the three greatest poets of liberty in England, and Swinburne is the greatest master of the English language living, wonderful in his power of expression and his controls of words. Language to him is what the beautiful musical instrument is to the musician—the violin from which he draws what tunes he wishes. No one in our times has written poems more full of the fervor for liberty and the strength of democracy, and no one singer has sung such delicate and dainty little songs. Where else can you find the refinement of feeling that there is in his poem:

> If you were what the rose is
> And I were like the leaf?[5]

Where such poems as his 'Garden of Proserpine' and his 'Hymn to Proserpine'?"

"You have been accused of imitating him," suggested the reporter. "Do you think it worth your while to make a defense?"

"That accusation of imitating someone has been brought against every English poet, and besides people forget that the first thing a young artist in painting or poetry should do is to study the great master. The only way to really original work is to acquire a knowledge of the style of all great teachers and to use that knowledge to produce an entirely new effect. No man in our age has studied Milton and Shakespeare so deeply as Swinburne, and yet from that study of Shakespeare and Milton he has produced a work entirely different from theirs. Take for instance the poems which appear in the periodicals through the country. Many of them show that the writers possessed feelings which, for lack of this study, they could not express. Hence their poetry is bad, although the idea is back of it. We of the younger school in England love Swinburne better than we love Tennyson, and consider him a much greater master. There is a breath, a depth to him which there never was to Tennyson."

"You have been questioned so much concerning your school that I had not intended referring to it, but since you yourself have spoken of it, tell me if you think that your designs are practicable?"

"Do you think that we, the young men of England, would give our youth, our energy and whatever of intellect we may possess to their fulfillment if we had the remotest intention of failing? If it were an experiment we should achieve success, but with us it is a matter of actual accomplishment. We have already changed the whole condition of English decorative art. Every handicraftsman in England is now working with the noblest designs and models before him, and as for the opposition that people sometimes make, particularly in America, you must remember that only one thing is opposed to beauty, and that is ugliness. Everything is always beautiful or ugly, and utility always goes with the beautiful—never with the ugly. Anything that is ugly is merely what a bad workman makes. The only way to get good work then in any trade is by means of good designs. If you have bad designs no good workman will work for you."

"Did you meet Emerson while in the East?"

"I did not have the opportunity to call on him, I am sorry to say, and I understand that he confines himself closely at home. It would give me much pleasure to meet him on my return. He is one of the most brilliant men of the nineteenth century—the only man of letters in America who has influenced the course of English thought."

"The American press has not given you fair treatment, Mr. Wilde," said the reporter, changing the subject suddenly.

"I think," he replied, "that the ordinary critic belongs to the criminal classes, and that in many cases the newspapers of America would employ people to write on art whom in England we would not consider qualified to report any case of petty larceny above the value of five shillings. I think that if American journalism continues to supply nothing to the public but slander that is shameful and jokes that are bad, they will cease to have the slightest influence and will merely increase the already too large number of comic papers which are not amusing."

"In New York," he continued, in answer to another question, "they wrote entirely fictitious interviews with me after having called on me. I think that they might at least have spared me the trouble of talking to them. In Chicago they put down what I said more exactly. We have no interviewing in England, but it is not so objectionable after if it is genuine."

"Does it not then strike you as objectionable that the details of a man's private life should be dragged before the public even in such small matters as his eating onions for breakfast?"

"The best answer that I can give to that question is perhaps the one I gave to a reporter in Washington who called on me and asked me to give him some details of my private life. I told him I wished I had one."

The conversation ended here, being interrupted by the entrance of his manager. Mr. Wilde stated before the reporter took his leave that he would lecture in Springfield Monday, and that he expected to be in Paris in May. It will doubtless be observed that in the interview, which is as near verbatim as it is possible for an interview to be given, the use of "aesthetic" terms which characterized the first part of it gradually disappeared as the speaker grew earnest, as when referring to Swinburne. The writer was forcibly impressed with it, and when he did leave the room he left it with a feeling that there was something under the sunflower and lily strangely akin to that practical system of metaphysics so unaesthetically styled "horse sense." And perhaps the young gentleman with the Sapphic speech[6] and the mane of Absalom[7] will not be so much ashamed of it when he has grown older and abandoned the lecture platform.

1. *Martin Chuzzlewit* (1843–44), the last of Dickens's picaresque novels, was set partly in America.
2. Joaquin Miller was the pen name of the American poet, essayist, and fabulist Cincinnatus Heine (or Hiner) Miller (1837?–1913). Miller hosted Wilde at dinner in New York on 4 February, a meeting that was widely publicized, as in "A Pair of Long-Haired Poets," *Boston Budget,* 5 February 1882, 1.
3. "Blades of Grass": this misconstrual of *Leaves of Grass* is the interviewer's error, and it betrays his ignorance of Whitman, which the subsequent deflection of the question suggests Wilde suspected.
4. Algernon Charles Swinburne included his long early poem "Laus Veneris" in *Poems and Ballads* (1866). This piece was challenged by critics for its eroticism, though *Atalanta in Calydon* (1865) had been received with enthusiasm. Wilde's point seems to be that he finds fewer instances of youthful extravagance and a greater commitment to politics in *Songs before Sunrise* (1871). Swinburne never published a volume entitled *Songs of Democracy,* but the third section of "Christmas Antiphones," "Beyond Church," is in Swinburne's terms "a foresong of democracy and humanity."

5. Wilde quotes lines from the first stanza of Swinburne's poem "A Match."
6. Sappho was a classical Greek lyric poet from the isle of Lesbos whose surviving
    fragments were much admired by Victorian and modernist poets.
7. In 2 Samuel 18:9 Absalom's long hair is caught in "the thick boughs of a great
    oak" when he rides under it.

---

24. "OSCAR WILDE," *CHICAGO TRIBUNE,*
1 MARCH 1882, 7

Mr. Oscar Wilde, the celebrated aesthete, arrived in the city yesterday morning from Springfield, Ill., where he lectured Monday evening. He registered
at the Grand Pacific Hotel, and was assigned to Parlor 11. About 2 o'clock
yesterday afternoon a *Tribune* representative called at the hotel to see the
apostle of the beautiful and to obtain his impressions of the Great West. The
reportorial card was returned by a bellboy, who also brought the information
that Mr. Wilde was asleep and could not be disturbed. A journey to his parlor
was then made, but a stalwart African stood guard at the door and would
allow no one to pass him. With the assurance that Mr. Wilde would arise in
an hour or so, the reporter repaired to the rotunda and waited.

About 3 o'clock a second tour was made to the regions above, and it was
discovered that the colored gentleman had abandoned his post. A rap at the
door brought forth a timid "Come in," and the reporter cautiously turned
the knob and entered. No one was visible, but the effeminate voice of the
aesthete, proceeding from behind a pair of lace bed-curtains, asked what he
wanted.

"The *Tribune* would like to see you, Mr. Wilde," said the reporter.

"Well, you can't see me now," he answered. "I am very tired after a long
journey, having come clear from Springfield, Ill., and I want to take a nap.
I'll see you in about an hour."

The colored gentleman entered at this point, and the reporter withdrew
while Mr. Wilde was giving his servant an angry talking-to for having de-
serted his post.

At 4 o'clock the newspaperman approached Parlor 11 a third time, and the
"Come in," in answer to his rap, was delivered in a firmer tone of voice. On
entering the room, Mr. Wilde was discovered sitting in a tastefully draped
chair near one of the windows. He wore a black velvet jacket, a pair of brown
breeches, a brick-red necktie and handkerchief, low shoes, and maroon socks.
His long hair fell gracefully over his shoulders, and his taper fingers toyed

delicately with a cigarette. He gave the reporter a cordial handshake and bade him be seated.

"When did you arrive in Chicago, Mr. Wilde?" asked the reporter.

"I reached here this morning from Springfield, Ill., where I lectured last evening."

"What cities have you visited since you left here?"

"I have lectured in Cincinnati, St. Louis, Detroit, Cleveland, Indianapolis, Fort Wayne, Springfield, and other places."

"Which one of the western cities are you most favorably impressed with?"

"In Cincinnati I was particularly pleased, not merely at the great love of art shown there, but the people are doing a great deal of beautiful work. Of course, old schools of art disagree when adopted by a young people, but experience will correct many faults. Still, a great deal of their work is very good, and they are going to work in the right way."

"How do you think the West compares with the East?" asked the reporter.

"The West interests us in England more than the East. You are making civilization by yourselves and for yourselves. So much in the East is a mere reflection of European thought, and so much of that a mere misunderstanding of it."

"What do you think of St. Louis?"

"I think that St. Louis has the best arranged museum of art I have seen yet. It does not contain very much, but all it does contain is excellently and brilliantly chosen. That is the first qualification of a good museum. Nothing in it could possibly lead a young student astray. Out of everything in it, oil paintings or plaster casts or etching, there is nothing but good to be got."

"But I think," continued Mr. Wilde, "that in America you are a little too exclusive in art matters—in fact, a great deal too exclusive. In your admiration for the modern French school, examples of English art seen in America all belong to the most dreadful period of English painting—the period of Benjamin West[1] and Haydon.[2] The wonderful modern school of English painting has no example here. I have not, for instance, seen in any of your public museums or private galleries any of John Millais's works. He is one of the greatest painters that England has ever produced and will be remembered along with Gainsborough[3] and Sir Joshua Reynolds[4] as one of the greatest portrait painters, and no man in my time in England, or indeed in the whole history of English painting, has done such a splendid amount of artistic work in styles so entirely different."

Here Mr. Wilde paused, drained a glass of lemonade, lit a fresh cigarette, and, having gained his second wind, continued:

"Millais, when a young man, belonged to the Pre-Raphaelite Brotherhood and was their greatest painter. His early pictures were full of the most beautiful imagination and most wonderful technical power, and his picture of 'Christ in the Carpenter Shop' is the only beautiful religious picture, with the exception of Rossetti's 'Annunciation,' that I have ever seen. From the pastoral sentiment of his pictures, when he chose his subjects from Florentine lyrics and sacred story, he passed with increased realism of technical power to motives drawn from the life of his own day. 'The Highland woman delivering the order of release to the jailer for her imprisoned husband' and 'the girl bidding good-bye to her lover going to the war' are great instances of how much splendid imaginative work may be got out of modern life. He then passed to landscapes, in which he is a really great master. His picture of 'Chill October' is one of the most pathetic and beautiful landscapes I have ever seen. And, lastly, his fame rests on his powers as a portrait-painter, in which he will rank, as I said, with Gainsborough and Sir Joshua Reynolds. No one has painted children with such delicacy and love of the beauty of childhood and perfection of treatment as he has since Sir Joshua Reynolds painted 'Penelope Boothby,' and no one has painted great men with such dignity and strength as he has. His portrait of Mr. Gladstone is one of the greatest pictures of the century, and he was painting one of Lord Beaconsfield at the time when that wonderful genius died.[5] Any modern gallery is quite incomplete without a specimen of his work."

"You call Millais your greatest painter, Mr. Wilde," said the reporter. "Who do you consider your greatest actor?"

"I call Henry Irving[6] our greatest tragedian, as he stands at the head of our Shakespearean actors. He has a curious and remarkable personality, with intensity and realism in his acting which was for us, in England, an entirely new departure from the more formal, declamatory style of Macready.[7] He is, in the matter of scenery and costume, as great as Charles Kean."[8]

"Is he thinking of visiting America?"

"I believe he is. If he comes here he will bring with him our most beautiful and fascinating actress—Miss Ellen Terry."[9]

"Mrs. Langtry is expected to visit this country soon. Is she as beautiful, do you think, as she is said to be?"

"She is one of the most beautiful women in the world," said Mr. Wilde, enthusiastically. "She is possessed of a figure molded like that of a Greek statue and is of a perfect artistic height. She has a beautiful stage voice, is joyous of manner, which is the element of all good comedy acting, and when she has studied her art more she will be able to act Shakespeare's Rosalind in a way in which most of us have never seen the part acted. There is not the slightest doubt of her dramatic genius. I truly believe that she is the most remarkable woman of this day in England."

"Have you seen any of our great actors?" asked the reporter.

"Oh, yes; I have seen those of your actors who have visited England, and others I have seen since my arrival here. I think Joseph Jefferson is one of the greatest actors I ever saw. I saw him play Rip Van Winkle in London and was greatly impressed by his acting."[10]

"Have you seen Edwin Booth?"

"I have, and I think him one of the greatest artists I ever saw. I saw him in all of his great parts in England, and I think he speaks English much better than almost any of our own actors. His perfect enunciation, his perfect delivery of blank verse, his knowledge of emphasis, and his consciousness that when one is speaking Shakespeare he is speaking music, was a source of the greatest delight to all of us in England. His King Lear I consider to rank along with Salvini's Othello[11] and Henry Irving's Shylock as the greatest thing in acting I have ever seen."

"What do you think of John McCullough?"

"I saw him the other night as Spartacus,[12] and I think he is very strong, exceedingly powerful, and a master of stage effect."

"Who of our actresses have you seen?"

"Clara Morris interested me enormously. Sarah Bernhardt told me there were two things in America worth seeing—one was Clara Morris's acting, and the other was some dreadful method of killing pigs in Chicago. She advised me to go and see both. I went to see Miss Morris immediately upon my arrival in New York City, but the other I have deferred quite indefinitely."

"You have what is called a Censor of Plays, I believe, in England?"

"Yes, we have. The Lord Chamberlain has control of that department, and the Censor of Plays reads all new works before they are produced. His decision is final. He has recently decided that the whole moral system of the British nation would be undermined if the French Palais Royal company acted 'Divorçons,' which he considers an immoral play. If we had a censor to prevent bad acting we all would support the office with every means in our power; but unfortunately there is no law to prevent men or woman from murdering great parts."

"Do you lecture in Chicago again, Mr. Wilde?" asked the reporter.

"Yes. I shall lecture at Central Music Hall Saturday evening, March 11, on the subject of 'The Decoration of Houses.'"[13]

"What are your ideas on that subject?"

"Well, it wouldn't be fair to tell you before I delivered my lecture. The subject covers an immense amount of ground, and I shall begin with the door-knocker and go to the attic. Beyond that is Heaven, and I shall leave that to the Church."

"Will you remain in Chicago long?"

"No, sir. I lecture every night now until I reappear here."

"How do you fancy making these one-night stands?"

"Oh, I don't mind it much. In fact I rather like traveling in this country."

"Have you seen any of our prairies in your travels?"

"What are they?"

"Why, vast stretches of rolling lands as far as the eye can see."

"No, I don't think I have seen anything like that. I have done most of my traveling in the night."

"How did the Mississippi River strike you?"

"Well, I think no well-behaved river would overflow as it has done, though I am quite ready to admit its beauty. I noticed a want of pure water in each city along its banks, caused evidently by the overflow. The streets are also in a dreadful condition in nearly all these cities, and this fact seems to indicate to me a serious want of provision against these extraordinary catastrophes. It is quite impossible to have any art unless you have good air, good water, and clean cities."

At this point Mr. Wilde arose from his recumbent position and extended his hand to the reporter. The hint was taken and a retreat was made in good order, while Mr. Wilde turned to the window and contemplated the sea of mud beneath him with a feeling, it is to be feared, that Chicago was not an art center.

1. Benjamin West (1738–1820), American-born painter who had a strong influence on the development of historical painting in England.
2. Benjamin Robert Haydon (1786–1846), English historical painter and well-known lecturer on painting and design.
3. Thomas Gainsborough (1727–88), an English landscape and portrait painter, was among the most famous artists of the eighteenth century.
4. Sir Joshua Reynolds (1723–82), English portrait painter in the grand style and a founding member of the Royal Academy.
5. In 1876 Benjamin Disraeli (1804–81), the British prime minister, statesman, and novelist, was elevated to the peerage as the earl of Beaconsfield. When Disraeli died, Millais was painting his portrait, which now hangs in the British Museum.
6. Henry Irving (1838–1905), one of the most famous stage actors of the Victorian era.
7. William Charles Macready (1793–1873) was an English actor in the tradition of Edmund Kean.
8. Charles John Kean (1811–68), the son of the actor Edmund Kean, was a well-known English actor.

9. Ellen Terry (1848–1928), born Alice Ellen Terry, was a popular English actress.

10. Joseph Jefferson (1829–1905) was among the most famous American comedic actors of the nineteenth century and star of a theatrical version of "Rip Van Winkle."

11. In his 1875 production of *Othello*, the Italian actor Tomasso Salvini (1829–1915) donned a turban, delivered lines in Italian, and growled savagely as he killed Desdemona.

12. Script by Robert Montgomery Bird (1803–54).

13. For a version of "The House Beautiful" reconstructed almost exclusively from extant newspaper accounts and a surviving five-page manuscript fragment, see O'Brien, "Wilde's American Lectures," 162–95.

---

25. "PHILOSOPHICAL OSCAR," *CHICAGO TIMES*, 1 MARCH 1882, 7

Oscar Wilde returned to the city yesterday from Springfield, where he lectured the night before, and is at the Grand Pacific Hotel. During his western trip he has occupied platforms in St. Louis, Detroit, Cleveland, Indianapolis, Fort Wayne, and other cities. He says he was particularly pleased with Cincinnati. Its people have not only a great love of art, but they are doing much beautiful work. All schools of design, he says, which are young and inexperienced commit many faults, but in Cincinnati the work is good, and the workers are going at it in the right way. As to the West, he says it interests the English more than the East, because its civilization is made by the people for themselves. There is so much in the East that is a mere reflection of European thought, and so much a misunderstanding of it, which is not met in the West. The reporter called attention to the reports that Mrs. Langtry and Henry Labouchère[1] were to come to America, and asked him concerning them. Of Mrs. Langtry he said:

"She is one of my greatest friends."

"What is she like?"

"Beautiful women are quite indescribable. The beauty of her face is in the extreme sweetness and loveliness of her expression and the wonderful delicacy and transparency of her complexion. The real wonder of her beauty to all of us who are artists is that whether one carved her in marble or painted her in color she is equally lovely, the lines of her face being as strongly worked and as definite in outline as a Greek bronze, and yet so perfect in proportion that the effect is one of the simplest loveliness. In acting, she has a wonderfully musical and well-modulated voice, a delightfully joyousness of manner, and real capabilities for her art. The part that, when she has had more study and practice, she will make her greatest success in will, I think, be Rosalind in 'As You Like It.'"

"Was her first appearance really good?"

"No art would be worth doing if it could be done easily the first time, but there has been no debutante on the stage in London for many years who showed such really remarkable power and such great promise. She is now going to study Frou Frou[2] to make a tour of England. She is very nervous about visiting America, but, like many of us, most ambitious to see your country and to make herself a position here."

"Are there many young actors of promise in England?"

"Yes; there are four or five now there on whom we all rest great hopes for the future of the English stage—Mr. Conway,[3] who will probably accompany Mme. Modjeska[4] on her return to America; Mr. Bellow,[5] whose father was well known as a reader in our country; and the Messrs. Forbes Robertson,[6] the elder of whom, besides being a most romantic and beautiful actor, is also a painter who has done most excellent work; and the younger, Mr. Norman Forbes Robertson,[7] who has made several brilliant successes with Mme. Modjeska and who is anxious to act over here."

"What about Labouchère?"

"He is one of the most brilliant conversationalists and the most brilliant journalist in England, one of the many democrats which the English aristocracy has produced. He is Bradlaugh's[8] colleague in representing Northampton and is a man of great importance to the radical party through his keen knowledge of all foreign affairs, having been attaché at all of the important courts. He is the only brilliant enemy I ever had in England. He has had more libel cases to defend than any man in England, and he always wins them."

"How old is he?"

"Men are always as old as they feel and women as they look, and I am sure that Mr. Labouchère feels eternally young, because he is always successful. But if we were obliged to go down to relentless facts, I should say he was a man of thirty."

"How do he and Bradlaugh work together?"

"Politically, he has been Bradlaugh's staunchest defender and has been most loyal to his brother member. The two best-written papers in England are *The World* and *Truth*. You have already heard the editor of *The World*, Mr. Edmund Yates,[9] lecture. A very brilliant lecturer he is. So I am sure Americans will be interested in hearing the editor of the other paper."

"How do you account for the radicalism of Northampton? The voters there are mostly poor and shoemakers, are they not?"

"I do not think there is any connection between poverty and radicalism, but there is between handicrafts and republicanism. I mean that to work at any handicraft produces that sense of individualism which is the key note of all republicanism. Then, in great cities there is a constant spirit of discussion and a certain clash of ideas which make men think for themselves, so that the political thought of England progresses always in the manufacturing towns and never in the agricultural places. An agricultural laborer's view of politics is founded entirely on the weather."

Mr. Wilde looks as if his western trip had agreed with him.

1. Henry Du Pré Labouchère (1831–1912), a radical and independently wealthy British politician, writer, and publisher, married the actress Henrietta Hodson in 1887. Hodson was Lily Langtry's teacher and promoted her career. Discussing his last Chicago interview in a letter he wrote to Mrs. George Lewis later in March, Wilde said, "I turned the conversation on three of my heroes, Whistler, Labouchere, and Irving, and on the adored and adorable Lily" (*Complete Letters,* 154). Ironically, Labouchère was the author of the so-called Labouchère amendment to the Criminal Law Amendment Act of 1885 (also known as "the blackmailer's charter")—the very law Wilde was convicted of violating a decade later. Wilde was given the maximum sentence the law permitted.
2. Augustin Daly adapted and translated Henri Meilhac and Ludovic Halévy's French play *Frou Frou: A Comedy of Powerful Human Interest, in Five Acts,* in 1870.
3. The English actor H. B. Conway (1850–1909).
4. Helen Modjeska (1840–1909), born Helen Opid, was a renowned Polish actress who specialized in Shakespearean roles.
5. Harold Kyrle Bellew (1855–1911), another English actor.
6. Johnston Forbes-Robertson (1853–1937) was considered one of the premier Shakespearean actors during his four decades on the stage.
7. Norman Forbes-Robertson (1858–1936), who acted under the name Norman Forbes, was a distinguished Shakespearean.
8. Charles Bradlaugh (1833–91), a popular English political activist and atheist, was elected M.P. for Northampton several times, but his refusal to take the religious Oath of Allegiance prevented him from serving as a voting member until 1886.
9. Edmund Hodgson Yates (1831–94), Scottish-born novelist and dramatist best known as the editor of *The World.*

---

26. "DAVID AND OSCAR," *CHICAGO TRIBUNE,* 5 MARCH 1882, 5

Mr. Oscar Wilde was in the city yesterday afternoon, and, understanding that he had something to say in answer to Prof. David Swing's criticism of him, published in a recent number of the *Alliance,* a representative of *The Tribune* called on him at the Grand Pacific Hotel. He lectured Friday evening in Aurora, appeared in Racine last evening, and discourses on the beautiful in art to the Philistines of Milwaukee this evening. As Milwaukee has been represented to him as a good town for Sunday shows, he thought he would try his Sunday experiment there first. He greeted the reporter in his usual cordial manner yesterday, and, in answer to a question regarding Prof. Swing's article, he said:

"While in Rockford, Ill., recently, I was informed that an important attack on me had been published by Prof. David Swing, of your city, in a paper called the *Alliance.* I was told that this article had so influenced the proprietress of a ladies' school there, who had purchased two tickets for my lecture—one for herself and the other for the best behaved pupil—that she returned the tickets to the box office in consequence of Prof. Swing's attack.[1] Of course I felt that any attack which would have such a marked and immediate influence on a whole city must be most remarkable and intellectual, and I quite looked forward to the pleasure of reading it this morning,[2] for, next to a staunch friend, the best thing that a man can have is a brilliant enemy. There is nothing more depressing than to be attacked by a fool, as one cannot answer and does not fight with the same weapons.

"I confess, however," he continued with a smile, "to have been greatly disappointed at what I read this morning, because if a man attacks one for the clothes that one likes to wear he should go for his answer to one's tailor, and if a man assails one for the flowers that one admires he should discuss the matter with one's gardener; and, as regards the learned professor's sneer at me for receiving a fee for lecturing, he is not the first clergyman that has visited me with such a bitter reproach, which derives all its sting from the fact that it comes from a body of men most of whom receive large salaries for preaching.

"As regards his remarks on me, omitting the aesthetics of mind and heart," said Mr. Wilde, "as I feel sure that he is too honest an antagonist to willfully misrepresent one, I can only conclude that he did not attend my lecture. Had he done so he would have seen that I divided my lecture into portions, in the first of which I dwelt on the necessity of teaching the handicraftsman to work not only with his hands, as though, indeed, he were a mere machine, but with his head and heart always, for unless a man does so his work will always be commonplace and poor and have no beauty at all in it. I dwelt on the moral education that working in every art would give a man—for all good art is founded on two things—truth and honesty. In the world of business, indeed, the liar and the cheat may escape detection all their lives, but in art it is not so. A workman who is dishonest in his labor or who tells a lie in his art, such as painting wood to represent marble, or staining paper to represent stone, or pretending that the thing is solid when it is probably merely a hollow sham, that man knows that in consequence of it his work is worthless and will not last for any time. So much for those who work in art.

"In the second part of my lecture," said Mr. Wilde, languidly knocking the ashes off his cigarette and throwing away all but the butt, "I treated of those who only look at art, and do not create, or the ordinary man and woman of life, and I showed of what value the refining influence of noble and beautiful art would be to them from their childhood to their manhood, and I spoke of what influence the arts would have in producing between all countries a common intellectual spirit, for no truth of history is clearer than this, that national hatreds are always strongest where civilization is lowest.

"And I acknowledge that I am surprised," continued Mr. Wilde, "to find that anyone with the name of David should be fighting for the Philistines. He should be taking a pebble from the river brook and hurling it at that monstrous Goliath of Chicago architecture, the water tower,[3] instead of praising it as being, as he calls it, calm and rational—two most unfortunate epithets.

"But perhaps I am wrong in taking the professor seriously, for, from what I have seen of American literature, I have found that the sermon of the divine is always humorous and the writings of the humorous always depressing. In my next lecture I hope to dwell at length on the relations between art and morality, which have been so much misunderstood. I lecture at Central Music-Hall in your city next Saturday evening on 'Interior and Exterior House Decoration.'"

"How have you been pleased with your reception in the smaller towns, Mr. Wilde?" asked the reporter.

"Very well, indeed. In Aurora, where I lectured last evening, they have recently started a decorative art school and are very enthusiastic."

"In any of the cities which you have visited have art schools been established as a result of your lecture?"

"Oh, yes. In Philadelphia and in some other cities."

"When do you leave this country?"

"I leave about the first of May and go to Paris to visit the salons and see the artists. I shall return to New England and lecture in Boston and some of the New England cities before I sail, however. On leaving Paris I shall travel through England and deliver lectures before the various art schools there."

"Have you ever lectured in England?"

"No, sir. I made my début as a lecturer in New York City."

"Have you ever delivered your Saturday evening's lecture before?"

"No, I have not. In fact, I have not completed it yet. I shall probably deliver it in Boston, but it is not a lecture to give a city at first—I think it best to start by giving the principles of art and then enter into the details."

1. In an article in the *Chicago Alliance* for 21 February (repr. in the *Chicago Tribune*, 23 February 1882, 8), David Swing (1830–94), an American Presbyterian minister, allowed that "having confessed Oscar Wilde to be sincere, we must add that his mind is of the small caliber, and makes more use of trifling forms of the beautiful than of any great ideas or works in that field."
2. Wilde soon dismissed Swing's attack: "I usually pay no attention to newspaper ridicule or criticism and have long ago learned to entirely disregard it" (see "Professor Swing and Oscar," *Chicago Inter-Ocean*, 6 March 1882, 8).
3. The Chicago water tower, designed in a gothic style by the architect William W. Boyington and built of yellowing Joliet limestone in 1869, was the only public building in the burned zone to survive the great Chicago Fire of 1871. The following year Wilde again referred to the water tower, this time in the *Pall Mall Gazette*, as an offense to good taste, calling it "a castellated monstrosity with pepper boxes stuck all over it" ("Mr. Oscar Wilde and the Unutterable Wheel," 7 May 1883, 11).

---

27. "OSCAR WILDE IN OMAHA," *OMAHA WEEKLY HERALD*, 24 MARCH 1882, 2

Mr. Wilde and his servant and Mr. Vale, his business manager, arrived in Omaha yesterday from Sioux City and ensconced themselves at the Withnell House. The day without the four walls of the hotel was blustering and the wind swept occasional eddies of dust along the streets, rendering it very disagreeable for anyone not habituated to the climate who should venture out.

Consequently when the *Herald* ambassador was admitted to Mr. Wilde's presence toward evening after sending up his card, he found that gentleman not prepared to speak advisedly upon the architecture or other salient points of Omaha and the conversation was rather general in its scope. *En passant*, it may be remarked for the edification of those who desire to know how Mr. Wilde exemplifies his ideas of dress in private life, that his negligee consists of a black velvet jacket, dark trousers, leather gaiters faced with yellow cloth, and that a maroon silk scarf is tied at his throat and a handkerchief of like color and material peeps from the breast pocket of his jacket.

One of the first questions put by the *Herald* representative was: "How do you find our western cities?"

"You have not the lower orders of the eastern cities," replied Mr. Wilde. "I find less prejudice and more simple and sane people." He added, however,

"The eastern part of America is really the part of the country that interests us in England less, because it seems to us that it has a civilization that you are not making for yourselves and by yourselves—not the complementary echo of British thought."

"You have pronounced ideas upon our architecture?"

"I find in all the eastern cities these general characteristics: the fault in American architecture is in an entire want of any definite conception of what style is suitable for your cities. The architecture should be as universal as the country and as easily understood. Most of the buildings are mere constructions of incongruous anachronisms."

"You have plans for future work, I presume?"

"For my life, do you mean?" and Mr. Wilde laughed merrily and lighted a cigarette as he threw himself back in his chair. "Well, I'm a very ambitious young man. I want to do everything in the world. I cannot conceive of anything that I do not want to do. I want to write a great deal more poetry. I want to study painting more than I've been able to. I want to write a great many more plays, and I want to make this artistic movement the basis for a new civilization."

"That is the highest and greatest of all your ambitions, I take it," said the interviewer. "But do you consider that there is an organized aesthetic school?"

Mr. Wilde replied: "There is a definite school of criticism and of attitude toward art. Up to this in England we have always had great artists, great portrait painters—for instance, in the last century—and the great landscape painters at the beginning of this age. But there has been an entire want of any concentration of artistic power. The great men stood, as it were, in a sort of sublime isolation, and their work was not understood by the common people and so not loved by them; and so both sides suffered, the artists missing the sympathy to which all artists are so sensitive and the people not understanding their work. We, on the other hand, are concentrating all the artistic genius of England, so that each art will gain and learn so much from its brother arts that the people will understand and love art more, for the decorative arts will indeed become part of their daily life. It will make beautiful the common vessels of the house, and it will become so natural to beautify their surroundings that even if the people wish to escape from it they will not be able.

"We also are making our artisans artists by giving them beautiful designs and noble models—for all the decorative arts of England have been falling into disuse and nothing that was made for the ordinary service of the house was either honestly made or beautiful. We look to this as the real strength of our movement. It is indeed to become a part of the people's life. It must begin not in the scholar's study—not even in the studio of the great artist—but with the handicraftsmen always. And by handicraftsmen I mean a man [*sic*] who works with his hands, and not with his hands merely, but with his head and his heart. The evil that machinery is doing is not merely in the consequences of its work but in the fact that it makes men themselves machines also. Whereas we wish them to be artists, that is to say men. Now you see what we want."

"How do your audiences in the West impress you?" asked the interviewer.

"I should never wish—and no man could—to have a better audience, more simple, more understanding, more quick in their appreciation than the audiences I had in Chicago, Cincinnati, and many of the western cities."

Mr. Wilde remarked that he had seen many men of marvelous physique and many beautiful women in the West and this elicited his opinion that "physical beauty is really, absolutely the basis of all great and strong art." He believes, too, that all true art work must be wrought by healthy and happy men and women.

---

28. "OSCAR WILDE: AN INTERVIEW WITH THE APOSTLE OF AESTHETICISM," *SAN FRANCISCO EXAMINER*, 27 MARCH 1882, 2

Oscar Wilde arrived in this city at noon yesterday by the overland train. The news that he was on the train induced hundreds of curious persons to go over to the Oakland depot in order to catch a first glimpse of this new lion. To these persons a cursory inspection revealed a tall, well-built, clean-shaven, eccentrically dressed young man with remarkable features, a somber, melancholy face, lighted up at intervals in the conversation going on around him and directed entirely at him, by a frank, pleased smile that came readily and passed away quickly, leaving the face in repose, as before. Wherever he moved the crowd, guided by a large, wide-brimmed, white slouch hat he wore, followed, not obtrusively, but quietly and respectfully. Mr. Wilde was dressed in a style that would attract general attention anywhere outside of an artist's studio or chambers, and there was no need for anyone to point in order to identify him. From beneath his large white hat fell long light-brown hair, reaching in somewhat straggling masses to the shoulders, half hiding a face inclined to sallowness. A close-fitting black velvet frock coat showed off strong, square shoulders, manly waist and hips. Pants dun brown, highly polished pointed shoes, a velvet waistcoat, low, wide collar, puce-colored tie folded wide, yellow gloves completed the appearance in dress of the outward man. A boutonniere, somewhat withered, made up of heliotropes, a brightly foliated daisy and a tuberose, decorated his coat front. A dark olive-green summer overcoat was carried carelessly over his left arm, and the right hand, when not resting lightly against the chin as if aiding the poet in thought, grasped a thick ivory cane. Thus the object of curiosity appeared to those who yesterday saw him crossing the bay to the city.

A quiet conversation with Oscar Wilde would have disclosed nobler material than dress anomalistic of the man. Unfortunately this converse could not be had yesterday in the rush of car and boat, each bend in their rapid onward flight cityward revealing to the ardent lover of nature scenes of picturesque beauty, silencing ordinary speech and thought; a changing panorama of soft murky outlines and hazy tints of color, the center always the sea-green bay, spangled with grassy Yerba Buena, and the gold of Alcatraz, which sparkled like brilliant splotches against indistinct backgrounds of black and indigo, coloring the far-off, woody mountain summits and curving shorelines; the Golden Gate lost in a sunlit mist beyond; San Francisco's hills, roadways, houses, dimly seen; at its feet a mist from which rose the tall, straight masts of merchant ships, tapering above the mist that hung over the wharves. Not alone the poet, but everyone ending the weary journey here were impressed by what to nearly all was the first view of the "uttermost Occident." Mr. Wilde was met at Port Costa by several persons, who, for one reason or another, laid a claim to his attention, among them an *Examiner* representative. All were met with the quiet, dignified courtesy of a gentleman and a man of the world. In speaking Mr. Wilde preserves a cold but polite and attentive air, and it is only when some favorite subject is touched upon that the face lights up and the gray-green eyes seek those of the person who has aroused his deeper attention, and smiles encouragement or appreciation. The long, rather thin face, the pointed chin and well-shaped nose seem to feel the influence of the smile, and an otherwise homely face appears momentarily handsome. A second later, the spurt of enthusiasm or interest having passed, the face becomes again immobile, the eyelids lower, the eyes grow dull with a faraway glance, or seek the ground as the tall body bends slightly to come to a nearer level with his companion.

Talking, Mr. Wilde speaks in a low, melodious tone, the broad English pronunciation being harmonized almost to rhythm. He gesticulates very little, and from constant practice has a habit of brushing loose hairs back behind his ears.

After apologizing for the intrusion, the reporter asked Mr. Wilde if the trip overland was a pleasant one.

"Partly," he replied, "but excessively long and tedious."

"Does the mountain scenery meet your appreciation?"

"Hardly; I saw it at an unfavorable time, I suppose. The view from the top of the Sierra Nevadas, however, was beautiful."

"Do you like our country, Mr. Wilde, or are you disappointed with America and Americans?"

"There is very much here to like and admire. The further West one comes, the more there is to like. The western people are much more social than those of the East, and I fancy that I shall be greatly pleased with California." Mr. Wilde merely smiled when told that California audiences would never think of showing him disrespect, and the only thing that might appear annoying to him will be the curiosity of all classes to see the man who has lately been so much read and talked about. "I like your country and its people," he said, as though apologizing for the latter.

"There is something quickening in the young life of a powerful nation. There is a wonderful opportunity for the growth and expansion of art in a country where a national life is unfolding. But there are too many amateurs here. Amateur art is worse than no art."

Reporter: "Mr. Wilde, do your admirers believe that you have created a new school of poetry?"

Oscar Wilde: "They certainly should not—that is if I have any admirers. The Pre-Raphaelite school, to which I belong, owes its origin to Keats more than to anyone else. He was the forerunner of the school, as was Pheidias[1] of Grecian art, Dante of the intensity, passion, and color of Italian painting. Later, Burne-Jones in painting and Morris, Rossetti, and Swinburne in poetry represent the fruit of which Keats was the blossom."

The turn which the conversation had taken had evidently aroused Mr. Wilde from apathy, for his face and manner showed that he was thoroughly interested in the theme. The reporter improved the occasion to remark: "Judging from the tenor of your own poems, I fancy that 'Charmides' (pronouncing the name with the soft accent) is your favorite poem, Mr. Wilde?"[2]

"Char—Charmides," he replied correcting; "yes, that is my favorite poem. I think it my best. It is the most finished and perfect. The people of America have taken very kindly to my 'Ave Imperatrix,' however."[3]

"Perhaps a feeling of nationality prompts this choice."

Mr. Wilde: "Probably so."

Reporter: "Does the 'Sonnet to Liberty' voice your political creed?"

Oscar Wilde: "You mean the sonnet beginning

Not that I love thy children, whose dull eyes
See nothing save their own unlovely woe,
Whose minds know nothing, nothing care to know—

No, that is not my political creed. I wrote that when I was younger. [Mr. Wilde
is twenty-six now.] Perhaps something of the fire of youth prompted it."

Mr. Wilde's recital of the lines was surprisingly impressive and pleasing,
a perfect modulation and an earnest, almost pathetic tone giving the recital
deep interest.

"If you would like to know my political creed," he said, after a short pause,
"read the 'Libertatis Sacra Fames'—I think it is the seventh sonnet." The sonnet referred to is as follows:

Albeit nurtured in democracy,
And liking best that state republican
Where every man is Kinglike and no man
Is crowned above his fellows, yet I see,
Spite of this modern fret for Liberty,
Better the rule of One, whom all obey,
Than to let clamorous demagogues betray
Our freedom with the kiss of anarchy.
Wherefore I love them not whose hands profane
Plant the red flag upon the piled-up street
For no right cause, beneath whose ignorant reign
Arts, Culture, Reverence, Honor, all things fade,
Save Treason and the dagger of her trade,
Or Murder with his silent, bloody feet.

"Mr. Wilde, one of your critics has denounced your poetry as impure and
immoral."

"A poem," replied Mr. Wilde, "is well written or badly written. In art there
should be no reference to a standard of good or evil.[4] The presence of such a
reference implies incompleteness of vision. The Greeks understood this principle and with perfect serenity enjoyed works of art that, I suppose, some of
my critics would never allow their families to look at. The enjoyment of poetry
does not come from the subject, but from the language and rhythm. Art must
be loved for its own sake and not criticized by a standard of morality."

The conversation turning somewhat upon his life, Mr. Wilde said that he
felt proud of his Irish birth and parentage. "I live in London for its artistic
life and opportunities," he said. "There is no lack of culture in Ireland, but
it is nearly all absorbed in politics. Had I remained there my career would
have been a political one."

"When do you expect to return to London, Mr. Wilde?"

"If lecturing does not kill me, very soon."

"Then you do not like lecturing?"

"Yes, I do," he responded quickly. "I like lecturing because it brings me face to face with those I desire should hear me. In England this is impossible."

By this time the train had run into the new depot on Long Wharf, and the passengers filed into the waiting room. Here the conspicuous figure of the coming lecturer attracted general attention. Even the shaggy fur overcoat, made famous by Du Maurier's sketches in *Punch*, caused a crowd to gather where the porter laid it with a valise in the corner.

On the ferryboat Mr. Wilde placed himself so that his back was turned to the crowd. The sights on the bay interested him greatly, and he asked many questions about the city, whose streetways, appearing like huge bleached ribs of a gigantic skeleton with the head pointing oceanward, were distinctly visible.

He asked many questions about the Chinese and had the Chinese quarters pointed out to him. Speaking of Chinese art, he said that it possesses no element of beauty, the horrible and grotesque appearing to be standards of perfection. "Their art and music," he said, "are extraordinary developments of national life. I have seen much that is admirable in Japanese art but nothing of excellence in Chinese art. When I was a lad I heard a Chinese fiddle, or so it was called, at the Paris Exposition, but I could discern no music in it. When the shah of Persia was in London the only music he cared for was the violin."[5] In answer to a question as to whether the harbor is fortified, Alcatraz and Fort Point were pointed out.

Mr. Wilde impressed all those with whom he came in contact as being "a very parfit gentil knight."[6] His manner is courteous, deferential, and self-possessed, his language clear and forcible, without ever descending to those excesses commonly attributed to him as daily talk. Nothing in his manner would attract unusual attention, and certainly not ridicule.

1. Pheidias, or Phidias (c. 490–430 B.C.E.), was an Athenian sculptor who created the most important religious images of the Parthenon and likely designed its overall sculptural decoration.
2. "Charmides" is a finely wrought and highly descriptive poem that narrates in 666 lines the "homecoming" of a drowned Grecian boy.
3. "Ave Imperatrix" is a poem of 124 lines in ABAB tetrameter quatrains. Ostensibly about English imperialism, it also addresses the idea of revolution against England, as the reporter insinuates.
4. Wilde initially developed this sentiment in his lecture "The English Renaissance" and recapitulates it almost verbatim as the eighth aphorism in the "Preface" to *The Picture of Dorian Gray*.

5. Nasser al-Din Shah Qajar (1831–96), the first Persian shah to visit Europe, visited the United Kingdom in 1873 and again in 1878.

6. Line 72 from Chaucer's "Prologue" in *The Canterbury Tales*.

---

29. "OSCAR WILDE'S VIEWS," *SAN FRANCISCO MORNING CALL, 27 MARCH 1882, 4*

Oscar Wilde arrived here yesterday on the overland train. A *Call* reporter who met him at Port Costa was introduced to a tall, large-faced man, with pleasant light brown eyes, winning smile, muddy complexion, and a charming manner. The two things about the gentleman which have given Gilbert's pen and Du Maurier's pencil such an amount of material to work upon are the use of extravagant and unusual adjectives in praise of art or anything artistically pleasing and an unusual style of dress. Gilbert has outrageously but brilliantly burlesqued the first; Du Maurier has faithfully reproduced the other, together with a heavy sensuousness in Wilde's face when in repose. On the train yesterday he wore a wide-brimmed white felt hat, a velvet jacket, concerning the fit of which he should have a word with his tailor, and ordinary trousers and shoes. The striking features of his costume were his cravat and handkerchief—so much of the latter was shown that it can be classed as part of his costume. They were both, apparently, from one piece of material, and were of a startlingly brilliant yellow. A bouquet of wild flowers pinned to the lapel of his jacket and his long straight brown hair completed the peculiarities of his appearance. Deprived of them he would be voted on sight by the average American "a strapping big clever fellow." The much advertised aesthete, in conversation, quickly showed himself to be a man of quick perceptions, deep insight, and practical views. In the hour and a half's trip in Mr. Wilde's company the reporter conversed with him on subjects ranging from Chinese art to the cause of the muddiness of the Sacramento River. Any subject he was already not familiar with he displayed a vivid interest in being informed about.

In the course of the conversation the reporter asked: "Have you been in this country long enough to have formed any general impression about it and its people?"

"Well, this country is too large to admit of its being comprehended in one general impression. In fact no one impression would answer for two regions of this country. I find not only different degrees but different kinds of development in different cities. My various impressions of them may be stated in detail in the future."

"What!" asked the reporter aghast. "You propose to write a book about us?"

"Human nature may be hardened to almost any degree of endurance," Mr. Wilde responded, laughingly. "I may even dare to write a book that mine enemies may read—and criticize it."

"If you are not yet prepared to give impressions regarding the eastern states, you, of course, are not regarding this state."

"Not regarding the state, certainly, but I must say that after the brown barrenness of the states and the endless snows of the mountains, it was very joyous to me to see the harmony of color Nature has painted upon the California hillsides and plains we have crossed today."

"Californians always expect that much praise—"

"Yes," interrupted Mr. Wilde, "and I have another pleasant impression about this state—the names of its towns. Now, in one of the states I stopped in a place called 'Griggsville.'[1] The aesthete shuddered. "Now, is not that the ultimate of vulgarity? Why not Griggtown, or Griggs? But Griggsville! Here you have beautiful names," and he ran over, with every evidence of delight, a score of the euphonious Spanish names of the coast country towns.

"But you have yet to visit the mountain counties, where they have Murderer's Gulch, Hangtown, etc."

"What are they compared to Griggsville? Proper. They at least convey an idea, an association, a—"

The reporter interrupted, in order to restore, if possible, Mr. Wilde's tranquility, and boldly asked: "What, Mr. Wilde, is your own definition of the English renaissance of art, concerning which we have been chiefly misinstructed by the satirists?"

"Yes, satire has paid the usual homage which mediocrity pays to genius, blinding the public to what is noble and beautiful."

"Then the satirists have not followed this subject sufficiently close to outline it?"

"Not only those who have written of it, but all those who have not asserted it, are supremely ignorant of the work that Morris, Rossetti, Burne-Jones, and Swinburne and Keats's admirers have undertaken. To know nothing about these great men is one of the necessary elements of English education, and to disagree with three-fourths of England on all points is one of the first elements of sanity, which is a deep source of consolation in all moments of spiritual doubt."

This savage sword thrust at his English burlesquers was delivered with a charming coolness.

The reporter, after a moment's admiration of the poet's vigorous prose, again returned to the attack, and said: "But your comprehension of the art renaissance, after all else that we have heard, will be doubly acceptable."

"Well," said Mr. Wilde earnestly, "the English renaissance has been described as a mere revival of the Greek modes of thought, and again as a mere revival of medieval feeling; rather, I would say, that to these forms of the human spirit it has added whatever artistic value the intricacy and complexity and experience of modern life can give. It is from the union of Hellenism in its breadth, its variety of purpose, its calm possession of reality, with the adventive, the intensified individualism, the passionate color of the Romantic spirit that springs out of the nineteenth century in England, as from the marriage of Faust and Helen of Troy sprang the beautiful Lady Euphonia.[2] The modern love of landscape dates from Rousseau,[3] and it is in Keats that one discerns the beginning of the artistic renaissance of England. He was the forerunner of the Pre-Raphaelite school."

"Speaking of the Pre-Raphaelites, what are they?"

"If you ask nine-tenths of the British public what is the meaning of the word *aesthetic,* they will tell you that is the French for affection or the German for a dado," said Mr. Wilde switching off slightly to give another vigorous slap at his scoffers. "If you inquire about the Pre-Raphaelites, you will hear something about an eccentric lot of young men to whom a sort of divine crookedness and holy awkwardness is drawing all the chief objects of art."

"Yes; but the Pre-Raphaelites?"

"Well," said the aesthete, smiling at the reporter's unaesthetic impatience, "in the year 1847 a number of young men in London, all admirers of Keats, were in the habit of meeting together and discussing art. They had determined to revolutionize poetry and painting. To do so was to lose, in England, all their rights as citizens. They had those things which the English public never forgives—youth, power, and enthusiasm. These young men called themselves Pre-Raphaelites, because as opposed to the facile obstructions of Raphael they thought they had found a stronger realism of imagination, a more careful realism of technique, and [an] individuality more intense. But of all things, it was a return to nature."

"Your explanation is, indeed, radically different from that humorous portrait of Gilbert's," the reporter said, vaguely conscious that he had taken down much more than he had taken in.

"But you must not judge of aestheticism by the satire of Mr. Gilbert any more than you judge of the strength and splendor of the sun or sea by the dust that dances in the beam or the bubble that breaks on the wave. Don't take your critic as any sure test of art, for artists, like the Greek gods, are only revealed to one another."

"You have found some savage critics in this country, have you not?"

"Yes, like a rainy day, such things are inevitable, but like a rainy day, I accept them as unpleasant in themselves, but not of a character to make me unhappy, if I only do not notice them."

"What have you found the American reviewers most object to?"

The aesthete was thoughtfully silent for a moment, as though trying to determine in his own mind which of the many American objections to his works had been the nearest universal.

Then he said, slowly, "Well, I suspect some of my verses have come in for the greatest amount of attack, and on the ground of their immorality, as set forth by one Higginson.[4] They insist upon an increased moral sense, or moral supervision of literature. Indeed, one should never talk of a moral or an immoral poem. Poems are either well written or badly written; that is all."

"Mr. Wilde, there is one point I know you could satisfy thousands of *Call* readers upon by telling me why it is that two certain flowers have become connected with the aesthetic movement in England, and said, I hope erroneously, to be the food of some aesthetic young men."

"Well, let me tell you that the reason we love the lily and the sunflower, in spite of what Mr. Gilbert may tell you, is not for any vegetable fashion at all; it is because these flowers are, in England, the two most perfect models of design, the most naturally adapted for decorative art—the gaudy leonine beauty of the one, the precious loveliness of the other giving to the artist the most entire and perfect joy."

Coming along the bay, Mr. Wilde frequently expressed his delight with its loveliness and the beauty of the surrounding hills.

On the train and boat he was the observed of curious hundreds, many of whom had apparently made the trip across the bay purportedly to see him. He hurried from the boat upon its landing, and with Mr. Locke[5] drove directly to the Palace Hotel.

1. When Wilde received a telegram asking him to lecture on aesthetics in Griggsville, Illinois, he archly responded, "Begin by changing the name of your town." He also joked with Mrs. George Lewis that he was now "sorry to say that an art-movement has begun at Griggsville. . . . At present the style here is Griggsville rococo, and there are also traces of 'archaic Griggsville,' but in a few days the Griggsville Renaissance will blossom: it will have an exquisite bloom for a week, and then . . . become 'debased Griggsville,' and the Griggsville Decadence" (*Complete Letters*, 149; see also appendix 1, "Impressions of America").

2. In part 2 of *Faust* Goethe's protagonist continues his association with Mephistopheles and has a love affair with Helen of Troy, with whom, in the third act, he fathers a son, Euphorion, "the spirit of poesy." Their son, an allegorical tribute to

the recently deceased Lord Byron, vanishes at the end of the third act. However, their union produces no daughter—euphonic or otherwise.

3. Théodore Rousseau (1812–67), French painter of the Barbizon school.
4. Thomas Wentworth Higginson (1823–1911), American author, abolitionist, and pastor.
5. Charles E. Locke, senior partner with J. Charles Davis in the theatrical agency of Locke and Davis, was responsible for bringing Wilde to San Francisco.

---

30. "LO! THE AESTHETE," *SAN FRANCISCO CHRONICLE*, 27 MARCH 1882, 3

The 8 o'clock ferryboat to Oakland yesterday morning carried a committee of reception, self-appointed, to meet Oscar Wilde, the apostle of aestheticism. The committee consisted of Manager Locke, several Bohemian Club men[1] and the usual flock of reporters that gathers on the railroad approaches to the city when some hapless celebrity is to be waylaid and ruthlessly rifled of his ideas of California. The committee having evidently had little more than forty winks of sleep, showed on its countenance the aesthetic pallor which bespeaks a true appreciation of utter beauty and a too joyous sympathy with poetic sentiment. Manager Locke, as the uncommissioned chairman of the committee, hastened to show that the aestheticism of his party was not merely skin deep by dashing instinctively for the lunch counter, where the too exquisitely utter cooking range was imbuing a plate of fried sausage with the exalted spirit of culinary art. The lofty example of the managerial aesthete, proudly poised on a stool as high and dangerous as a Norman charger and wielding half a yard of steel with the vigor of a thirteenth-century Crusader, was instantly followed by the committee, and the range flowed and flamed in the intensity of its industrial zeal until the sun-kissed citizen in front of it looked like a spot on a harvest moon. Before the refreshed aesthetes laid down their napkins and readjusted their sunflowers, the ferryboat had touched the Oakland side and been made fast. This is especially worthy of note, as it is the first instance on record where anything but a collector was made fast by touching at Oakland.

As the committee filed out to the train for Port Costa an opportunity was given to note the aesthetic beauties of their attire. Manager Locke, who had evidently been studying a cut of a medieval saint, had donned a dark-blue coat and a bright yellow necktie, which contrasted so violently with the unsubdued hue of his mustache that he looked like Julian Rix's sensational picture of the "Redwoods on Fire."[2] Each of the Bohemian Club men sported a large breastpin, on which a one-legged silver stork gazed pensively on a bronze frog, as if deliberating whether to go hungry or risk the terrors of strangulation and dyspepsia. The reporter of a morning journal which caters to the aesthetic aspirations of Jessie and Natoma streets[3] and keeps the police department and the aristocracy of Minna Street mutually intimate,[4] boasted that in humble recognition of the coming aesthete he had shaved off his mustache. On careful examination this was found to be a fact. The other journalists who found themselves attached to the tail of the committee of reception had contented themselves with the most ordinary attempts at aesthetic adornment, and by their sameness of color helped to distract public attention from the party and save it from a suspicion that it was the advance guard of a milliner's picnic or the board of trustees of the Oakland cockpit.

The run to Port Costa was pleasant and rapid. Flying over the broad fields, green as the imagination of an aesthetic poet, and whirling along the pebbly shores of the bay, with its sparkling waters, blue as the theatrical managers who have not dug into the bonanza of aestheticism, the committee of reception met the overland train and Oscar Wilde at 10 a.m. Marcus Mayer,[5] formerly of the Democratic party of San Francisco and now the agent of the divine Patti, conveyed to the committee from the fore platform of the train the pleasant news that the poet had breakfasted.

"He was presented with a magnificent bouquet of sunflowers and camellias by Mr. Woodson at Sacramento," said the cheerful agent, unconscious of the intimation which the remark conveyed.

The medieval splendor of manager Locke's attire gained him an immediate audience with the poet, who was in the rear portion of the sleeping car, paying his morning devotions to a pansy presented by a Benician aesthete. The moment the manager entered the floral sanctuary the door was closed by the poet's colored valet, and the committee was left to its own envious thoughts. After minutes which seemed liked hours to the anxious aesthetes, the door of the sanctum was opened and the manager came out hurriedly and looked as if he had been worshiping a thistle or paying a compliment to a nettle.

"I ought to have known it myself," said he, bitterly to Mr. Vale, the poet's traveling agent, and he took a poster out of his coattail pocket and exposed the offensive advertisement.

"What," gasped the terrified agent; "is that the way you've billed him? A plain yellow poster, without sandhill cranes, or lilies, or sunflowers—not even a line in old English text."

The guilty manager look utterly woebegone.

"Not even a marguerite or a frog on the border," continued the agent, with a withering glance at the offender.

The manager groaned and hung his head.

"You haven't shown it to him, I hope," gasped the agent.

The manager nodded despairingly.

"Great Caesar," exclaimed the agent, and he bounded into the poetic retreat.

The alarmed spectators were about to follow, but the valet closed the door and faced the crowd grimly. Presently the agent reappeared, looking very pale.

"Where's that camellia that was presented us at Reno?" he anxiously inquired.

The valet fished the precious souvenir out of a silver tea-pitcher, and the agent, snatching it, dashing into the sanctuary once more.

"Bring them violets," he yelled a moment after to the valet.

While the colored servant was climbing over the baggage on the rear platform to reach the box of violets on the roof of the car, the audience heard a deep sign of relief from the sanctuary.

"Ah, that is so beautiful, so joyous. Put it away, Vale. I feel much better already."

"Take another sniff," replied the sturdy voice of the agent, and immediately the painful suspense of the audience was relieved by hearing a long-drawn inspiration, followed by another exclamation of aesthetic gratification.

"How delicious; how sweet; how surpassing and too utterly sweet is the incense of the wild flowers in the joyous spring time."

"I guess so," replied the soulless agent, as he handed the poet his cherished bunch of violets, and came out to announce that Mr. Wilde would immediately appear to the visitors.

In a few moments the eminent aesthete stepped through the doorway of the sanctum and, bowing to the group of admirers, advanced to the middle of the car. The poet was still pale from the effects of the severe shock to his sensibilities, but the sight of the distant hills purpling in the morning sun completely restored him.

"They looked nice," remarked a prosy admirer.

"Ah—y—e—s—how utterly lovely—how exquisitely beautiful—observe the softness of the outline so full of the grace and perfect harmony of Nature's handiwork."

Having delivered himself of this rapturous compliment to the wooded peaks of Marin, the poet clasped his hands and gazed out of the window for some moments, lost in the too utterly joyous abstraction of the aesthetic.

While the poet's eyes were fixed on the environments of the hoary Tamal-pais[6] the *Chronicle's* representative was making a mental sketch of the midday dreamer, and found, when the picture was completed, that it was an odd one for this outlying post of civilization. In an older community, the aesthete might have passed with slighter attention, but his figure was certainly one calculated to excite the most intense curiosity in California.

He did not look more outlandish than a trapper from the wilds clad in the trophies of the clime, but the outlandishness was of a kind to which western people have not been in the smallest degree accustomed. Mr. Wilde's hat was of the sombrero pattern, light brown, pliable, and of itself would not astonish the Californian. The poet's face was almost boyish, and the closer we examined it the more juvenile it seemed. It was the face of a man of twenty-one years; a long face made up of a pair of eyes set rather deeply, a large aquiline nose, full lips and a decidedly heavy chin. The dress of the poet was not less remarkable than his face and consisted of a short velvet coat, rose-colored necktie and dark-brown trousers. The lower garments were cut with utterly sublime disregard of the latest fashion, but the aesthete had yielded sufficiently to his shoemaker to allow that worthy artisan to fit him with the newest production of his last. The poet wore the perennial sunflower in his buttonhole, and allowed his brown locks to float over his shoulders and just show enough ambition to curl to prove that they shared the wearer's hatred of the rigidly straight. The amount of ink that has been expended in England and America to prove that Mr. Wilde in the dress of aestheticism is a very remarkable person is the best proof that his figure is sensationally uncommon.

The *Chronicle* man had expected to meet an odd-looking person, and pre-pared himself against surprise, but, as the poet lounged into the railroad car and leaned out of the window to revel in the picture of blue sky and purple hills, the reporter forgot his resolution and stared and stared again in mute astonishment. What was particularly mystifying was the fact that this strange being, who looked as if he had no part in the everyday affairs of our prosy life, could not only talk of the matter-of-fact when he pleased like a man of education and refinement, but like a man who was capable of deep thought and vigorous conclusions.

As Marcus Mayer, who has carefully watched the aesthete for days, el-egantly remarking in forming his estimate of the poet: "Anyone who picks him up for a fool will get left, and don't you forget it."

Though occasionally willing to show his ability to discuss the affairs of the world of man, the aesthete could with difficulty be kept from raving over the world of art. He appeared to be able to give points to Ruskin in artistic rhapsody, and to discount everyone but Charles Warren Stoddard,[7] whom he so greatly resembled in manner and sentiment that the Bohemian Club men could scarcely believe that the poet of Hawaii had not come back in disguise to greet them with a poetic and tender embrace.

"I like your names here so much," said the poet, after he had fed his soul to satiety on the purple of Tamalpais and the blue of the sky over San Rafael. "How delightful it is to hear such names as San Antonio, San Pablo and San Lorenzo, after one's ears have been horribly shocked by such terms as Griggsville."

The poet shuddered as he thought of the presumptuous borough of the East which has proudly taken to itself the title of Griggsville.

"The fierce suggestiveness of your western names, such as Bloody Gulch and Murderer's Bar, have in them something of interest," he continued, "but in such a name as Griggsville there is nothing but utterly, unmitigated, and offensive vulgarity, ugh," and again the aesthete's velvet coat shook with the violence of his emotions.

Coming to a stretch of green meadow, enriched by the wealth of wild flowers, the poet exclaimed with the enthusiasm of a woman, and not a very strong type of western woman at that:

"How joyous it is to see a spot of green after one has grown so weary of the desolate stretches of brown and gray! The lack of color in your American landscapes has been to me a source of much regret. In the old countries neither the winters nor the summers make much difference, for the landscape is always green—always full of color. It is a garden throughout the year, and there one can at all seasons appreciate to the fullest the beauty and the perfection of nature."

When asked how he felt towards his critics of the East the aesthete sighed for those sordid and shortsighted persons, who in the blindness of their ignorance of aestheticism know not the rapture that they miss.

"It would be more profitable," said he, "to listen to the sighing of the wind, for that tells of the power of the infinite, but to listen to those who can only see in the well of truth the reflection of their own substantial ignorance would be time misspent."

The poet refrained from speaking the kind words of the American people and expressing the unstinted praise of California which distinguished visitors generally bestow before they have reached the Oakland wharf.

"I find in the eastern states," said he, "too much of a reflex of English manners and customs, and reflections of themselves are not admirable. What I like best is the civilization which the people of the West have formed for themselves."

At this stage of the aesthete's recovery an English admirer thought it advisable to drag him into a controversy on the Land League,[8] the poet having several times intimated that the St. Patrick's Day celebrations throughout the country had greatly interested him.

"I read of a great demonstration in San Francisco on the 17th of March," said he. "You had an oration and a magnificent parade, and a poem. Who, by the way, was the poet?"

"Don't mention it," said one of the paraders. "He is already dead."

"The Land League," said the poet, "is the most remarkable agitation that has ever taken place in Ireland, for it has, through the influence of America, created a republican feeling in Ireland for the first time. The agitations that preceded it would, if successful, have resulted in the establishment of a monarchy. Now, success would mean the foundations of a republic."

"Do you think so?" said the British aesthete, with a glare.

"I don't think so; I know it," said the poet, with so much energy that a second after his nervous system utterly collapsed, and hastily apologizing he staggered back to his sanctum, and for half an hour had to be treated to fresh applications of violets, with an occasional whiff of the Reno camellia and Mr. Woodson's floral offering.

On arriving at the Oakland ferry and during the passage the poet was the observed of all; but though his strange appearance provoked many smiles, he was treated with the courtesy of silence by the curious crowd. The only question he deigned to ask about the city, which he viewed from the upper deck of the steamer, where he stood poised on one leg like the decorative fowl of aestheticism, was: "Have you no old ruins in your city?"

When told that the Mission Dolores[9] boasted of an old church and a number of adobe shanties, the poet's face brightened, but the joy was short-lived. Presently, borne on the wings of the western wind, came the odoriferous offers of the waterfront, churned into aggressive life by the ferryboat, and the poet, with an appealing look at Mr. Locke, turned and fled to the cabin. On arriving at the San Francisco side the poet was adroitly whisked into a carriage and driven to the Palace Hotel.

He will remain some weeks on this coast, and meditates a visit to Japan. His fellow-passengers, including John Howson,[10] the actor, speak of him in the kindest manner and tell sorrowfully of the reception which he got at Corinne, where forty bogus aesthetes, with big sunflowers and a terrible brass band, serenaded him.

1. The Bohemian Club, founded in 1872, was modeled on New York's Century Club.

2. Julian Waldbridge Rix (1850–1903), American painter, illustrator, and landscape artist who studied at the School of Design in San Francisco.

3. See the *San Francisco Daily Chronicle*, 30 March 1882: "The aesthete's bitter sarcasm against the plastering ability of the present day caused quite a flutter in the middle section of the hall, where a large number of sunflowers were dancing in the bonnets of the Jessie and Natoma Street aristocracy."

4. According to the *San Francisco Daily Chronicle* (30 March 1882), Wilde "dealt a most unchivalrous blow" to a "delegation of Minna and Sixth Street dressmakers" by scorning modern millinery in his lecture.

5. Marcus Mayer (1847–1918) was an American producer and manager.

6. Mount Tamalpais, a popular subject in California landscape painting, is the highest peak in the Marin hills, just north of San Francisco's Golden Gate.

7. The poet Charles Warren Stoddard (1843–1909) coedited the *Overland Monthly* and celebrated same-sex love in such books as *South-Sea Idyls* (1873).

8. The Irish National Land League was founded by Michael Davitt in 1879, just prior to the Land War of 1880–82, as an instrument to abolish "landlordism" and help poor tenant farmers own the land they worked. Wilde praised the work of the league at greater length in "A Home Ruler," *St. Louis Globe-Democrat*, 27 February 1882, 6.

9. The oldest structure in San Francisco, the Mission Dolores stands on a site dedicated in 1776, half a block from what is now the corner of Sixteenth and Valencia.

10. John Jerome Howson (1842–1887), an Australian-born actor, played Reginald Bunthorne to great success in the Comley-Barton company's touring production of *Patience*.

---

31. "OSCAR ARRIVES," *SACRAMENTO RECORD-UNION*, 27 MARCH 1882, 3

As a fitting introduction to the apostle of modern aestheticism, a *Record-Union* representative yesterday morning met Oscar Wilde at the depot with a bouquet of the choicest flowers that could be culled from Sacramento's floral wealth, and being received by that gentleman with cordiality, the twain sat down to breakfast and had a chat, which, being unconcluded when train time was up, the apostle and the news-gatherer, having found themselves upon pleasantly debatable ground, continued the conversation in the cars as they went Bayward. Mr. Wilde is one of the best talked about men of the day. This cultured young English poet is, his friends claim, the most misrepresented of foreigners that ever visited the country. The Oxonian, who is a genial companion and an admirable conversationalist, showed no disinclination to unbosom himself, and the determination being announced to give him for once a perfectly "fair show" in a representative American newspaper, responded to the questions propounded to him with ready fluency and sincere earnestness. He is scarcely twenty-six years of age, very tall and quite slender. This "build" gives him the appearance of slightly stooping in the shoulders when he addresses men of ordinary stature. He dresses plainly, to severity, indulges in a broad turn-down collar, a simple knotted scarf without jewelry, and wears a broad-brimmed white sombrero decidedly Spanish in style. His clean-shaven face is long, broadest at the lower jaw, with a full, round and oversized chin; a large and well-developed nose, a broad mouth, with full lips opening over large, prominent teeth, the upper lip a shade too short, and eyes very full, large and handsome and an apology between gray and blue, are arched by delicately lined eyebrows. His forehead is high, narrows as it ascends, and on either side his straight brown hair, which from a middle parting falls to a level with his chin in unstudied negligence, and shades a neck rather long and with a tendency to crane slightly forward.

The expression of his countenance is very amiable, and a constant smile of perfect content rests upon his overfull features, which are almost effeminate in apparent lack of vigor and force, but which in that respect belie the man, whose conversation proves him to be shrewd, perfectly self-possessed, and entirely able to take care of himself in this world. With a Chesterfieldian bow, he returned his thanks for a button-hole bouquet a Sacramento lady sent by the newsman for "the lover of the beautiful," and the aesthete settled himself in the cushions of a palace car and signified his readiness to be put upon the categorical rack.

The news-gleaner opened the ball: "Are we to correctly understand you, Mr. Wilde, that your belief is that a true love for art for its own sake, and in its highest development, marks the best forms and systems of civilization most easily attainable?"

The Aesthete: Yes. Life without industry is barbarism; industry without art is barren. We should first teach the people to use their hands in the work of art. All that is artistic must begin in handicraft.

"You have been quoted as pronouncing the devotion to beauty and the production of the beautiful as making a man's life immortal. Would you be understood as erecting that into a creed of a religion of culture?"

The Aesthete: The best service of God is found in the worship of all that is beautiful. Such a worshiper can do no wrong willfully. We should remember that all things worthy should be satisfying. The religions of the world too often tell us to love the Creator without keeping in view the created things. How starved is such a belief—it sees the Creator and is blind to His work; it teaches of Him but makes no effort to teach of His work's beauty and grandeur.

"In one of your addresses, Mr. Wilde, you speak of the necessity of every household possessing the things that give pleasure to the user and were a pleasure to the maker. Do I understand from you by that, that if we surround ourselves and children by beautiful things, and keep both within, as you put it, 'the atmosphere of fair things,' that we will soonest bring the race to the purest state, and to despise and utterly forsake the vulgar and coarse and wicked?"

The Poet: Yes, indeed. The man who lives in such an atmosphere must be a better man, a better workman, a better citizen, and there will follow such a better civilization. The mistake in our educational systems has been that we have sought to teach truth abstractly. Great special truths must grow up in us. Truth comes to the child through the atmosphere of his surroundings. Purify that, and you purify him. Surround him by the beautiful, the useful, and the good, and what must result? The theory of beautiful surroundings that finds expression in Europe is true of nations. The life of every nation is influenced by its surroundings. Taine,[1] in the history of literature, is constantly turning to the hills and the valleys—to the scenery of England. He could not resist it nor disassociate them from his theme. Formerly the products of the man's mind were treated abstractly—and not as to his surroundings. The first thing to teach the boy is to use his eyes, his ears, and his hands. But we are always trying to educate his mind before we give him a mind, for mind is creative. The child is endowed with intellectual faculties, but the mind is the result of growth; and I need not say to what extent we control that. To a child the teaching of abstract truth is folly.

"You conclude one of your lectures with the words: 'The secret of life is in art.' Would you add a word and tell us how the masses can best attain a knowledge and love of art?"

Mr. Wilde: I hope that the masses will come to be the creators in art. That is what I mean—that art will some time cease to be simply the accomplishment and luxury of the rich but the possession, as it is the rightful heritage of all, poor and rich alike. The difficulty I have felt and met in America is not that there is a lack of interest in art; not that they do not love it; not that they are not receptive—no, they have a great love for the beautiful—but the difficulty is that they do not hold the handicrafts in greater honor and respect. I would dignify labor by stripping it of its degradation, and that by developing all that is beautiful in the laborer's surroundings and opening his eyes to it. Ah! I would speak to the hard-working people, whom I wish I could reach through the prejudice that shuts them and me away from each other. Why, it is to the mechanics and workers of your country that I look for the triumph that must come. Why, back here in the West I met a railroad-repairer—a man working out on the line at a hard, laborious task. It was his daily business. He talked with me, wanted to know what we are trying to do. Why, that man quoted Pope[2] to me, analyzed his method, discussed my positions with me, understood me, and where he doubted gave his reasons in homely phrases, but unmistakably and clearly. He took an interest in the best of life; was keen, kindly, receptive, and pugnacious in need, withal—altogether a charming fellow. Now, in England, in men of his class such a conversation would be simply impossible. Here I learn that a man is fairly representative of a myriad.

"Mr. Wilde, the decorative art rage, as it is called, is thought by many to be indulged in to the extreme. Do you think there is a danger to true art culture in the rush and push in the former line, or is it one of the signs of our renaissance?"

The Poet: Oh, of course; for the people have not had the opportunity, in all respects, as yet to get on well, so they are constantly going wrong. Still the desire to go at all is something, and much has been and is being accomplished. But if this desire is to culminate in anything great, it must be by the affectionate study of art and beautiful things. The truth about decorative art, like all in art, is to be revealed to those who are receptive of the beautiful. The present revelation is the cause of the revival in decorative art.

"There is one question I much desire to ask you, whether you think the drama most popular now, the spectacular and the class that appeals more to the fancy and the eye and the emotions than to the intellect and the reason—whether it is not a stumbling block in the path to higher art culture?"

Mr. Wilde: No, no. So far from that being the case, the fault I find with the modern stage is the departure from the true spirit that intended it for the pageant. In this modern life, where we have given up so much of color, so much of the beautiful, let us leave on the stage all we can in beauty of dress, in richness of scenery, in graceful groupings. The trouble is the controllers of the stage belittle these spectacular effects by sensational scenes of the most improbable kind, and work up all sorts of morbid situations, with flying trains and sinking steamers, and all that. The stage is art in action. See how much we have fallen away from that ideal. On the stage we should see all we can of rich color, beautiful drapery, and grouping, and all things that will cultivate a taste among the people for beautiful and chaste things. When they thus see how beautiful things can be made by their surroundings, they will look to their own and discover possibilities before unknown to them.

"In your first address in America you spoke of the perfection in your movement that you felt there was in America, because we are 'young.' Do you mean by that that the absence of the influence of the architecture, the art schools and culture of Europe, etc., is no drawback to our people in art advancement?"

Mr. Wilde: No art is better than bad art. I'd sooner the people studied no art than some of the bad art of Europe—they would be more receptive of the true when it does come to them. Why, sir, architecture in England is deteriorating. The handicrafts are falling into disrepute. Against this it is to be said that England has had great examples and eminent exemplars, but they have isolated ones, like Turner.[3] They were surrounded by masses that did not appreciate them. They had admirers, votaries, supporters, but not in the masses. Against this nonappreciative spirit we are fighting. So I say that a new people, not under a dead weight of crowded Europe, give hope for quicker appreciation of the true and the beautiful. As I have said, "the very absence of tradition with you is the source of your freedom and strength."

"You have been much caricatured, and your theories much satirized. How has that affected your judgment of the American people?"

Mr. Wilde: I rarely think of it; when I do, I think nothing of it. It does not in the slightest degree represent to me the strength or the sanity of a great modern nation. One must always remember that wisdom does not brawl upon the street. The voice of folly is always shrill and very loud, but it passes away. Of one thing I am convinced, and that is, the fool has no influence; he may for the moment—that is all.

"*Harper's Monthly* criticizes you in a little dash this month,[4] and dislikes your extravagance and eccentricities."

Mr. Wilde: Do you call that a little dash? I call it as cruel as it is unjust. Suppose it is true—admitting it for argument's sake only—that people come to hear me out of curiosity? Well, I get a hearing, and still hope to do some good in my day. But it isn't true. I've found in America truly appreciative audiences. True, caricature and misrepresentation have excited curiosity. Why, in Chicago I had an audience of 3,000 people, and spoke for an hour and twenty minutes, and only one man left the room before the close, and he came to apologize for the necessity requiring it. That speaks of appreciation, at least for respectful hearing. I think the West is very fair to those who address it."

"So you do not fear ridicule?"

Mr. Wilde: Indeed, no. I want what I have to advance to stand on its merit. I ask no quarter. I have not the remotest doubt as to which side will win. I think the school I am in will win, because it represents great principles, and they are working for us, no matter what I may do.

"But has the press given you a fair show?"

Mr. Wilde: Oh, the papers! They run in grooves a good deal. They might just as well take the other side. The praise of the man who can't understand me is quite as injurious as the abuse of any enemy can be. There is no limit to the nonsense some men will write if it raises the circulation of the paper from one to two.

"What do you think of this country so far as you have had opportunity to observe? Does it come up to or fall below your preconceived ideas?"

Mr. Wilde (with a merry twinkle of the eye): My dear sir, I was sensible enough (pardon me) not to have any preconceived ideas about it. I came to see and learn. Well, thus far I find more independence of thought here than in Europe.

"You are reported as saying that the commercial spirit in England is killing nobility and purity. Coupling this with your expression of hope for art culture in America, are we to infer that you think this nation of traders less sordid than your people?"

Mr. Wilde: I mean the spirit of commerce is misunderstood. Some of the most beautiful cities have been built by commercial men, as Genoa, Florence, Venice. But in England men have been made machines, quite as soulless and ignoble as the whirling wheels of machinery. I don't speak now of the flood of bad patterns and ugly designs as resulting; but I speak of the injury to the workmen themselves, so deep that they cannot realize the nobility of life. In America I don't think it goes to that extent. I don't think the American workman will submit to such a position.

"I have read in Emerson's essay on 'The Poet' these words: 'The beautiful rests on the foundations of the necessary.'[5] Do you agree with that sentiment, Mr. Wilde?"

The Aesthete: The moment art becomes a luxury it loses, for it must arise out of necessity. All art is the expression of the noble and joyous in life. Luxury gives us the gaudy, the vulgar, the transient. It may help but it never creates art. For instance, luxury gives great prices for French landscapes of the modern school. Now, while I admire French landscapes, the indulgence by luxury in them does not dignify American handicrafts at all, or help home effort.

"But, Mr. Wilde, if surroundings have so great an influence, does not the architecture, the great models, the atmosphere of art in Europe account for preference?"

Mr. Wilde: Familiarity with the beautiful in architecture does not belittle it with him who appreciates it. It grows on you. Italy is the loveliest country of Europe, but Italy gives you no landscapes from her studios. You speak of the broad field for the study of the lofty and the beautiful and awe-inspiring in California. Well, it is not necessary to have great natural wonders at home to develop art. It is in the eye and the heart of the artist that we find the secret of success. The landscapes of Italy are all-satisfying, and so the Italian artist does not reproduce them. You must go to the cloudy, the misty lands, for great landscape painters—the blue and the golden light of Italy is unapproachable.

"An American woman, Mr. Wilde, has written of beauty in lines with which you will accord, I presume: Mrs. Sarah J. Hale. Never heard the lines? They are:

> Beauty was lent to nature as the type
> Of Heaven's unspeakable and holy joy
> Where all perfection makes the sum of bliss."[6]

Mr. Wilde: Yes, certainly.

"By the way, Mr. Wilde, what do you in England think of the international copyright question?"

The Poet: That a country gets small good from a literature it steals.

"But you are retaliating now?"

Mr. Wilde: Very little. It doesn't change the principle. Why, in all your cars I find newsmen selling my poems—stolen! I never can resist the impulse to read out a lesson on the heinousness of the offense.

"But there is a genuine American edition?"

Mr. Wilde: Oh, yes! By a Boston house.[7]

"I heard you were getting out a work in America."

Mr. Wilde: That is a volume of poems by a friend, Rennell Rodd,[8] an English officer. It will appear in Philadelphia.

"Why not issue it in your own country?"

Mr. Wilde: I desire to introduce the author to the American public. I think it will appreciate him. It will have an introduction that I have written. In that I point out the strong quality of this young man's work and show how the artist can best use the life around him. Young workers in art are apt to go too blindly in. They perceive too often without rule or principle and don't cultivate our sense of beauty. They are slow to perceive how all art is a desire for perfection.

The conversation was continued at much length. What has been given exemplifies its tone and character.

Wilde has an apparently affected drawl in his speech, but it is evidently his normal style of delivery. Divest him of his flowing locks, add crispness to his enunciation and vigor to his tone, and there would be nothing about him to give ground for ridicule, except, perhaps, his expressive and languidly poetic eyes, the almost boyish fullness and effeminacy of his face, and the full lips that speak of the possible voluptuary. His friends on the train complained bitterly of the rudeness of the crowds at small stations on the road beyond the Sierras—especially of the attempt at Corinne, Utah, of a grotesquely accoutered crowd, with a band, that sought to invade the car.

Some of the crowds will probably be chagrined to now learn that the Oscar

Wilde many of them saw was not *the* Oscar Wilde, but was that inimitable comedian John Howson, of the Comley-Barton Opera Troupe, who, being on the train, several times put on his "Bunthorne" wig, contorted his features into an admirable resemblance of the ever-dwelling smile on Oscar's countenance, and showed himself at times to save his friend and to have a bit of fun on his own account.

At Sacramento there was no embarrassing staring at Wilde, and no crowd gathered about him. He was not subjected either to any vulgar inquisitiveness by the great crowd on the Oakland ferryboat. The people hunted him out, glanced at him and passed on without offensive staring.

Mr. Wilde expressed often his warm admiration for what he had seen of America and its people. In all his conversation many will be disappointed to learn he never used the words "superlatively beautiful," "ravishingly beautiful," "too utterly utter," "too too," or any phraseology to which ridicule and satire have given point as to aesthetes.

Concerning the sunflower, which is in the popular mind connected with Wilde's name, it may be added that he has himself explained about in a lecture, in these words:

> You have heard, I think, a few of you, of two flowers connected with the aesthetic movement in England said (I assure you erroneously) to be the food of some aesthetic young men. Well, let me tell you that the reason we love the lily and the sunflower, in spite of what Mr. Gilbert may tell you, is not for any vegetable fashion at all; it is because these two lovely flowers are in England the two most perfect models of design, the most naturally adapted for decorative art.[9]

The poet, aesthete, and Romantic philosopher will remain on the coast three weeks, and will put in one day at Sacramento, when all the curious can for themselves see the present lion of curiosity.

These things impressed the press representative yesterday after a long conversation with Mr. Wilde and after observing him in a great crowd of representative people and making note of their expressions. He is scholarly, studiedly polite, a gentleman, shrewd, fearless, observant, self-possessed and of poetic temperament. He has been considerably misrepresented and unduly ridiculed. He is apparently sincere and earnest. He is, however, ludicrously odd to the American eye in personal appearance; is eccentric (or affected) in this regard, and lacks the manifestations of manliness in his countenance, and frequently in his manner. If he was more an object of curiosity than respect to Californians yesterday, it was due to the latter causes, to the ridicule showered on him at the East, and in part to the present public conception of the tendency of his teachings.

1. Hippolyte Taine (1828–1893), French literary critic and historian.
2. Alexander Pope (1688–1744) was an English poet of the neoclassical, or Augustan, period who wrote highly refined verse, often of a didactic or satirical nature.
3. J. M. W. Turner (1775?–1851), eminent English Romantic landscape painter.
4. Wilde refers to George William Curtis's comments in the "Editor's Easy Chair," *Harper's Monthly* 64 (Apr. 1882): 790.
5. The complete quotation: "Arising out of eternal reason, one and perfect, whatever is beautiful rests on the foundation of the necessary. Nothing is arbitrary, nothing is insulated in beauty. It depends forever on the necessary and the useful."
6. These lines, then very famous, are from "Beauty," by the American poet Sarah Josepha Hale (1788–1879).
7. The Boston publishing house Robert Brothers brought out an authorized American edition of Wilde's poems in 1881.
8. James Rennell Rodd (1858–1941), English diplomat, politician, scholar, and poet.
9. These lines are from the conclusion to Wilde's lecture "The English Renaissance."

---

32. MARY WATSON, "OSCAR WILDE AT HOME," *SAN FRANCISCO EXAMINER*, 9 APRIL 1882, 1

The English language is popularly supposed to be a vehicle of expression that was perfected long ago. It is intended not to conceal but to express thought, and only persons who labor after originality, like Robert Browning,[1] for instance, give themselves the trouble to twist its words into new meanings. Yet, strange to say, there are two words in the English language which of late are employed as frequently as any other two that could be named, if we make due exception of "charming" and "awful," and they are "aesthetic" and "utter," about the signification of which there seem to be no general agreement; yet all concede that they apply to an unknown quantity in artistic niceness, and at once the more complex form of intensified aestheticism in the shape of "utter" presents itself. The most agreeable and perhaps the most effective solution of the much-used word outside of dictionarial definition would be to get the meaning from the fountainhead, that is, from the apostolic source of aestheticism, Oscar Wilde himself. I saw the lion in his lair, saw him stirred up, poetically speaking, and an interesting process it was. It took place at the Palace Hotel,[2] where the young poet resided during his stay here. Without further preliminaries I will endeavor to picture Oscar Wilde's at-home manner and how he exists in so unaesthetic a caravansary as the Palace Hotel. Fortunately, there was plenty of time to get a good look at the room and peer about without transgressing any social rules, for when I arrived, as per appointment, there was no one but his servant at home, and the opportunity was afforded to get an uninterrupted few moments and jot down whatever there was remarkable. Between the fear of not seeing everything and of his sudden arrival, I could only get cursory glimpses of all the peculiarities the room offered, and had little time to think of what I was to ask him when he did make his appearance. At any rate, all the questions that I had in my mind in reference to Mr. Wilde flew from me when he entered a few moments after I did.

His lazy manner and my hard effort to explain in a depressed sort of way, occasioned by my feeling of strangeness, soon made matters rather one-sided. He talked, and talked well, and soon I regained my ordinary frame of mind, but with still a misgiving as to how to broach my subject; but his action in throwing off his circular cloak, the quick and well-rehearsed movement of the servant, who reached the center of the room just at the right moment to catch the outside wraps of the poet, and his subsequent position on the sofa, partaking rather of an easy posture, half reclining, half sitting, set me quite at ease; and the poet, whom I had expected to lead me in the empyrean ways of poetic fancy, for which I was half prepared, made me believe so utterly in the mere commonplace that I felt a sense of disappointment, for it is so awful to believe in a man's superiority and then find him out. The rooms were of the usual hotel order, with the walls as innocent of cheerfulness as the sunless light which filtered in from the window. It suggested a question and I haphazarded it.

"How do you manage to live in these rooms without any surrounding signs of the beautiful?"

Quoth he, with an accompaniment of a rather comfortable shudder, "Don't mention it."

Since the request of not mentioning it was so vigorously put to me, I dropped the question of the beautiful in art, or whatever else was in my mind pertaining to the subject, and naturally did what ninety-nine people out of every hundred, when a lack of material for conversation occurred, would do. I spoke for myself.

"Is not this something new for you, Mr. Wilde? You have never met a lady reporter."

"No," replied he, smilingly; "I have not. We do not have them in our country."

I looked toward the bay window, wherein was placed a table, and on it a vase with a large bouquet of white flowers, beautifully arranged, and, to give it effect, a silk handkerchief had been thrown carelessly across the two lower branches, and the air coming from the window swayed the ends in graceful movements. Glancing from the top of the table to the floor, the pile of newspapers met my gaze, and naturally suggested the next question:

"Are you pleased at the newspaper reports of yourself and the reporters' interviews?"

Evidently this had struck a rich vein, for he looked up with a peculiar and hearty smile; but, evidently remembering that his questioner was of the same genus as the subject spoken about, he seemed to restrain himself but replied, with a laugh:

"Frankly, then, I read them all, and not only here but all over America I have been quite amused at the struggle each of the gentlemen have had to write what I did not say; but I have the most sympathy with the writers of the articles which strive to be what is called here in the United States 'funny.' Their hard work has been so apparent."

From this on the conversation was quite easy, and Mr. Wilde displayed a fund of shrewd common sense hardly to be expected from an art enthusiast and a poet. The conversation on his part which followed gave me full opportunity to memorize the disposition of every article in the room, and that a certain eccentric individuality of the man was displayed in every phase of the furniture could not be gainsaid. There were three tables in the room, the one mentioned in the embrasure of the bay window, one inside the room and one about the center, and all in a row. The sofa on which the poet was reclining was on the left hand and the mantel on the right. On the table where the striking posy of white flowers was placed were also strewn in confusion scraps of paper, letters, books, etc., and at the foot the newspapers, which fortunately suggested the opening of a conversation which by this time was flowing along smoothly enough. On the table in the center of the room was also a lot of papers and cards from various business houses, evidently intended to convey to the much advertised aesthete the pleasure every merchant would have in showing him his wares, to be used in the future as an advertisement no doubt. On the table near the window and about four feet from the other was a large silver fruit dish, filled with oranges, two plates and a knife, and placed there innocently enough as a living example of an effective and suggestive picture of still life. On the sofa was carelessly thrown a dark brown rug with a pillow, over which was thrown a crepe shawl of the same color, with long fringe to match. During our conversation several cards were handed in, and among other things the servant brought in an autographic album with someone's compliments and a request for Mr. Wilde's little contribution to the general collection. He arose, seated himself at the table with the open book before him, and in a posture which excellently expressed "thought," he tried to evolve something for the inevitable autograph hunter and great

American nuisance. The inspirational mood was not on him then. He arose, gracefully spread his arm over an almost impossible distance, and, with an admirable breadth of reach, got hold of a copy of his own poems, set down again and said to me:

"One sometimes forgets one's own lines."

The struggle was short and had to be given up, so he bade the servant— "Tell the messenger to leave the album, as I am too much engaged just now." This with a glance at me.

A few moments later, another autograph album was sent in and the message repeated—without the glance, however. He then wheeled the sofa in front of me and threw himself upon it—not, of course, lying down, but in a careless posture, with his arm thrown carelessly over the pillow. I got a good glance at his necktie, and I noticed that the handkerchief in his coat pocket and the scarf were of exactly the same tint of satin—a peculiar shade of live bronze.

Among the other questions, and they were legion, I asked him:

"At what hour of the day do you find it most convenient to write?"

"At no particular hour. In writing a verse I sometimes wait for the exact mood, and it takes weeks at times before I get the right word to express my thought in the completion of a sentence or a line. Sometimes a subject is presented to me when I least expect it, perhaps in a company of friends, perhaps traveling, or in a crowded street."

In an animated conversation, and especially about himself, Mr. Wilde, in a youthful sort of way, becomes quite enthusiastic. From the conversation which followed I gathered that he was born at No. 1 Marian Square, Dublin, and that his mother, of whom he seems very proud, inspired him with a desire to become a poet. He showed me her picture, and, from her portrait, she seems to be a handsome woman of about forty-seven, with a clear sunny expression of face, and not at all like a woman who is given to writing poetry. Mr. Wilde does not resemble his mother a particle, although there seems to be a deep bond of sympathy between them. He assured me that until the age of eighteen he never thought of writing a line; and in proof that others have the same enthusiasm, and entertain the same views of poetry, art, and literature as himself, he pointed out the fact that a young classmate of his has written a volume on the same subject and dedicated it to Mr. Wilde himself. Mr. Wilde is now having it published and it will be out shortly. He showed me a bit of manuscript which he declared he appreciated and valued above anything which had ever been given him. It was the original manuscript of "An Ode to Blue," written by Keats in a handwriting peculiarly dainty and small. The manuscript, old and yellow, was presented to Mr. Wilde on his recent visit to Louisville.[3] While there, he received a note from a young lady asking him to call, signed simply Miss Keats. It was from this lady, to whom the poet was a relative, that the young disciple received his treasured ode. That Mr. Wilde is not sure of his ground, nor has he a fixed idea, is best illustrated by his reply to a question relative to his new book. He said: "My other book may be a perfect contradiction of the first"; and, on being asked about his return to England, he said: "I don't know. I never made plans, but go whither my feelings prompt. I wish, however, to be back in time for the salons."

Mr. Wilde regrets exceedingly that he entered into a contract with Sarony, the New York photographer,[4] not to have any one else take his pictures while in this country. He admires the pictures produced by some of our local photographers, and, in an art sense, apparently believes in the superiority of San Francisco workmanship to that of New York. He had some fine specimens from the principal photographers of the city. On being asked as to the age expressed in the last words of his poem, which interest all women—

> I have made my choice, have lived my poems, and though youth is
>   gone in wasted days,
> I have found the lover's crown of myrtle better than the poet's crown
>   of bays![5]

he replied: "Sometimes one feels older at twenty than he will at forty."

During his conversation about his poems he certainly evidenced a belief in them and gave way to his enthusiasm by frequent gestures. His voice, in ordinary conversation, does not partake of the same tone as that used on the rostrum, nor are the same unpleasant monotones employed with all their faulty intonations. Youthful fervor carries with it a sense of truth, and if the word "utter," as expressed by this aesthete, means ardor, coupled with a sense of art and what is beautiful in the world, it is a good word and ought to be a welcome one in our vocabulary, which, after all, is not replete with adjectives expressive of things that are beautiful, as a lady reporter can testify.

1. Robert Browning (1812–1889), British dramatist and poet famous for his innovation in style, especially with regard to the dramatic monologue.
2. San Francisco's luxury Palace Hotel was built in 1875 and destroyed in fires that followed the earthquake of 1906.
3. Emma Speed, Keats's niece, presented Wilde with the original manuscript of "Sonnet in Blue" in Louisville, Kentucky, in March 1882. In his letter of appreciation, Wilde calls Keats the "supreme and perfect artist" (*Complete Letters*, 157).
4. Napoleon Sarony (1821–96), a Canadian-born photographer and lithographer, held exclusive rights to Wilde's photographs during his 1882 lecture tour. One of his portraits of Wilde, used for advertisements without Sarony's permission,

became the subject of a U.S. Supreme Court case in which the Court upheld the extension of copyright protection to photographs.

5. The poem is "Flower of Love" (1881); this is the last of its fourteen verse paragraphs.

---

33. "OSCAR WILDE," *SALT LAKE HERALD,* 12 APRIL 1882

Our reporter called upon Mr. Oscar Wilde on Monday and was received by the distinguished aesthete with characteristic courtesy, Mr. Wilde speaking of his American experiences with the utmost candor.

No part of America it appeared has struck Mr. Wilde so favorably as California, but as he said, "I have still to see Colorado." Whatever may be the effect of Denver and Leadville, it is at present certain that San Francisco and the West Coast have captivated the poet, for Mr. Wilde intends to return there next year with a party of friends, "in the capacity," as he described it, "of a private gentleman traveling for his own amusement and not as a public lecturer condemned to go on the platform at every place he stops."

Of the results of his tour, financially, the apostle of art decoration spoke very contentedly, and proposes devoting a portion of the proceeds to a lengthened visit to Venice and a leisurely study of Italy.

But it was when he came to speak of his reception by the American public that Mr. Wilde was most interesting. "I am," he said, "more and more astonished and pleased every time I lecture at the courtesy with which I am received by my audiences. Everybody, they say, laughs at me and says I am a fraud, yet not only do they fill any place I choose to lecture in, but they sit out all I have to say with surprising good humor and patience. I am quite conscious that much of what I say may be annoying, but after all I came to America to say it, and so long as audience with such breeding allow me to strut my brief hour upon the stage,[1] I should be singularly stupid not to take advantage of the opportunities given me of trotting out my hobbies. I have no doubt that tonight there will be many people present, perhaps even most of them, who, after they have seen me and satisfied their curiosity as to my costume and my long hair, would be glad to go away again without sitting through a lecture on a subject that does not interest them; but at the same time I have no doubt whatever that they will, out of pure courtesy, sit it out to the bitter end. Sometimes I am inclined to laugh at this kindness, knowing that my audiences often laugh at me, but I really consider my opportunity

so splendid a one for saying what I wish to say that I only wish my delivery
and my language were better than they are. Yes, you are right; my delivery
has often been criticized *very* severely, but I confess it is abominable. But I
cannot help it. I have never studied elocution—but I shall when I return to
England, probably under Vezin.[2] As for my costume, I have several reasons
for it, but the more important are these: that the present evening dress of
gentlemen is the most objectionable possible, and then I should be glad to
do something towards introducing a better. As it is, the prince of Wales[3]
and some of his friends have already pronounced in favor of the velvet coat,
ruffles, knee breeches and silk hose, and it is quite possible that in another
year or so all young England may be dressed as I am. Indeed, in New York,
one very charming lady has ordered knee-breeches as *de rigueur* at her recep-
tions, and New York has cheerfully submitted to her delightful tyranny. But
another reason for my wearing this costume is based on a principle, for live
poets have principles, and that is that one should do as one preaches. Now
William Morris, the author of that exquisite *Earthly Paradise,*[4] is propheti-
cally proclaiming the doctrine of artistic dress as a preliminary to a revival
of true art, but he goes about himself in the very shabbiest and ugliest of
nineteenth-century clothes. I do not agree with this, so that when you call
upon me as you do now, you find me dressed in aesthetic colors. My coat is
a pearl grey velvet, my necktie Venetian green, and you see that I spread a
fur robe over this hideous sofa before I sit down on it. Tonight, for the same
reason, if you come to the theater, you will find me in black velvet lined with
purple and wearing the ruffles and seals of the regency."

Mr. Wilde then went on to speak of the American poets, expressing that
special preference for Joaquin Miller and Walter Whitman, which he has
so often tried to vindicate in opposition to other opinions. For Longfellow,
he did not entertain so much reverence for the poet as love for the man.
"Longfellow," he said, "was himself a beautiful poem, more beautiful than
anything he ever wrote." Emerson's prose he considered poetry; the poetry
of certain others he considered prose. But as he said, "We rhymesters are
without number; the real poet has not come once in a century." Mr. Wilde
then quoted favorite sketches from Aldrich, Holmes, Lowell, and others,
showing an intimate acquaintance with American literature that justified
his undertaking to criticize it. Of our novelists he places Howells and James
easily first; "indeed," he said, "they are your only two."

Much more that Mr. Wilde said might be of interest to our readers, but
our space compels us to be brief. To sum up, he appears to be thoroughly
satisfied with the financial results of his tour, and more than satisfied with
the good taste and courtesy of the audiences that have listened to him, and

among the personal friends he has made in America, there are many who have exacted the promise that he will return to the country next year. "And so I will," said Mr. Wilde, "when I have got more to say and learnt a better style of saying it."

1. Wilde paraphrases Shakespeare's famous speech on transience and life from *Macbeth,* act 5, scene 5, lines 24–26.
2. Hermann Vezin (1829–1910), American actor, writer, and teacher of elocution.
3. The prince of Wales is a title typically given to the heir apparent to the British monarchy, in this case George V (1865–1936).
4. William Morris (1834–96), an English writer, artist, socialist, and principal founder of the arts and crafts movement, began writing his popular long poem *The Earthly Paradise* (1868) in 1861.

34. "OSCAR WILDE," *DENVER ROCKY MOUNTAIN NEWS,* 13 APRIL 1882, 8

The aesthete has come. The man whose life and talents are devoted to the study and cultivation of the beautiful, and the business of making money, has arrived in this prosaic city, where dollars and cents rank high, and where beauty is valued only for its money value.

Last evening's train over the Cheyenne division was delayed about half an hour, and seated in the drawing-room car of the train was the much talked of Oscar Wilde, who manifested some regret and annoyance at the unexpected delay. The aesthete is not handsome, and yet he is remarkably fine-looking. About his person there is an air of refinement, culture, and grace that makes a striking contrast to the typical American man.

Oscar Wilde is tall and elegantly proportioned. His head is not large, and yet it is good-sized. His hair, a dark brown, is parted nearly in the middle and is worn long, giving him a somewhat peculiar appearance. His face is long and oval in shape. He wears no beard or mustaches, his mouth is rather large and the lips are full and as bright colored as a girl's. His teeth are large and not particularly handsome, his forehead is low. His eyes are extremely beautiful; they are blue and very large. His nose is long and thin, and if breeding and blood are indicated by the nose, Mr. Wilde can lay claim to a large quantity of genuine "blue." His complexion is so clear and beautiful that the maidens may well grow green with envy, for no balm or powder can give to their cheeks the peculiar beauty of the aesthete's complexion.

His hands are well-shaped, his fingers long and tapering as if made to handle beautiful objects or wield the pen while the poetic mind dictates words of fire. His feet are large and well proportioned to his body. Taken all in all, Mr. Wilde can be truly called an elegant-looking gentleman. His looks would indicate that he was the descendant of a well-bred, fine, old English family, and his conversation marks him as a man of sense, strength, and sympathy. During repose his face might be called plain, but when conversing his eyes grow bright, the color rises to his cheeks, his gestures are free and easy, and he is the picture of animation.

On the train last evening he wore a pair of dark brown trousers, well cut and neat fitting, and a black velvet coat, rather after the fashion of a sacque. It was cut high in the neck, leaving visible only the necktie, which was a cream-colored silk scarf tied in a large bow. His collar was of fine white linen, and was not noticeably large. He wore a long heavy overcoat of *gen d'arme* fine cloth, lined throughout with fur, a broad fur collar and deep cuffs finishing the outside of the handsome garment. Around his neck, a gold-colored embroidered scarf hung untied. The ends were fringed. Upon leaving the ear, the scarf was carelessly drawn close about the neck under the overcoat. Upon his head Mr. Wilde wore a large black, or deep blue, slouch hat. Upon the third finger of his right hand he wore a large handsomely carved intaglio ring which was his only ornament.

After shaking hands with the *News* representative Mr. Wilde at once entered into conversation with an ease that is not ordinary even among public speakers. His voice is pleasant to listen to and gives one the impression of much power, yet he always talks in a monotone which must grow tedious. He talks rapidly, uses beautiful language and pronounces his words in a way which Americans will be very apt to call affected. His gestures during conversation are graceful and yet very emphatic.

Sinking back into the seat and assuming a comfortable position, Mr. Wilde said: "Yes, I am very sorry about the delay. I fear I shall be obliged to keep the audience waiting."

Upon being asked how he was impressed with the country through which he had recently passed, he said: "Oh, everything looks so brown, bare, and disconsolate. You know I have just come from California, which is a garden of beauty. Oh, it is so lovely! The cities of the Atlantic Coast look bare and dreary at this time of the year. You know, at home, in England, it is always green. We have only the little island and it is well tilled, every inch of it. It is always beautiful. For five months I have been longing for that garden spot, and California was such a delight to me. The green was such a rest to my weary eyes. It is the most restful of all colors. The California people are delightful; I disliked to leave San Francisco and I should love to visit it again.

Mr. Wilde then asked a question which is only natural, considering what the ride from Denver to Cheyenne is. He inquired: "What is there beautiful in Colorado?"

Being desirous of obtaining the aesthete's views of the cities he had visited, the reporter said: "Mr. Wilde, if it is not impertinent to ask, which city of those you have visited have you found the most aesthetic?

Mr. Wilde, smiling a little sarcastically, replied: "You cannot ask an impertinent question of me. But really I cannot specify any one city. New York being so near Europe has many of the characteristics of a foreign city. Boston and Philadelphia both are paying considerable attention to art. But what especially pleased and interested me were the cities further removed from the Atlantic Coast. Cincinnati has an art school and a good one, a school of wood-carving. Chicago people are very enthusiastic over art. I had large audiences in that city. I talked to about 3,300 people, who listened with the closest attention to all I had to say. St. Louis, too, is full of people who are interested in art, and San Francisco—"

Here Mr. Wilde was interrupted, but it is safe to infer all he had to say was in hearty praise of the aesthetic movement among the dwellers in the city of the golden gate.

"You would bring art into the humblest houses, would you not? You would have art among the multitude? Is that your doctrine?"

"It is. Art, but not poor amateur art."

Here Mr. Wilde shook his head in a disgusted manner and said:

"We had better have no art than bad art. We can live without art but we cannot live with bad art. Let our architects build good substantial houses and let them be beautiful if they can. Let our chairs and tables be made first for use and second for beauty. Aestheticism should begin with the handicraftsmen, and when it does we will have more beautiful homes than we have at present."

"What about aestheticism in dress?"

"Women's dress at present is too somber. More bright colors should be worn. In England these ideas are being adopted rapidly. The milliner is being done away with, and the draper is taking her place. What is prettier than drapery, stately folds for the matron and becoming curves for the maiden? The milliner does away with graceful folds and gives us awkward bows instead."

Speaking of places of amusement, he said: "There should only be two things consulted in building a theater—first, the audience, then the actor. The trouble with too many theaters is, we have blue skies, red seats, green hangings, a great display of gilding, and then what is the actor to do? His costumes fall flat. Instead of this the house, the scenery, and the stage should be only a setting; let the woods used be dark and rich looking. Let the hangings be of oriental materials, for they are the best example of correct tone in coloring. I was delighted with the Chinese quarters in San Francisco. Their theater was plain and the stage was devoid of ornamentation. Those Chinese quarters fascinated me. I wish those people had a quarter in London. I should take pleasure in visiting it often.

"Common things should be made beautiful. When I was in San Francisco, at the hotel I was obliged to drink my chocolate or coffee out of a cup an inch thick, and I enjoyed going down into the Chinese quarters and sitting in a pretty latticed balcony and drinking my tea out of a cup so dainty and delicate that a lady would handle it with care. Yet this was not an expensive place for wealthy people to go to. It was for the common people. The laborers on the railroad came here, with pick and shovel, and drank their refreshing beverage out of a pretty cup of the two beautiful colors blue and white, while I was thought unworthy of anything better than a cup so thick that it suggested the idea that it was intended as a weapon, to be hurled at the heads of those seated at the next table. Beautiful things for everyday use are what we want. The child is not taught by books and lessons alone. We know how we used to throw our books aside and rush out into the air and sunshine. The child must be taught by constant association with beautiful things. Beauty should be as free as the air and water, and then it cannot fail to leave its impression on all minds."

Talking of beauty in men's dress, Mr. Wilde said: "We dress without the slightest regard to beauty or even comfort. When a man is going to walk, or row, or perform feats which require a display of strength and muscle, the trousers are done away with and knee-breeches are worn. Then again black broadcloth is chosen for dress suits, and no material can be more devoid of beauty than broadcloth. Velvet should be chosen instead, for it is a material which is always becoming."

Mr. Wilde believes that there will be a complete revolution in gentlemen's wearing apparel within the next few years; but for the sake of those gentlemen who are not of stately build it is to be hoped that knee-breeches will not become fashionable.

Mr. Wilde, speaking of the press, said: "When I read the papers and see what they say about me, it gives me a peculiar sensation. I feel as if I was traveling about in a country of barbarians."

The aesthete spoke enthusiastically of the cordial way in which he had been received. Being asked how long he would remain in America, he shrugged his shoulders and said: "If I survive, I shall remain until June." So it is evident Mr. Wilde has not fallen desperately in love with America.

Of American women he said: "In this country I see any quantity of beautiful young girls, girls whose faces are charming with the flush of youth, whose eyes are radiant, and whose forms are full of beauty. But there are few handsome matrons in this country."

Speaking of his first appearance in this country, Mr. Wilde said: "With the exception of speaking at an occasional wine supper at Oxford, I had never spoken in public until I lectured in New York. I then found out what a difficult task I had undertaken. Americans are natural orators. I never heard a spontaneous burst of oratory until I came to America and listened to an American."

35. "ART AND AESTHETICS," *DENVER TRIBUNE*, 13 APRIL 1882, 8

The train which brought Oscar Wilde over the Denver Pacific railroad last night was thirty minutes late, on account of a delayed connection at Cheyenne, and for this reason alone he was exactly thirty minutes behind the usual time for raising the curtain at Tabor Grand Opera house. He arrived in the midst of a spell of weather that is not specially palatable to aesthetic taste, and for that reason only there was not an overflowing audience, but the parquet and dress circle were filled.

The train arrived just five minutes ahead of the time announced by telegraph, and baffled the designs of a large crowd of unaesthetics whose curiosity caused them to gather about the platforms, or take refuge from the snowstorm in the sitting rooms of the Union depot. Even the enterprising advance agent, Mr. Locke, was thrown off his guard by the premature movement of the train and was two minutes late, while Mr. J. S. Vale, the manager of the athletic-looking aesthetic, was out prowling around in unknown places for the agent.

A reporter for the *Tribune* had taken precaution against the uncertainties of telegraphic reports or railroad time, and having waited beside the track for half an hour, boarded the train the instant it landed. While the passengers of the palace car were hurrying to and fro with their baggage in the usual unaccountable haste of the railroad passenger to be first out of the narrow door, the reporter was elbowing his way through, eagerly scanning the face of every man for a recognition of Oscar Wilde. At the rear end of the little smoking room the distinguished poet was found all alone, standing and waiting for somebody to receive him. The reporter, feeling that this duty devolved upon him in behalf of the city, introduced himself to Mr. Wilde, welcomed him to Denver, and relieved his uneasiness by the information that his carriage was waiting at the front of the depot. Mr. Wilde was dressed for the evening's entertainment, but covered with a pair of loose trousers and a large, heavy overcoat with a broad fur collar. A muffler was wrapped about his neck and he wore a broad-brimmed felt hat. He was conspicuous for his splendid physique, his long hair and singular cast of features, which in repose would be that half of man and half of woman. In every movement of the man it was easy to detect a something which gave an effeminate shade to his masculinity, bearing a striking resemblance to the *Scribner* portrait of George Eliot. But behind and beyond all that was unusual or eccentric, to a man of observation, the strength of manhood and the character of genius.

When the reporter introduced himself Mr. Wilde received him cordially and began to say a great many pleasant things, which he ended by declaring that his trip had been very tiresome. Just then Mr. Vale and Mr. Locke entered the car and conducted the poet to the carriage which was waiting for the party. A large crowd had gathered on the platform, and there were many young men who have not the slightest conception of the poetry that lives in the sunflower or the beauties that grow in the lily [who] followed in the footsteps and almost trod upon the heels of the aesthetic apostle. In still greater numbers they blockaded his way and surrounded his carriage, till the pressure of the crowd became disagreeable and even an annoyance. Some of them said such things as

"Hello, Oscar!"

"Let us see you, Oscar, old boy!"

"Put your head out the window, Oscar, for we know you're in there!"

And this they continued till the carriage drove away. One fellow was so anxious to see the famous poet that he pressed his nose against the glass window till he got the full benefit of a peep into the carriage.

"I supposed this scene is familiar to you, Mr. Wilde," remarked the *Tribune* reporter, as the horses were turned and started off in a brisk toward the opera house.

"Yes; it is so everywhere," answered the poet artist, with a happy smile, which at once revealed a happy, philosophic disposition and a handsomely-formed and well-kept but somewhat irregular set of teeth. In such a smile there is less of the spiritual in the eye and a gentility of expression which makes the nose and the mouth a part of the index to a brain that is as practical as it is sentimental.

"Yes, such scenes *are* familiar," said Mr. Wilde. "This is simply curiosity, you know. It is the evidence of an unfinished civilization."

"But do you now find such curiosity universal?"

"Oh, yes, curiosity I find a universal characteristic; but in Europe the people are less curious about public characters, and they are not rude."

Mr. Wilde was evidently pained by the familiarity of the young men who called "Oscar."

"Did you have many such experiences on your California trip?"

"Oh, my!" ejaculated the young man as he threw up his hands with a half-languishing smile. "In daytime, at almost every station, they crowded the platforms, besieged the car windows and would become actually angry if I did not make an appearance. But," said Mr. Wilde, "this was only a manifestation of idle curiosity." He mentioned a few exceptions among those he met en route. One was that of an old gentleman who wrote him one of the most delightful letters he had ever read and then met him on the train. There were some evidences among the men he met of deserved culture among the people of the West, but he had not had the time to cultivate them.

The carriage stopped at the stage entrance of the opera house at ten minutes after eight o'clock. The audience had already gathered. He was ushered into the private dressing room, where especial preparations had been made for his reception. While making his toilet he ordered a small bottle of Piper Heidsieck,[1] which he touched quite temperately, leaving fully one-half till after the lecture.

• • •

At the close of his lecture Mr. Wilde, accompanied by the *Tribune* reporter, walked into his dressing room, remarking as he came off the stage, "Well, this is somewhat jolly; to travel in the close atmosphere of those coaches six hundred miles on a stretch and then give a lecture before resting.

"I suppose it must be very tiresome."

"Oh, no; not the lecture, but the miserable travel," and Mr. Wilde emptied the remaining half bottle of Piper Heidsieck into a goblet. After refreshing himself, he talked away to the reporter about art and poetry, art schools in Europe, and the lack of them in America, and said many pleasant things as chirrupy as though he had just awakened from a refreshing sleep upon a bed of posies.

Then the carriage was ready, and Mr. Wilde and his attendants were whirled off to the Windsor Hotel, where all things were prepared for his quiet reception. Taking the elevator to the second floor, he was escorted straightway to his room, succeeding in escaping the crowd which had awaited all evening to see him. Only three gentlemen and three ladies who were promenading the hall caught a glance of the stalwart aesthete as he passed on to his room. There everything was prepared for his comfort and convenience. First of all was his supper, which was spread upon a small table. It was not by any means an extravagant bill of fare. There was a plate of fish, a dish of potatoes, an omelet, a pair of mutton chops, relishes, bread, butter, and a cup of tea. Throwing off his overcoat Mr. Wilde sat down at once to the table.

"Take away this tea and bring me a bottle of this wine," said he, pointing to the wine list. "With the glasses," he added.

The servant quickly returned with a bottle of Grave Bordeaux.[2] Mr. Wilde took one bite of the broiled fish and then ordered the plate removed. Just as he cut the first morsel from a mutton chop (after a glass of wine) and tested the bread and butter very sparingly, there commenced a series of raps on the door. Mr. Wilde abandoned his meal for the time, though he was almost famished, and gave himself to the duty of entertaining. Governor Tabor[3] was among his visitors, and in the course of the interview, among other things, arranged to treat the poet to a visit to the Matchless mine at Leadville after his lecture tonight.

Mr. Wilde expressed himself delighted, for he said of all things that which he desired most was to see a mine.

When his visitors had ceased calling, Mr. Wilde resumed his meal and the *Tribune* interviewer again unfolded his notebook.

"When will your new book of poems appear?" asked the reporter.

"Not until after I return to Europe. I hardly think it practicable to write it here. There are so many things which I had intended which are impracticable, you know."

Mr. Wilde then related that in leaving Europe he left his preface to the work with a friend. He said he could not write in America. His subjects would form a new departure, and he could not find either the time or the surroundings in America suitable to his themes. Besides, there were so many new experiences crowding upon him in his travels that he could only take notes. "When I return to Venice," said he, "I will begin to write, and whatever I have seen to impress me in America, whether of the beauties of nature or of men and women, I will write and give America credit for it."

As to his drama [*Vera*], which has been prepared for two years past, he had little say, except that it would soon be produced upon the stage.

"How were you impressed by your trip to California?"

"How can I tell you? I could talk to you all night about it. California is an Italy without its art. There are subjects for the artist, but it is universally true that the only scenery which inspires utterance is that which man feels himself the master of. The mountains of California are so gigantic that they are not favorable to art or poetry. The scenery for definite utterance is that which man is lord of. There are good poets in England, but none in Switzerland. There the mountains are too high. Art cannot add to nature. There is no imitative art."

Mr. Wilde continued to illustrate by showing that the only landscape schools of art in the world were situated in countries where the scenery was less attractive and vice versa where the beauties and grandeurs of nature existed the schools were devoted to faces and figures.

"What class of people do you think are the most susceptible to the impressions that inspire poetry and art?"

"That depends upon the nationality. All classes of the Celtic race are the most susceptible to these finer touches of nature. With these people it matters little about their station in life. They are naturally sympathetic and their impressions are manifest in art and poetry."

Here Mr. Wilde finished one mutton chop and the omelet, pushed the dishes aside, and took another glass of wine.

The conversation was just beginning to assume a delightful form and Mr. Wilde, though weary, had become enthused with his favorite theme, and his words were pouring forth in a fluent stream of poetic beauties when he was abruptly arrested by a question as to the Mormons of Salt Lake and his impression of them.

"Oh, I could tell you a great many things. I was entertained by the president, Mr. Taylor.[4] I found him a courteous, kindly, and charming gentleman. The house had a good deal of feeling in it in the way of pleasing works or art and good furniture. But the tabernacle has the shape of a soup kettle and the decorations are suitable to a jail. It was the most purely dreadful building I ever saw. There was not even the honesty to tell the truth, because they painted sham pillars. There are no pillars in the building. In the house of God, I think, no lies should be told. The city interested me because it was the first city that ever gave a chance to ugly women,[5] and so with feelings of philanthropy [I] looked with kindly eye upon it; it is a city of execrable architecture, and yet I felt that it also robbed life of a great deal of its romance, for the romance of life is that one can love so many people and only marry one. The people, as a body of humanity, have the most ignoble forms I ever saw, and the women are commonplace in every sense of the word."

Mr. Wilde was asked what he thought of the American people in comparison with the Europeans. He answered:

"I came with only one idea about this country, and that was that it was free from prejudice. To us in Europe, America is looked upon as a nation simple and grand, and I thought that the moment they heard what I had to say they would understand me and realize what I meant by life and art. I find that I was wrong."

Mr. Wilde spoke further of the prejudices of those who criticized, from ignorant views of the position he maintained, but he always felt that in every audience there were some intelligent listeners. He had found audiences in the West which listened with more simplicity, more real interest and desire to know what he had to say than in many audiences of the eastern cities, showing that the West has kept itself free and independent, while the East has caught and spoiled itself with many of the flirting follies of Europe.

Mr. Wilde at the conclusion of the interview referred to the many foolish and unjust things which have been said of him by the newspapers, and then turned himself to a great pile of letters, which he glanced over, and many of them he threw away, saying, "If only I should read all of these I would not rest much tonight."

"And if you were to read all the letters you receive you would become pretty well acquainted with the people of America."

"Well—," and Mr. Wilde significantly shrugged his shoulders for a reply, when the reporter extended his hand and bade the gifted young gentleman an affectionate adieu.

1. Piper-Heidsieck is a prestigious champagne house founded by Florens-Louis Heidsieck in 1785.
2. Wines designated Graves, a region of Bordeaux, include a celebrated white wine.
3. Horace Austin Warner Tabor (1830–99), an American prospector, businessman, and politician also known as "Silver Dollar Tabor" and "the Bonanza King of Leadville," was the lieutenant governor of Colorado from 1878 until 1884.
4. The English-born John Taylor (1808–87) was the president of the Church of Jesus Christ of Latter-day Saints from 1870 until his death.
5. Wilde's comment about Mormon women echoes chapter 14 of Mark Twain's *Roughing It:* "With the gushing self-sufficiency of youth I was feverish to plunge in headlong and achieve a great reform here—until I saw the Mormon women. Then I was touched. My heart was wiser than my head. It warmed toward these poor, ungainly and pathetically 'homely' creatures" (Twain, *Roughing It,* ed. Harriet Elinor Smith et al. [Berkeley: University of California Press, 1993], 97).

---

36. "WHAT MR. WILDE SAYS ABOUT HIMSELF," *MANCHESTER EXAMINER AND TIMES [MAY 1882];* REPR. *NEW YORK TRIBUNE,* 11 JUNE 1882, 9, AND *CHICAGO TRIBUNE,* 17 JUNE 1882, 3

Mountain climbing is not a subject of general interest, and some of my readers may be glad to turn from Pike's Peak to hear a word about Oscar Wilde the Great. I met Mr. Wilde a few days ago in Kansas and had a long conversation with him. In the eastern cities his photograph was most conspicuous, and Mr. Wilde told me that the demand for it far exceeded any possible supply. He was enthusiastic about the kindness he had received in many of the western towns, particularly Cincinnati, Chicago, and San Francisco, and spoke most highly of the culture and intelligence of the leading people he had met in those cities. In New York he had a reception given to him such as in England is rarely given to a prince, and he has a promise that on his return an evening party shall be given in his honor, when all the gentlemen shall discard the odious trousers of dull respectability and assume the more becoming substitute of the aesthetic future. Mr. Wilde told me that in the West people had traveled long distances and waited weary hours at railway stations to see him pass. He was compelled, even when fatigued, to show himself on the platforms, and I presume the farmers went back to work cheered and refreshed by the phantom of delight on which they had feasted their hungering eyes. What the American press appears to resent is that Oscar Wilde should have achieved such a position in their country without his being generally looked up to at home. The idea that he is fooling their public seems to irritate them extremely, but in my opinion this is a most erroneous opinion. Oscar Wilde's message is one which is really wanted in the United States, and without some grotesqueness and exaggeration he would not have secured a hearing.

He gave me a remarkable illustration of the Californians' detestation of the unforgivable crime of horse stealing. Where murder is looked on rather as a fine art, a horse thief is regarded with universal loathing, and Mr. Wilde had dined with a gentleman in California who owned to having fired eleven shots at a predatory poet and who could not be convinced that he had been guilty of want of respect for literature in so doing. When Mr. Wilde was lecturing in Chicago he received a present of a beautiful little bas-relief, quite precious in its delicacy, from a struggling sculptor. Upon which the lecturer rebuked his Chicago audience for allowing such an artistic man to be unrecognized. "And instead of being offended," said Mr. Wilde, "they sent the young man more commissions than he could execute in two years." He said that he had no more attentive audience than the miners in Leadville. His intentions for the future are to lecture in Australia and New Zealand, and, above all, to visit Japan, and remain for two months at least in that wonderful country, contemplating its artistic treasures, while attired, if possible, in that grand old national Japanese costume which the natives themselves are so foolishly casting aside.

37. "AESTHETIC: AN INTERESTING INTERVIEW
WITH OSCAR WILDE," *DAYTON DAILY*
DEMOCRAT, 3 MAY 1882, 4

A representative of the *Democrat* paid Mr. Wilde a visit in his room at the Beckel House just after he had finished his dinner yesterday. A more opportune moment for an interview could not have been chosen, for the old truth, well known, that a man's sociability and talkativeness are at their best when the inner man has been supplied with all that nature demands or culinary skill can supply was here amply proven, and promptly in answer to the reporter's card sent up from the office came the invitation to walk in.

There sat the great Oscar Wilde, half reclining on a sofa, a small table before him bearing writing materials in the use of which he had evidently been interrupted by the entrance of his visitor. Papers were strewn about his feet in profusion. The remains of his dinner stood on another table beside him, and the whole character of the room presented an air more of comfortable utility rather than orthodox neatness. Mr. Wilde himself was in perfect keeping with these surroundings as he sat there, whiffing a fine cigar. His face is well known to our readers through the thousands of pictures that have been scattered over the country since his arrival upon American soil. He looks exactly like these pictures with his long scraggy brown hair, wiry and oil-less, falling over his ears and neck, about his shoulders, his mild blue-grey eyes, his graceful nose but large lips, his soft effeminate flesh, but withal his very large, massive head and graceful form. He is odd and eccentric in his dress and style, but it is an eccentricity which loses its conspicuousness in the charm of his conversation, the depth of thought, and brilliancy of expression. Eccentric, it is true, but it is the eccentricity of a great man and not the eccentricity of affectation, or else he could not have won for himself the commendation of the greatest artists and literati of this continent and the old world as it undoubtedly has done ere he has reached the age of three decades.

His dress was peculiar, although he did not wear his much talked-of knee breeches. He had on a mouse-colored, corduroy blouse with grey worsted pantaloons.

About his neck was tied an old silk tie of a warm green hue while from the left breast pocket of his coat protruded a silk handkerchief of the same color.

"How do America and American institutions impress you, Mr. Wilde?" asked the reporter by way of opening conversation after self-introduction and cordial greeting had passed.

"Oh, what is the use of generalities? This country is much like other countries; we do not find much difference. I think the West is grand. I was far more interested in that part of America than in the East. The East is much more like the countries of Europe. But in California I was perfectly delighted. Everything is so new and novel and interesting. I was charmed with California and the West. But what a dreadful barrier of desert separates you of the East from the West. It seems as though nature had exhausted her resources on the West and had nothing left for those prairies. Oh, it is so dreary, so dissolute with those miles and miles of level plain sweeping across the country with not a tree, not a flower, not even an animal."

"I presume, however, that you do not find as much art in the West as in the East?"

"No, but still there are some good artists out there. We do not want to teach the people how to become great artists. We do not want to take a fine Italian masterpiece and put it in the workman's shanty. He would not appreciate it. He could not be made to appreciate it. It would give him no pleasure. What we want to do is to teach the people that they can have beauty in everything, teach them to open their eyes and look at nature, teach them to see the glorious panorama of color that is going on every day in the skies above their heads and in all nature about them. We want to get them to quit using these horrid forms of furniture and household utensils and make them understand that there can be beauty in the meanest vessel. We want to educate them to despise these dreadful combinations in color in the wallpapers. Either they are now ignorant and insensible to these outrages to taste or else they are existing in utter misery. Now look at that chair. Can anything be more horrid in form? Where it curves in it should curve out and where it curves out it ought to curve in. It will not last, either; it is badly put up.

"All over the country, in all the hotels I stop at, they give me cups like this to drink my coffee or chocolate from. See how thick and clumsy it is. It is at least half an inch thick and so barbaric in form that one would think it was made in a barbarous, savage age and intended to be used to hie at the head of an enemy as a weapon of defense. It disgusts me to drink from it. Such rude things make men rude who use them. We ought to have things of beauty in everything about our house. Let children when quite young be accustomed to see and handle delicate things and they will become refined. I was impressed, while out West, in going among the Chinese, to see these navvies who work hard all day on the railroad, shoveling dirt, go home at night and drink their tea out of cups of fine porcelain as thin and delicate as the petals of a white rose, so delicate, indeed, that our ladies even are afraid to handle them for fear of breaking them. That is what we should have for ourselves here. I would place things of beauty, things of delicacy, in the houses of all our mechanics as well as of the wealthy. This is the first hotel that I have been in for two or three weeks where my room did not have that horrid dreadful thing called a stove in it. I think the way people make stoves now is an outrage. If we must have them in our houses with their black iron bodies and ugly coiling pipe, let us have them plain and unornamented. But no, they insist upon decorating them, and so they put a garland of roses around the bottom—black, grimy horrid machine-made cast-iron roses! What a desecration! And then on top they put a something that so much resembles a funeral urn that we think we are living in a cemetery or sepulchre all the time. Why not make them plain? Then they can be accepted simply as a disagreeable necessity."

"Mr. Wilde, do you think that this present so-called 'aesthetic craze'"—?

"Oh, *do* not call it a craze. It is no craze. You Americans have such a way of treating serious things as a joke. And yet you are not a joyous people. In society there is all brilliancy and apparent joyousness, but on the railway trains I do not see happy men and women. Everybody has a troubled anxious look, and everybody is pushing forward in some business project. But the people do not appreciate art and so they call it a craze. But it will live and spread its influences and be continuing in its good, and it is no craze."

"You have answered just the question I was going to ask. I should rather have used the term 'revival.' Do you think the present great revival of interest in art will pass away after a time or will its benefits be lasting?"

"Art and true beauty can never die. There may be a wave of barbarism sweep over Europe by an Asiatic invasion, but true art will not be lost."

"Pardon me for asking it, Mr. Wilde, but I have a great curiosity, as many other Americans have, to know why it is you have selected the lily and sunflower as the emblems of beauty. You know it has been only since your arrival in America that these flowers have really been discovered by Americans."

"I love the lily and sunflower," answered the great aesthete, laughing, "because of their perfectness of form and adaptability for decorative purposes. What is more beautiful than the gracefully flowing outlines of the lily and the symmetry of the sunflower with its large round disk of rich reddish brown surrounded by its beautiful rays of yellow? Then with the lily there is such a purity of color, and it has so many beautiful legends associated with it. And the sunflower's fidelity to the great source of warmth, and light, and truth. It always looks to the sun, never drooping its head toward the cold shadows of earth. The lily is so beautiful for decorating [a] room, but the sunflower is too gorgeous for indoor decoration, unless the room is full of richness and color. The rose is a beautiful piece of color, but it has no beauty of form and is not adapted for decoration."

"Do you think, Mr. Wilde, that you Pre-Raphaelites of the present day, while tending to wean art away from the old heroic style of Michael Angelo and introducing more of the realistic and more of nature as it is, are bringing it more within the power of appreciation of the masses than it has been hitherto?"

"Why, what could be more realistic than Michael Angelo? The truth is we are only beginning to appreciate the classic art. The infinite beauty of Greek art is only being discovered. But it is a mistake which the Americans so often make, to confuse me with the Pre-Raphaelite. While I owe much to Mr. Ruskin and to Pre-Raphaelite teaching, I do not class myself with that school but I belong to a very different school entirely."

"Whom do you consider the greatest living painter?"

"I think Mr. Whistler is by far the greatest artist living, and I am glad to be able to say he is an American, although he lives in England."[1]

"Have you found any artist in America whom you consider equal to your great painters of England?"

"It is hard to institute comparisons between artists and especially between men of genius, because to be a genius a man must possess certain qualities which are exclusively his own, and the value of these qualities cannot be compared with the value of qualities possessed by another. I think Mr. Duveneck of Boston is the greatest painter in America.[2] He and Mr. Whistler are the leaders in this new school which I champion."

"Are there any other great artists who have become allied with this school you speak of?"

"No, it is followed now only by the younger class of artists."

"What are the characteristics of the school?"

"Simplicity of treatment and the rendering of subjects taken from scenes of the present day in preference to the old subjects of history. The Pre-Raphaelites estimate the worth of a picture by the story it tells. We do not consider that. It does not matter so much *what* you paint as *how* you paint it. Our school lays greatest weight on the importance of color. A picture badly colored is not a picture at all. Unless, as you approach a picture from a distance, the eye is pleased with the beautiful scheme of color, it is not a good picture no matter how good a story is told.

"I believe that art has a province of its own without invading the provinces of literature. If we want a poem, let us go to a poet; if we want a story, let us go to a storyteller; but if we want a picture, a representation of the wonderful beauties around us, then let us go to the artist. Whistler has adopted this idea of the importance of harmony of color that he paints his pictures and names them solely with this in view. He paints symphonies in color. You may laugh at the idea of a man painting a symphony, but he does it, and he names his pictures 'Symphony in Blue and White' or 'Symphony in White.'

"Why, the most beautiful picture I ever saw is Whistler's 'Symphony in White.' It is so simple and yet so lovely. A gray sky lightly flecked with delicate white clouds, a grey sea dotted with white waves. And in the foreground is a white balcony with all the varying shades of white, from the pearly white marble to the rich yellow-white of ivory. Upon the balcony are three little girls, oh! so beautiful, all dressed in white, and one is reaching over and tearing the petals of white blossoms from a tree, and they are borne away upon gentle zephyrs, like little white snowflakes. Could anything be more exquisitely lovely? What purity! What beauty! And then would you turn from this to some dreadful picture of 'Mary, Queen of Scots, about to be beheaded,' painted by some artist who ought to have been beheaded himself before he ever was allowed to paint such a picture?

"That is the kind of art that is destined to win the day in this present age. We are tired of these bloody, ugly dreadful pictures we have had so long."

"What do you think of America, Mr. Wilde, viewed from an artist's standpoint?"

"It will never produce great landscape painters. It will be greater in figure painting than in landscape. But it will be greatest in sculpture. The country is new. People look upon the forests from a commercial point of view and do not appreciate them artistically. Men at hard labor in the mines or at agriculture form excellent subjects for figure painting, while men who are confined in large cities become stooped and ungraceful. But no county which has the clear atmosphere and the cloudless sky that America has or that Switzerland or Italy have can be good for the landscapist. The great landscape painters of the world have been in Holland, France, and England, where the hazy, damp atmosphere lends a charm to the view not seen in clearer air."

"Well, I must express my thanks to you, Mr. Wilde, for this interview. I presume you have found us newspapermen a great annoyance since you have been in America."

"Oh, no, not at all. I never allow anything to annoy me. If I don't want to see anybody I tell them so." Soon after this, the carriage drove up which had been provided by Professor Isaac Broome, through whose efforts Mr. Wilde was brought to Dayton, and by the courtesy of Mr. Wilde and Professor Broome representatives of the *Democrat* and *Journal* accompanied these two gentlemen on a trip of sight-seeing.

1. James Abbot McNeill Whistler (1834–1903), an American-born painter and etcher, championed "art for art's sake."
2. Frank Duveneck (1848–1919), an American realist painter, sculptor, etcher, and art teacher, helped to overturn the reigning tradition of the Hudson River school in the 1870s.

---

38. "OSCAR WILDE'S RETURN," *NEW YORK WORLD*, 6 MAY 1882, 1

Mr. Oscar Wilde arrived in New York early yesterday morning and went to the Grand Hotel, where, yesterday afternoon, a *World* reporter found him.

"After I left the East," said Mr. Wilde, "I found a people that struck me as more representatively American than those in the other states. It was west of Chicago that I found America. Here in the older country the people are very closely akin to the English. I arrived at last in San Francisco in the spring. The peach trees were in bloom in the orchard, the apple trees blossomed in the close, the beautiful sky was bright, and the warm ocean, flooded with light, was pouring in through the Golden Gate. Oh, it was most beautiful, and for the first time I understood why nature had so clothed itself in green. It is because it is the most restful of all colors, and after yearning for it for three months I found it in San Francisco. Moreover, the place itself is most attractive; the people are warm and generous and are cultivated. I lectured four times there and twice in Oakland, a little place just across the bay."

"Of course, I have no desire to enter into a political discussion, but I found the Chinese quarter in San Francisco most interesting, and, in my opinion, the Chinese have a decided artistic value, which I think Congress should consider in discussing the Chinese question. Their quarter is full of artistic motives, and they have a constant eye to the value of color. We do not value color sufficiently—we do not recognize the element of joyousness that color brings into life. The Chinese have two theaters in San Francisco, and every actor is most nobly and beautifully attired, so that their plays are pageants, as every play ought to be, because the stage should be art in action. I learned many things from the Chinese."

"How did the rough manners of the West impress you?"

"There, now; I object to that word 'rough' as applied to miners.[1] They are cordial and generous and not at all rough. One of my best and most interested audiences was composed of Leadville miners. One reason I liked them was because of their magnificent physiques. I spent a night in a silver mine, and it was one of my most delightful experiences. The most unintellectual audience I had was in Salt Lake. The Mormons are the most unintellectual people I have met in America, because they have the worst physiques I have seen; and a people must have good physiques in order even to comprehend art. I found President Taylor charming. I went to his house, and he and his three wives occupied a stage box at my lecture. The Mormons' tabernacle is the shape of a teakettle and is decorated with the ornaments of a jail."

"In Chicago I had delightful audiences. I was particularly struck with the courtesy of the western audiences, which the tone of the press did not lead me to expect. In every city where I have been I have either found an art school—crude, to be sure—or, if they had not one, they started one on the occasion of my visit, so that I cannot doubt that my coming to America has had an effect. In the smaller cities most of the people have never seen any art whatever, and the idea of design is bad. The idea I had of America when I landed has been very strongly confirmed; it is that what this country needs principally is not the higher imaginative art but the simple decorative art that can make beautiful for us the commonest vessel of the house. If an article is beautiful, it must have been made by a good workman, because only a good workman can make a beautiful thing."

Mr. Wilde said that his costumes described in the *World* of Thursday were an experiment. They were very beautiful; so simple, yet so artistic.[2] The age of Francis I, the era when the costumes such as he had ordered were worn, was an era of simplicity. He did not know whether he would wear them in public, but he would if he wore them at all. On Thursday afternoon next he will deliver a lecture at Wallack's Theater on "the practical application of aesthetics to house decoration, dress, and morals." He thinks it probable that he will go to Australia, as a strong pressure has been brought on him to do so. If he concludes to go he will sail from San Francisco on June 31 [*sic*], after having first visited Canada. He will remain in and about New York until he leaves for Canada.

1. Wilde mishears the question.
2. See "The New Costume," *New York World*, 4 May 1882, 5.

---

39. "OSCAR WILDE IN MONTREAL," *MONTREAL WITNESS*, 15 MAY 1882, 8

Few men, at least of his age, have been so much talked about, and certainly none so much laughed at, as Oscar Wilde. Curiosity as to his personal appearance has been by no means abated by the many descriptions published, for readers at once recognize the fact that in some cases the most vivid language is useless to convey a correct impression, and Oscar Wilde has been considered a sufficiently unique personage to be one of those cases. Consequently, when a *Witness* reporter was ushered into the poet's room at the Windsor Hotel this morning, his personal as well as professional curiosity was somewhat disappointed to find no poet visible. He was there, however, and his apparent absence was only due to the tobacco smoke which hovered ethereally about his poetic form, and through which his countenance was presently revealed. Reclining in an armchair in the midst of anything but artistic, not to speak of aesthetic, surroundings was the apostle of art and aestheticism. Mr. Wilde, as he rose and extended a large, gentle hand to the visitor, showed to full advantage. Tall and well proportioned, his large figure was clad in graceful garments of soft homespun.[1] The absence of knee-breeches and hose was at first a painful shock, but the effect was partly removed by a glance at the massive throat; the broad turned-down collar was decidedly "all but," while the aesthetic dull red necktie, baffling comprehension as to the manner of its putting on, can only be described as "quite consummately too." But attention could not remain long fixed on the attire. Mr. Wilde's face, surrounded and framed by a mass of long, untamed, tawny hair, is massive, almost colossal, and at the same time very pleasant in feature and expression, especially so far as the poetic eyes are concerned. But mere description, as was before hinted, is of necessity somewhat powerless.

Mr. Wilde, who speaks with the accent generally credited to the higher classes of London society, and by no means uncommon in the region of Pall Mall, showed no objection whatever to being interviewed, and kindly refrained from making any of those unpleasant remarks about journalists which his experience with them would seem to justify. When asked what opinion he had formed of the probable results of his campaign, he at once said that after all the nonsense written about him had been forgotten, good and lasting results would remain. In the cities where he had been, decorative art societies had been started, and old societies had been brought into more prominence. His immense correspondence was entirely on this subject. "Here," said Mr. Wilde, "is a letter only received this morning, referring to the effect of my visit to Philadelphia last week." The letter was from Charles Leland, the famous "Hans Breitmann,"[2] and a member of "the school," thanking Mr. Wilde for the good he had done in connection with the teaching of art principles to the young. These results are being seen in the increase of orders given to the art societies. Mr. Wilde mentioned an incident which showed the way in which he was able to help on native art. In Chicago he came across a young American sculptor of really extraordinary power and genius, but unknown. He spoke about him, and told the people that they could not really appreciate art if they neglected the native talent in their own city. Now, that young sculptor has ever so many commissions.

The questioner asked how the British and Americans compared in their reception of his teachings. Mr. Wilde could hardly give a definite answer. "In America, you see, I have for the first time been face to face with people who have never seen any good art; as to their reception of what I say, while, no doubt, many come to hear me just from curiosity, yet afterward I am continually getting letters from these people saying how they have been pleased with this or that point in my lectures. The great thing is to get them to come, for when they come they always see what I mean. And," said Mr. Wilde, "what one really wants is not to be either blamed or praised but to be understood."

"You have been all over the United States now, have you not, Mr. Wilde?"

"I have been all over the states except in the South, and I suppose, though it is difficult to guess, that I have spoken to some two hundred thousand people. I have found the people very willing and ready to listen and appreciate."

Mr. Wilde has been in California, and is quite enthusiastic over it; "it is Italy without art," was his judgment of the Hoodlum city. Only he objected to its being called the Hoodlum city. He said, "No, it is the city of fine men and beautiful women! San Francisco has the most lovely surroundings of any city except Naples. I lectured there six times and had the most delightful and appreciative audiences. People's appreciation of beauty depends so much on what they are accustomed to see around them. It might be thought otherwise from those who live in beautiful places not speaking about beauty, but they have no need to talk about it. That is our object. We want to see the homes of the people beautiful, and when that is the case people will no longer talk of the beautiful at all. We are forced to do so now because there are so many ugly things in the world. In the ideal state of art there will be no art lecturer."

Mr. Wilde went on to speak of the knowledge of art in the different countries, England and America. "In England, now, we have the great advantage of models of art always with us, in the cathedrals, in the colleges of Oxford and Cambridge, and in many buildings of the finest architecture. In America the great want is of absolute models of art. The art which is learned from books is very worthless at best." Speaking of the aims of the movement with which he is identified, Mr. Wilde urged strongly that people should occupy a good deal more of their time with simple things. "It is all very well to devote time to little flower vases; they do for ladies' drawing rooms, but that is not touching the people. It is the people we want to touch, and this can only be done by beginning with simple things. The least things, every household article, should be made beautiful, and I had far rather that, instead of designs for flower vases, a good design should be produced for a simple jug and basin, instead of the coarse pottery, inartistic in color and outline, which is now common."

"What do you think is the present position of the movement in England, Mr. Wilde?"

"Well, you may best understand that from the fact that Mr. Morris has just received from government the contract for the decoration of St. James's Palace.[3] The movement is one that must be recognized. We have entirely altered the condition of society in respect to art, and no one will now furnish a house without having regard to art principles."

Mr. Wilde said all this with a simplicity of language and manner and a hearty sincerity which were quite refreshing after the caricatures which we have sometimes been led to imagine were imitations of the Arch-Aesthete. During the whole conversation, "stained-glass" attitudes were conspicuously absent, and languid lackadaisicality was also entirely wanting. Once, indeed, the lithe-limbed poet sank into a position recalling in a faint degree certain creations of Du Maurier's imagination, and few could produce so aesthetic a yawn as once occurred in the intervals of puffing a cigarette. But these were evidently too natural to suggest even the ghost of a smile to the most risible. And then the visitor withdrew, leaving Oscar Wilde to plunge again into the wisdom of Mr. Shorthouse's sudden-famed *John Inglesant*,[4] and thinking as he went that behind the closed door there reclined neither a Postlethwaite, a Lamber Stryke, nor a Reginald Bunthorne, and that Messrs. Du Mauier, Burnand, and Gilbert had all done him a grave injustice.

1. This description is meant to be arch. Garments of homespun are plain, homely, and of "rude" texture; they are neither "graceful" nor "soft" (*OED*).
2. Charles Godfrey Leland (1824–1903), an American humorist and folklorist, was the author of the comedic *Hans Breitmann Ballads* (1871).
3. St. James's Palace was until 1837 the official residence of the sitting monarch, and the royal court is still formally based there. William Morris's company completed its initial contract to redecorate the palace's armory and tapestry rooms in 1867, and in 1880 the company was once again commissioned to decorate the palace.
4. Joseph Henry Shorthouse (1834–1903), English author of *John Inglesant* (1881), a religious "romance" of "free invention" set in mid-seventeenth-century England.

40. "OSCAR WILDE: THE ARCH-AESTHETE ON AESTHETICISM," *MONTREAL STAR*, 15 MAY 1882, 3

Mr. Oscar Wilde arrived at the Windsor Hotel yesterday, where he very kindly received our reporter this morning. He was found amid the ruins of a substantial-looking breakfast, and there was nothing in his appearance to indicate that he had been sitting up all night with a lily, unless, indeed, the fact of his breakfasting late might suggest something of the sort; but then again, the fact of his breakfasting at all refutes such a supposition. Some of Mr. Wilde's critics, in addition to caricaturing his principles, have gone so far as to accuse him of affectation to an offensive degree, and as these statements have found their way into print it is but the merest justice on the part of our representative to say that if affection exists there, it is most artfully concealed and therefore can scarcely be offensive. To the tap of the Ethiopian lily who announced our representative, a remarkably musical voice replied, "Come in," and as the door opened a tall, well-built gentleman with a very pleasing countenance arose from the breakfast table and advanced with extended hand and a smile of welcome to receive his early visitor. He was dressed in a delicate sage-green velvet coat and light cloth continuations of the Philistine order of architecture. A red necktie blended well with his dark complexion, which was thrown into striking relief by a profusion of long black hair surrounding it. The costume was decidedly indicative of good taste, and his movements, like his conversation, were easy and graceful.

"I am afraid, Mr. Wilde, that by this time you must look upon all newspaper men as a great nuisance," said our reporter, apologetically.

"Not at all," was the hearty response. "I am very pleased to see you."

"We have heard so much lately of aestheticism, have seen it so abundantly caricatured, and really understand so little about it that I am glad to have an opportunity of conversing with you on the subject."

"There is nothing I like talking about better."

"Do you think the aesthetic movement in England has arisen from a genuine appreciation of the principles you teach, or is the general adoption of aesthetic principles in decoration and dress a fashion in itself, one fashion being simply superseded by another?"

"It is not a fashion at all; it is a return to the right principles of art. This movement has entirely altered the whole character of ordinary English decorations. It would be impossible for anyone now to furnish a house without reference to our principles of design and decoration. Not merely are the ordinary houses of London so embellished, but when the government wanted to decorate St. James' Palace last year, they at once gave the work to Mr. William Morris, one of the leaders of aestheticism."

"You think, then, that this very general adoption of aesthetic principles has arisen entirely from a genuine appreciation?"

"I don't think anyone adopts beauty out of consideration for fashion. If a thing is beautiful, one cannot help liking it. People will adopt the *bizarre* for the sake of fashion, but not the beautiful. Even if they did, they would come to see it was beautiful after being with it for a time."

"May I ask, what is your conception of beauty?"

"In the last century, people were fond of finding an abstract definition of beauty. I am quite content to put that off for my old age, if lovers of art have an old age."

"Do they die young then?"

"No! But art is always youthful. I am quite content if I am able to surround myself and others with beautiful things. That is the difference between our aesthetics of this century and those of the last century. The German philosophers of the last century were content to live in the midst of the most dreadful surroundings, provided they could call beauty long names. We want to produce beautiful things, which is very much more practical. It so happens that within the last two years fashion has been with us, and as you suggested just now many people may have adopted our principles for fashion's sake, but those principles will never leave them. They educate the taste in color, for instance."

"Are English tastes improving?"

"In music, the taste of the English people has enormously improved. Ten years ago the fashion happened to be for German music and consequently for good music. Now all the works of Beethoven and the other great masters are loved and appreciated. When you can bend fashion to the service of anything good or beautiful, it is of immense importance."

"What do you consider the principal element of beauty in music? Is it in association?"

"The charm of all art is founded entirely upon the senses. One of the uses of art is to cultivate the senses. The ears of people who do not often hear good music become very coarse. They have not cultivated the sense of hearing, a sense capable of infinite refinement. One of the great faults of all the education of children is the trying to educate the mind, when probably they haven't got one, instead of trying to educate the senses, which everybody has. We all have eyes, ears, and hands, but most people never use either eyes, ears, or hands. Any right theory of education, it seems to me (and by the way I want to write upon that subject), must be founded on a principle of educating the mind, not directly, but through the means of the senses. What universities have you here, and what are they like? I take great interest in universities everywhere."

Our representative, having briefly explained a few of the characteristics of the Canadian universities and the educational system generally, evoked several expressions of approval from Mr. Wilde. "Yes," said he, "it is better for the country to have a good general standard of education than to have, as we have in England, a few desperately overeducated and the remainder ignorant. One of the things which delighted me most in America was that the universities reached a class that we, in Oxford, have never been able to touch, the sons of the farmers and people of moderate means. These are the people to whose wants the university should adapt its curriculum and expenses so that it should be able to reach them."

"Is not Gower Street (i.e., London University)[1] a move in that direction?"

"Yes, Gower Street and Owens College, Manchester, are a move in that direction. Really half of any good that comes from university life comes from the indirect influences from fitting the boy to live by himself; it teaches him independence of mind and common sense, too."

"But under our system it is possible for a young man to earn his living while obtaining his education."

"I do not think any university which does not require residence on the part of its undergraduates is anything more than a good day school."

Mr. Wilde very much dislikes our bare walls, and called our reporter's attention to the white breakfast service with the nearest approach to disgust he had yet exhibited.

"Do you recognize any primitive and intrinsic beauty in color?" asked our representative.

"Color! It is the greatest enjoyment of my life, from the rising of the sun till the setting."

And this was the first and last time in the interview that he became enthusiastic or "intense." His conversation was earnest, but practical and sensible. The arrival of a second visitor, many more being in the background, terminated a most agreeable interview.

1. In 1826 London University was founded on Gower Street in Bloomsbury, central London, as a secular alternative to the religious universities of Cambridge and Oxford. It acquired degree-awarding powers when it joined with King's College London in 1836 to create the new University of London.

41. "OSCAR WILDE," *TORONTO GLOBE,*
25 MAY 1882, 3

Mr. Oscar Wilde arrived in the city yesterday morning on the Grand Trunk express from the East. A deputation of gentlemen belonging to the city was at the station to receive him and escort him to the Queen's Hotel. By previous engagement he attended the lacrosse match between the Torontos and St. Regis Indians in the afternoon. He arrived on the grounds a few minutes before the game commenced, and when the grandstand and other available seats were densely packed. As he passed through the gate someone shouted, "Here's Oscar Wilde." The intelligence soon passed along the rows of seated spectators, and all eyes were at once strained to catch a glimpse of him. The juveniles were inclined to be boisterous at first, but they soon ceased their shouting, as Mr. Wilde appeared not even to notice their demonstrations. He was escorted to the space on the grandstand reserved for the lieut.-governor, where he was introduced to Miss Robinson and a lady friend. Without noticing the sensation his arrival had created he reclined his head gracefully on his hand, assumed the aesthetic attitude, and gazed earnestly into the field, where the teams were preparing for the fight. He was dressed in a grey tweed pair of trousers and cobweb-coloured velveteen coat and vest; his necktie was a dark green in colour, tied loosely around his neck, and covering his shirt front. He wore a handkerchief to match. He had a flowing coat, with a deep velvet collar, and secured to his form by a tasselated cord, which passed across his chest. He wore a black felt hat of unusual proportions. The earnest or intense expression of his almost feminine face, his long flowing hair, and his tall, handsome figure, and graceful movements gave him a striking appearance, producing immediately a favourable impression. When the game was started he evinced the most lively interest, and as it progressed his enthusiasm seemed to keep pace with the players, for he laughed heartily when any of them went unceremoniously to "grass," or clapped his hands when a good piece of play was done. He left the field shortly before the match was completed. On being asked by a *Globe* representative how he enjoyed the match, Mr. Wilde said, "Oh, I was delighted with it. It is a charming game. That was the first opportunity I ever had of witnessing your national game, and I enjoyed it so much—but can you tell me who that tall, finely built man, that played defence for the Torontos, is?" broke off Mr. Wilde.

"That's Rors Mackenzie, one of the best lacrosse players in Canada."[1]

"I admired his playing so very much," said Mr. Wilde. "He appeared so thoroughly at home in the game. Lacrosse is so far ahead of cricket for physical development, and then everyone seems to get an equal share of the play, or hard work as I should term it. But don't you think," Mr. Wilde asked, "that the Indians, or at least the Indian umpire, should have been dressed in a manner to impress one with the position he occupied? I think he should have been dressed, say, in war costume, with his face painted, armed with a tomahawk, and wearing a headdress of feathers. I was greatly amused at the gesticulations of the Indians, and I wondered what language they were speaking."

After asking some questions about the Indians and the original of the game, Mr. Wilde said he was much pleased with the appearance and dress of many persons he had seen on the ground; "and," he continued, "I could not help admiring the dress of a little girl who sat in front of me. It was charming—such a beautiful blending of colour that corresponded so nicely with her rosy cheeks."

"What is your opinion of Toronto and Toronto ladies, Mr. Wilde?"

"I have seen so little of the former that I have scarcely formed an opinion, but I judge from the appearance of your principal business street that it is a bright little town, and I have no doubt it is a commercial centre. But I cannot help wondering why your citizens build their houses with that horrid white brick when red brick is the same price. I think white brick such a shallow colour—in fact, it spoils the effect of the architecture. I see the same fault here that I noticed in all Canadian cities. The colour of the stone and other building material completely spoils the effect of the good architecture, which I could not help admiring in Canadian cities. As to the ladies, I think some of them are very nice and dress exceedingly well, but I will have a better opportunity of judging hereafter. I am gratified sometimes to see the monotony of an audience relieved by the presence of at least one well-dressed lady."

1. Rors Mackenzie (d. 1897) once threw a lacrosse ball 422 feet, a world record that remains unbroken.

---

42. "THE AESTHETE AT THE ART EXHIBITION," *TORONTO GLOBE,* 26 MAY 1882, 6

Mr. Oscar Wilde visited the exhibition of the Ontario Society of Artists yesterday afternoon, where he was shown around by Mr. T. M. Martin.[1] The aesthete spent about an hour there, criticizing the different works freely and with a quickness of perception which showed him to possess clear and well-defined ideas of true art. Portraits and object painting, containing nothing idealistic, he passed over as unworthy of notice. He especially admired Mr. Watson's works,[2] finding in them considerable "soul" and "feeling," expressing the opinion that the artist was "an exceedingly clever fellow." Dull grey sky and rocks always attracted his attention. Upon glancing at a miniature painting of Mrs. Cornwallis West,[3] he remarked that miniature painting was dead. After enquiring as to the working of the society, Mr. Wilde took his departure. He visited the university in the afternoon.

1. Thomas Mower Martin (1838–1934), English-born Canadian artist and a founder of both the Ontario Society of Artists in 1872 and the Royal Canadian Academy in 1880.

2. Wilde dubbed the Canadian landscape artist Homer Ransford Watson (1855–1936) the "Canadian [John] Constable" based on similarities between the painters' subject matter and style.

3. Mary ("Patsy") Cornwallis West (née Fitzpatrick) (1835–1917) was a beautiful Irish-born English socialite and the second wife of William Cornwallis West.

43. "OSCAR WILDE TALKS OF TEXAS," *NEW ORLEANS PICAYUNE*, 25 JUNE 1882, 11

"There are in Texas two spots which gave me infinite pleasure. These are Galveston and San Antonio. Galveston, set like a jewel in a crystal sea, was beautiful. Its fine beach, its shady avenues of oleander, and its delightful sea breezes were something to be enjoyed. It was in San Antonio, however, that I found more to please me in the beautiful ruins of the old Spanish mission churches and convents and in the relics of Spanish manners and customs impressed upon the people and the architecture of the city. America is so full of youthful vigor and vitality that one sees those relics of a past age in the midst of so much that is new with a positive sensation of surprise and pleasure. Those old Spanish churches, with their picturesque remains of tower and dome, and their handsome carved stonework, standing amid the verdure and sunshine of a Texas prairie, gave me a thrill of strange pleasure."

These were the words of Oscar Wilde as he stood by the window of his parlor in the St. Charles Hotel on Saturday evening on this return from a brief pilgrimage to the Lone Star State. Mr. Wilde was looking fresh and bright, and he expressed the pleasure with which he had viewed the striking and picturesque scenery of the swamps in Louisiana and Texas. The giant cypress trees towering above the dense jungle of undergrowth and tangled vines, while long streamers of gray moss waved in the wind from the great branches which the trees thrust forth into the sky, attracted the poet's attention, while he had much to say of the alligators, which sprawled and yawned in the sunshine on the trunks of fallen trees and on the muddy banks of the bayous and the great morasses.

Nothing in the way of animal life, however, seemed to please the poet and art reformer so much as the young negroes.

"I saw them everywhere," he said, "happy and careless, basking in the sunshine or dancing in the shade, their half-naked bodies gleaming like bronze, and their lithe and active movements reminding one of the lizards that were seen flashing along the banks and trunks of the trees."

"You were in Texas long enough to acquire a military title. A week is quite sufficient, and I have no doubt I would be justified in addressing you as Col. Wilde," said the reporter.

"Oh, yes: I am a colonel by all the rules and regulations of a Texas brevet. I was dubbed 'Colonel' in Galveston and was fully invested with the title by the time I got to Houston. I shall write home to my friends of this new rank and promotion."

After some further conversation the reporter spoke of Mr. Wilde's reported intention of visiting Hon. Jefferson Davis on the way from New Orleans to Mobile. Mr. Wilde said he had an intense admiration for the chief of the Southern Confederacy. He had never seen him, but had followed his career with much attention. "His fall, after such an able and gallant pleading of his own cause, must necessarily arouse sympathy, no matter what might be the merits of his plea. The head may approve the success of the winner, but the heart is sure to be with the fallen."

"The case of the South in the Civil War was to my mind much like that of Ireland today. It was a struggle for autonomy, self-government for a people. I do not wish to see the empire dismembered, but only to see the Irish people free, and Ireland still as a willing and integral part of the British Empire. To dismember a great empire in this age of vast armies and overweening ambition on the part of other nations is to consign the peoples of the broken country to weak and insignificant places in the panorama of nations; but people must have freedom and autonomy before they are capable of their greatest result in the cause of progress. This is my feeling about the southern people as it is about my own people, the Irish. I look forward to much pleasure in visiting Mr. Jefferson Davis."

The poet had an engagement to go out for the evening, and he shortly took his departure with a party of gentlemen, as it was reported, to witness some mysterious and curious ceremonies of the devotees of voodoo, which were to inaugurate the recurrence of St. John's night,[1] June 24.

Mr. Wilde will lecture on Monday night at Spanish Fort, on the internal decoration of the home, and on Tuesday will depart for Mobile, stopping at Beauvoir,[2] the residence of Jefferson Davis, to spend a day with him.

1. According to legend, the birth date of John the Baptist.
2. Beauvoir, in Biloxi, Mississippi, was the last home of Jefferson Davis (1808–89), the U.S. politician who became the sole president of the Confederate States of America.

---

44. "OSCAR WILDE: ARRIVAL OF THE GREAT AESTHETE," *ATLANTA CONSTITUTION*, 5 JULY 1882, 8

When Oscar Wilde reached Atlanta yesterday from Macon, he disembarked from the train and stalked with measured tread to the Markham, flanked by his valet; when he entered the arcade of the Markham, he advanced to the radiator and came to a halt. There he posed; one hand sought the spot where the heart was supposed to be and the other hung by his side. His head was thrown back, his long locks fell over his shoulders, and he gazed upon the frescoing in the ceiling apparently oblivious of the curious gazes that were directed toward him. His able secretary advanced and put his autograph upon the register, and then Mr. Wilde was shown to a room on the second floor facing to the west, kept especially for aesthetes. Mr. Wilde had scarcely had time to be dusted by his valet before a *Constitution* reporter sent up his card. The response was an invitation to the young man to "come up at once," and accordingly after a brief lapse of time the *Constitution* was rapping at the door of the room of the great aesthete. A deep voice from the inside called, "Come in," and the reporter turned the knob and entered. The room was rather narrow and one end opened by two windows upon Loyd Street.[1] Almost right under the window the colored people were yelling and shouting in true Fourth of July style. The spectacle that met the astonished gaze of the reporter was one long to be remembered. In the farther end of the room, seated in a large rocking chair, was the great aesthete. His appearance was striking in the extreme, so odd he appeared. His hair was long and fell about his shoulders. It was parted near the middle and was rather stiff and in great abundance. His face was large, his lips exceedingly so, and his nose prominent. He would weigh evidently about 180 pounds. His dress was not the court costume which he wears while on the stage, but it deserves especial mention. His coat was a black velvet jacket. He wore a white waistcoat with gray woolen pantaloons. A monster moonlight green tie surrounded his throat. His socks were exquisite silk and his shoes dainty gaiters. On a table near him lay a very fine cloth cloak with silk lining. On the bureau lay a large wide-brimmed hat and near it an ivory cane. On a table lay a bouquet of sunflowers. Around the poet lecturer lay scattered several books, novels, and books of poetry in French. The *Constitution* was not long in making known its business. Mr. Wilde appeared to be irritated by the yelling outside, and rising said:

"Oh, the patriots, the patriots; let's shut down the window and shut out the noise."

"This is the first Fourth of July you ever saw in America?"

"Yes."

"What do you think of it as you see it now?"

"I don't think that anything so fine as the Declaration of Independence should be celebrated at all if it cannot be celebrated in a very noble manner. Amongst the most artistic things that any city can do is to celebrate by pageant any great eras in its history. Why should not the Fourth of July pageant in Atlanta be as fine as the Mardi Gras carnival in New Orleans? Indeed, a pageant is the most perfect school of art for a people. It shows them what otherwise they would not have a chance of seeing, noble costumes, beautiful colors, and sculpturesque grouping. It would be quite impossible to overestimate the influence on art that any celebration of the kind would have, for in an age like this, where there is such a growing feeling for what is merely grotesque and consequently ignoble, I think the people need to be reminded of the dignity of pure beauty. Amongst the many signs in Europe of a growing feeling for art, perhaps one of the foremost is the revival in so many cities of the beautiful pageants of the past. But I am afraid that the only pageants that most American cities have a hope of seeing are the glaring processions of their traveling circuses, and I feel that they deserve something very much better."

"You have been to see Mr. Jefferson Davis lately. Tell me something about your visit to him."

"He lives in a very beautiful house by the sea, amid lovely trees. He impressed me very much as a man of the keenest intellect, and a man fairly to be a leader of men on account of a personality that is as simple as it is strong, and an enthusiasm that is as fervent as it is faultless. We in Ireland are fighting for the principle of autonomy against empire, for independence against centralization, for the principles for which the South fought. So it was a matter of immense interest and pleasure to me to meet the leader of such a great cause. Because although there may be a failure in fact, in idea there is no failure possible. The principles for which Mr. Davis and the South went to war cannot suffer defeat. I had read Mr. Davis's book,[2] which is a masterpiece, although to us in Europe the elaborate detail of military maneuver is at times a little burdensome. But there are passages in which he dwells on the principles of the southern confederacy that were read by us with the keenest interest and delight. It is impossible not to think nobly of a country that has produced Patrick Henry,[3] Thomas Jefferson,[4] George Washington,[5] and Jefferson Davis. Besides its great men I admire in the South the wonderful beauty of its vegetation. I have seen no forests in Europe more wonderful, no flowers more exquisite in perfume or in color. It is worthwhile to come over here merely to see the magnolia in full blossom. It should be—the South—the home of art in America, because it possesses the most perfect surroundings; and now that it is recovering from the hideous ruin of the war, I have no doubt that all these beautiful arts, in whose cause I will spend my youth in pleading, will spring up among you. The South has produced the best poet of America—Edgar Allan Poe;[6] and with its splendid traditions it would be impossible not to believe that she will continue to perfect what she has begun so nobly. The very physique of the people in the South is far finer than that in the north, and a temperament infinitely more susceptible to the influences of beauty."

"Tell me something about your sunflower ideas."

"Oh, yes! I have some here that were sent up to me. The reason that we value the sunflower so much is because it is so perfectly adapted for decorative art. Many flowers will merely be beautiful in color, without having a definite form, such as the magnolia, for instance. But this flower is best suited for decoration, because its form is definite and perfect, and of all flowers, perhaps, the sunflower is the one which art has made noblest use of. It appears constantly in the medallic and tapestry of old Europe and is found all through eastern art. Besides its beautiful form, the imagination of the world has surrounded it with a halo of beautiful legions as golden as the halo of its own golden rays. I have been very pleased to find since I came to America that the people have come to see and to appreciate its wonderful splendor far more than I think they did before, and indeed that is one of the noblest uses of art. It takes up some flower which people have thought common and shows them how beautiful it is."

"How do you find art in America?"

"The feeling of art and the admiration of beauty is, I think, more general than I expected. I found a greater appreciation of art in Boston, New York, Cincinnati, St. Louis, and Chicago than anywhere else."

"What do you think after your American tour?"

"With regard to my American tour, I may say that nothing could be more interesting to any young man than to have the opportunities that I have had of studying the civilizations in many cases very fine and in many cases incomplete of this new world. I have found a greater feeling for art than I expected, but far less knowledge of it, a great feeling for beauty and beautiful things, but a very vague idea about how a nation could acquire them. The real question that I have found in America standing in the way of its right artistic developments is that the ordinary handicrafts are not held in their proper honor. So many young men whom I have met in railway cars and elsewhere, young men of a great deal of brightness of intellect being contented to select as a profession the occupation of clerks in stores, and the like, which in many cases means so little more than a form of salaried idleness, and on seeing how much finer it would be for them to select a profession in which they could use their hands and really do useful and good work."

"When will you return to Europe?"

"I shall not be in Europe for a year. After my tour through the South, I shall go to Canada, where I have to deliver ten more lectures. I will then return to California, a part of America which I admire enormously—will go from there to Japan. In Japan I intend to study the method and the education of their ordinary artisans and to try and understand how it is that every ordinary Japanese workman has got this delicacy of hand, this feeling of beauty and this perfectly masterful power of design which are characteristics of their work. I am a wanderer by nature and I hardly know when I will be in Europe. I will sail for Japan about the 15th of August."

1. Loyd Street is now Atlanta's Central Avenue.
2. *The Rise and Fall of the Confederate Government,* Davis's nearly eight hundred-page history, was published in 1881.
3. Patrick Henry (1736–99) was a prominent figure in the American Revolution, best remembered for the speech in which he proclaimed, "Give me liberty or give me death."
4. Thomas Jefferson (1743–1826) was the third president of the United States and the primary author of the Declaration of Independence.
5. George Washington (1732–99) led America's army in the Revolutionary War and served as the nation's first president.
6. Edgar Allan Poe (1809–49), American poet, writer, critic, and editor.

45. "OSCAR DEAR, OSCAR DEAR!" *CHARLESTON NEWS AND COURIER*, 8 JULY 1882, 4

The arrival of the apostle of modern aestheticism was an event which would have been marked by something of a demonstration, but for the fact that very few people knew at what hour the apostle would reach the city. A few moments after 1 o'clock yesterday an open carriage stopped in front of the ladies' entrance to the Charleston Hotel. From this emerged first a small but good-looking American citizen, a little off color; then a dapper little red whiskered man; and finally two hundred pounds avoirdupois of aesthetic human flesh and bones done up in a mouse-colored velveteen shooting jacket and salt and pepper small clothes. The head was ornamented with long ambrosial locks of very dark hair, and capped with a broad-brim, dim-colored slouch hat, something after the style of Buffalo Bill or Texas Jack.[1] "That's him," cried Ingliss, the barber, who had come out to see the sight, and there was a rush of the few persons who were loafing about the hotel in the direction of the show, while the storefronts in the immediate vicinity were speedily adorned with idle salesmen and drummers. The door of the ladies' entrance being locked, the two hundred pounds of aestheticism posed about on the doorsteps, grim and dusty, and uncomfortable, but looked all the same like a magnified photograph of Geo. Denham in the role of "Bunthorne."[2] There was no mistaking his identity. The face, form, figure, attitude and movement of the man brought "Bunthorne" forcibly to mind, and caused the spectators to look at once for the "Twenty love-sick maidens" who invariably accompany that aesthetical hero. The reporter who had been sent to describe the event caught himself whistling the refrain which has of late become so popular:

> Oscar dear, Oscar dear,
> How utterly, flutterly utter you are;
> Oscar dear, Oscar dear,
> I think you are awfully wild, ta-ta.[3]

The door being at length opened, Mr. Wilde was ushered in by an army of waiters, while his manager went around to the main entrance followed the crowd and wrote upon the hotel register, "Oscar Wilde and servant of Ireland." The apostle was then hurried into the elevator and was soon comfortably put away in room 3.

An hour or two afterward the reporter sent up his card and was ushered into the awful presence of the founder of aestheticism, the apostle of decorative art, the only genuine Oscar Wilde. The off-colored *valet de chambre* "of Ireland" stood sentry at the outer door. To his knock came in sweet accents the answer to "come," and the reporter entered the room now rendered famous.

The great aesthete was "lolling" upon a sofa, his ambrosial locks parted in the middle resting upon a pillow, and his feet, ornamented with red-striped socks and sharp-pointed shoes, occupying the other end of the sofa. Mr. Wilde wore the same mouse-colored velveteen shooting jacket which he wore on entering the hotel, and the same pepper-and-salt small clothes, but his person showed evidence of a bath and the minor details of his costume were more attractively arranged. The ferocious "Buffalo Bill" slouch hat had been laid aside. From his collar there hung the ends of a salmon-colored silk neck handkerchief, while a pale violet-colored kerchief peeped out from the breast pocket of his coat. In front of the sofa upon which he lolled was a cane-bottom chair upon which stood a large tumbler filled with a liquid of some kind, and out of which protruded the end of two straws which ever and anon were conveyed to the lips of the apostle. Sundry pieces of lemon in the tumbler suggested lemonade, but the color of the fluid, a bright yellow, suggested "sunflower seed tea."[4] A few moments later a gentle aroma of rum floated through the air, and at that moment the reporter found himself in the hands of the great aesthete, who inquired very sweetly and solicitously after his reportorial health, at the same time requesting him to be seated. Then the business of the interview began. The apostle resumed his lolling attitude on the sofa and gave himself up languidly to the task of answering the questions that were put to him.

Mr. Wilde looks like an enlarged and magnified "lah-da-dah" young man and speaks with the "don't-you-know" yawp of the day.

"Ya'as," he said, "it was a very dusty journey don't you know, but the kentry is fine, a beautiful wooded kentry all the way from Augusta here."

R. You've seen a good deal of the southern people. What do you think of their capacity for aesthetic culture?

W. Well, you see, one can travel through a country, and see so very few of the people. It's awful when one realizes how *few* people one knows in the world; but upon the whole I'd rather travel through a country rapidly. I like the southern people, although you have let the northern people get ahead of you in art. I think you are more adapted to the cultivation of art, I mean decorative art. You are of a warmer temperament and of a more imaginative turn of mind, don't you know. I should think you would turn your attention more to art. You have magnificent forests, beautiful flowers. What you want is more diversity. I saw in your paper today that two carloads of furniture had been bought for an infirmary here and brought all the way from Chicago. Now, why shouldn't you make that furniture here in Charleston? The aim of our school is to educate the people into the love of the beautiful and to apply it to practical use in the manufacture of useful articles.

R. Let me ask—if you won't think the question trifling—why is it that you are always pictured as posed with a sunflower or drooping over a lily?

W. Certainly I'll explain. (With a smile and a change of posture.) When the few of us young men got together to organize this movement we selected the lily and the sunflower for several reasons—as emblems of aestheticism. In the first place the outlines of these flowers are distinct and easily reproduced for wallpapering and other proper uses. Now, there's your beautiful and fragrant southern magnolia. Nothing could be more beautiful or more fragrant; ah, but you can't draw or paint the magnolia. Its outlines are not distinct, don't you see. And then the lily has always been associated with art in Italy and the sunflower with reverence and worship in the East. In Japan the worship of the lily is the foundation of religion; its emblem, the pure white flower springing from a bed of dross. The sunflower, too, is the emblem of the sun worshippers.

R. The sunflower, as you know, grows wild in this land, and the people of Charleston, white and black, are affected with the craze. I saw a number of colored women on the Fourth of July parading the streets with huge sunflowers in their dresses and hats. Do you think this is owing to the love of the beautiful?

W. Who can say? To live one's life is to love the beautiful. I think the people are awakening to a sense of the beautiful. As you say, you have lived all your life among sunflowers, and never until now noticed anything beautiful in them. That is the mission of true art—to make us pause and look at a thing a second time. At Atlanta all the girls that passed the hotel wore sunflowers, and at Mobile an enterprising little boy made twenty-five dollars selling sunflowers to the people who came to my lecture. That boy will be a congressman yet—who knows? It was a fortunate and harmless speculation for him. I wish all other speculations were as harmless and as innocent—(this *a propos* of nothing).

R. It is printed in the newspapers that you are engaged to and will marry a young lady of Boston. It would interest the ladies of Charleston and the South to hear whether this is true or not.

W. Ah! (with a smile.) That, you know, is one of those things which must always remain a vast mystery. But if a man is engaged to be married, he shouldn't come to the South (this with an air which suggested "taffy").

A gentleman who was in the room here suggested that the fair sex of Boston were hard to beat for beauty, to which the aesthetic apostle replied that that was true, but the women of the South were, upon the whole, much more beautiful than any that he had seen in this country. Their color and features, he said, were richer and more regular, and at this point the manager entered to bring an invitation to the apostle to visit the Charleston Club, and the reporter seized the opportunity to take his leave and bow himself from the too awfully awful presence of the mighty aesthete.

1. William Frederick "Buffalo Bill" Cody (1846–1917), a soldier and showman, was one of the most colorful figures of the Old West. John Wilson "Texas Jack" Vermillion (1842–1911) was a Confederate Civil War veteran, gambler, and gunfighter.
2. George W. Denham was an American star of opera and light opera.
3. Lyrics by M. H. Rosenfeld, "Oscar Dear!" (1882).
4. Sunflower seed tea is the only green tea produced in China without leaf stalks; this is, of course, more likely a jab at Wilde's love of sunflowers than a comment about his drink.

46. "LOVELINESS AND POLITENESS," *NEW YORK SUN*, 20 AUGUST 1882, 5

The following extract from the *New Orleans Times* was shown to Oscar Wilde by a *Sun* reporter in a parlor car of the Long Beach Railroad on Wednesday evening:

THE MOST BEAUTIFUL WOMAN IN AMERICA.

Oscar Wilde pronounced Miss Alsatia Allen of Montgomery, Ala., the most beautiful young lady he had seen in the United States.

Mr. and Mrs. Steele Mackaye[1] were in Mr. Wilde's party, which was returning from Long Beach. Mr. Wilde was dressed in a light gray suit of Irish frieze, with a high-crowned slouch hat of light gray. He removed his hat as he read the paragraph, allowing his abundant long hair to descend about his face. Then he chuckled gently and said:

"This is a remark, my dear fellow, I supposed I have made of some lady in every city I have visited in this country. It could be appropriately made. American women are very beautiful, and some of the finest types of beauty I have ever seen I found in the South. But it is in the decay of manners that the thoughtful and well-bred American has serious cause for regret. I have repeatedly said this, but I am told in reply, 'We are still a young country. You must not be too severe upon us. Where we are raw and crude now these finer arts will come with time.' 'Ah, yes,' I answer, 'but when your country was still younger its manners were better. They have never been equal since to what they were in Washington's time—a man himself whose manners were irreproachable.' I believe a most serious problem for the American people to consider is the cultivation of better manners among its people. It is the most noticeable, the most painful defect in American civilization.

"I shall spend some weeks more in this country," Mr. Wilde continued. "I shall lecture at Long Branch, Cape May, and several other watering places. I meet at these summer resorts people who are interested with me in these matters. Of course, there are many disadvantages in lecturing in summer hotels. The lectures are apt to be badly managed, the rooms are often difficult to speak in, and there is an inevitable bustle and confusion, which nobody can help, and for which nobody is to blame. From America I shall go to Japan, the most highly civilized country on the globe. Nowhere else do good manners so universally prevail among all classes. The culture and attainments of these people are little understood in this country.

"Next to Japan is France, where, in spite of frequent revolutions, good manners have reached a strange degree of perfection. If you visit France do not waste your time in Paris, among the ruined monuments of the empire, but go into the villages and the remote country hamlets, and note the instinctive politeness of the peasant, who will convince you that you have honored him and honored his country by coming into it.

"The Englishman abroad is in the main a man of good manners and an agreeable companion. I am a Celt, but I can tell the truth about him. At home the average Englishman is arrogant, ill-tempered, and tied down by prejudices which nothing will induce him to lay aside."

1. James Steele Mackaye (1842–94), American actor, producer, and theatrical manager.

---

47. "THE APOSTLE OF BEAUTY IN NOVA SCOTIA," *HALIFAX MORNING HERALD,* 10 OCTOBER 1882, 2

The afternoon train from St. John on Friday brought beauty's latest evangel to our province. He came not surrounded by a halo of blue and purple glory, not in a carved car, not in a Greek urn. He rode on the engine. He saw the little hills rejoicing merrily. He saw Moncton, and noticed the irradiant wonder of the *Transcript* editor. He took in the Pre-Raphaelism of Dorchester. He rejoiced at the preciousness of Westcock, and was enraptured at the gaudy leonine beauty of the Tantramar.[1] Oscar praised the railroad and liked the appointment of the cars. He smoked the cigar of peace as he crossed the Missequash, but he took no interest in Fort Cumberland,[2] as the battles fought there were not fought for love of beauty but for love of territory.

At Amherst he shook hands with the engine driver, gaily wished him a good day, gave him a stray cigar, and leaped lightly to the platform, declining the proffered help of a hand kindly outstretched to assist him. The station platform was crowded with citizens trying to get a glimpse of "wild Oscar," as they called him, and these were anxiously watching the door of the car where the Evangelist might be supposed to be, while he was quietly getting into a carriage and getting under way for Lamy's. The first impression on looking at Oscar is that he looks like his pictures. You have seen that picture before and are ready to turn over a leaf.

A *Herald* representative called upon Mr. Wilde in his room at Lamy's. He was received with a polite friendliness that was winning. The Apostle had no lily nor yet a sunflower. He wore a velvet jacket which seemed to be a good jacket. He had an ordinary necktie and wore a linen collar about number eighteen on a neck half a dozen sizes smaller. His legs were in trousers such as Greenfield might have made,[3] and his boots were apparently the product of New York art, judging by their pointed toes. He wore a ring with a seal of great size. A consensus of the opinions of Amherst people decides that Oscar's hair is not good. It is the color of straw, slightly leonine, and straight as an Indian's. It is faded and bleached looking, and when not looked after goes climbing all over his features. Mr. Wilde was communicative and genial. He said that he found Canada pleasant. He liked the scenery of New Brunswick, as it lent itself readily to art. There were no towering mountains and deep gulches such as he had seen in the West. There were no large rivers, but the scenery was always changing as one passed through. Every turn in the road brought a small surprise. The streams wound attractively through the land, and there were innumerable hills and valleys of all conceivable forms.

Had our autumn forests finer colors than those in England?

Well, he would not say that. Our timber was finer, but its beauty was of a different sort.

Mr. Wilde uses the word "timber" in a sense that he thinks American. He talks about the leaves on our timber, etc.

The conversation turned on newspapers.

"The editor of a paper," said Oscar, "has an advantage over all other writers. He never waits for his audience, and he is sure that what he writes will be read."

(Oscar sighed here, doubtless thinking of his poems.)

"American journals are in many respects better than the English. I think the American newspaper is the journal of the future. It is filled with news. The reader of the large New York papers knows everything that goes on in the world that is worth knowing, and much more. Still there is a want of dignity, and an amount of scurrility in the American newspaper which one gets in smaller towns that is terrible."

"Did they not discuss your appearance and your lectures in a somewhat unsatisfactory way?"

Oscar at this stage had brought in to him a cup of tea and having asked your representative to partake with him he laughed quietly and pushed his hair behind his ears, as he replied: "They talk in an incredible obtuse manner about my message and my work. I think nothing whatever about the criticisms now. It does not interest me as it did at first. I understand the people who say those things about me and I cannot bring myself to care what they say. I cannot possibly do it. At first it surprised me. I came out here, never having spoken in public, in earnest about my message, strongly feeling what I was saying, and I talked seriously to those people. They heard me and went away and talked about my necktie and the way I wore my hair. I could not understand how people could do such a thing. I thought it inexpressibly stupid."

This last with a sigh and a look of half-wearied pity at the thought of these critics. He said "stupid" with a strong accentuation on the last syllable.

"The English Journals," he went on, "are much more serious and earnest in their tone than yours. But a man who has a name that is valuable will not be an English journalist. English newspaper articles are written anonymously. A good writer can get no credit for good work, and so will not write for an English paper. The proprietor is everything, the writer nothing there. In France, where the writers sign their names, better men become journalists."

"But as a matter of fact you can tell who writes many articles in England."

"Yes, in some cases you can. There is George Augustus Sala.[4] (This name was uttered with a weary look, as if the physical effort of articulating it was nearly too much, and the last syllable of Sala was clearly accented.) You can always tell what Sala writes. No other human being can write such intolerable English."

Oscar made enquiries about the institutions of Amherst.

"Do you tell me that it has only three thousand inhabitants? Why (lying back luxuriously on his bear skin rug and sipping his tea,) I never spoke in a town so small as that. Mr. Townshend has driven me about the village and I consider it a beautiful little place."

He spoke of our style of government, of democracies generally, of sociology, of Herbert Spencer, whom he had read and admired greatly.[5] He found nothing in his work or in any other work on evolution which differed from

Plato and Aristotle. "There is nothing in art or philosophy in which we are as wise as the Greeks. Spencer has prosecuted enquiries which have led him to verify the Greek philosopher. No, we should *not go back* to the Greek; we should to get up to the Greek. All that remains for us anywhere is to corroborate the Greeks in everything. They reached a level the summit of which we cannot yet see. True, they had simpler problems. Their common people were less stupid. It is a wonder we do not have twice the trouble we do have, with the elements that go to make up the countries we now live in. Our conceptions of beauty may reach the Greek conception some time. There is nothing higher to hope for."

"Yes, I have found America pleasant. Out in the West, delightful. At Denver I met the most interesting people I have ever seen."

"Rough and ready I suppose?"

"Ready, but not rough. They were polished and refined compared with the people I met in large cities farther East. Yes, I *did* see the common people. I spent a night in a silver mine. I dined with the men down there. They were great, strong, well-formed men, of graceful attitude and free motion. Poems every one of them. A complete democracy underground. I find people less rough and coarse in such places. There is no chance for roughness. The revolver is their book of etiquette. This teaches lessons that are not forgotten. I wish I could have gone to Winnipeg. I like free people without the resources of civilization. They are freer and more artistic in their surroundings because they follow nature."

"Speaking of ladies (he had spoken of them), do you consider American or European ladies the finest looking?"

"That I cannot answer here. I shall wait till I get in midocean, out of sight of both countries. If I were to answer you I should find it to my advantage to be anything but candid."

Your reporter intimated that the last remark was a sufficient answer.

Oscar, smiling and drinking more tea, proceeded: "Your women are pretty. I never saw so many pretty women as I have seen here, especially in the South, but the prettiness is in color and freshness and bloom. A truly beautiful woman never grows old. The most of your pretty ladies will not be pretty in ten years."

"I believe you discovered Mrs. Langtry?"

A look of rapture came to Oscar's face. He flung his locks from where they clustered around his nose, and with a gesture, the first of the interview, he said:

"I would rather have discovered Mrs. Langtry than have discovered America. Her beauty is in outline perfectly moulded. She will be a beauty at eighty-five.

"Yes, it was for such ladies that Troy was destroyed, and well might Troy be destroyed for such a woman. Perhaps it may be true—they say it is—that the siege of Troy was brought about by a quarrel about a harbor, but they thought they fought for a woman; they had the conception that it was for beauty, and that is the same as if it was. It would be a fine thing if nations went to war with each other now over such questions as to which had the most beautiful women. How much better that than the senseless dispute about getting Egypt and possessing Arabi.[6] Now that we have caught Arabi we do not know what to do with him. When I was young I thought the Wars of the Roses were to decide whether a red or a white rose was the most beautiful. I learned afterward that it was a vulgar dispute. The right of one or two men to a crown or something of that kind."

This last was spoken in a tone of injured susceptibility, as though York had thrown soup on Oscar's coat, or Lancaster had smoked a black pipe over Oscar's dinner.[7]

"What do I think of your American Literature? I think you have had a great poet in Poe. He is your greatest poet. His sense of form and exquisitiveness of touch are intense. His gold is not to be gilt and his lilies are unpaintable. Joaquin Miller is also a beautiful poet. 'Arizonian' is a poem of great artistic excellence. Fawcett,[8] a new poet, whom we had not heard of when I left England, has written some of the most perfect poetry which I have seen. Walt Whitman if not a poet is a man who sounds a strong note. He writes neither prose nor poetry but something of his own that is unique. He is one of your greatest men."

"No, I do not care for the 'Commemoration Ode' of Lowell.[9] It has no harmony in its conception. It is oratory of the strongest kind, and is eloquent, but does not meet my idea of poetry. Lowell has written a poem on dedication which is delicate poetry. You must like it: You have poets with you. In New Brunswick a young man, Mr. Roberts, has published a little book. You have heard of it."[10]

The reporter had read Roberts's published poems and was delighted to find that Mr. Wilde met and liked them.

"And Mulvaney of Toronto,[11] a countryman of my own, a man once well known at Trinity College. He is a man of taste. Fréchette,[12] I believe, is however your best poet.

"Wordsworth was undoubtedly a poet. I do not read the poems he liked best of his. I do not care for his 'Idiot Boy.' 'The Excursion' is nothing to me."[13]

Your correspondent intimated that the poem was too long for what poetry it contained, which reduced the average too low.

Said Mr. Wilde, "I do not like to hear poems spoken of as too long. 'The Excursion' is shorter than the *Iliad*. I would not have one line less in the *Iliad*.

But I like Wordsworth's Sonnets. That beginning: 'Milton thou should'st be living at this hour,' is fine, as is that which commences: 'The world is too much with us.'"[14] As your representative rose to go, having declined a cup of tea, which was again politely offered, he was asked about Halifax, the nature of the people and the style of the town. Mr. Wilde had met Sir John Macdonald and his lady.[15] "Sir John (and Mr. Wilde sighed as he said it) was a man of the world, but his lady was charming and so was he."

And your correspondent left. There was other talk about the classics, about the French idea of the dramatic unities, about Shakespeare and Wordsworth and Keats and Rossetti, but this was of a nature too confidential to be communicated to everybody. It will be remembered that Mr. Wilde begins one of his sonnets with this line: "I stood by the unvintageable sea."[16] Your correspondent thought of this as he was leaving, and remembering that the Tantramar was very muddy as the aesthete passed over it, he asked, "Do you consider the Tantramar vintageable to any extent?" The apostle laughed gaily at this proof of the presence of a Philistine, but contented himself with praising other streams of less leonine beauty.

1. The Tantramar River in New Brunswick borders on marshes of the same name.
2. The construction of Fort Beauséjour, also referred to as Fort Cumberland, began in 1751 on a ridge overlooking the Tantramar marshes.
3. Jacob Greenfield's famous haberdashery was located on Second Street in New York.
4. George Augustus Henry Sala (1828–95), an English journalist, wrote approximately ten articles a week for London's *Daily Telegraph* over a quarter-century beginning in 1857 and served that newspaper as a foreign correspondent for nearly two decades.
5. Herbert Spencer (1820–1903), English philosopher and classical liberalist political theorist.
6. Ahmed Arabi, also known as Arabi Pasha or Ahmed Arabi Bey (1841–1911), was an Egyptian dissident, former colonel in the army, and representative of the native "National Party" who was branded a rebel and traitor by England.
7. The Wars of the Roses (1455–87) were civil wars fought over the British throne by adherents of the House of York (whose badge was the white rose) and the House of Lancaster (represented by the red rose), both of which were branches of the Plantagenet royal house.
8. Edgar Fawcett (1847–1904), American novelist and poet.
9. James Russell Lowell's turgid "Ode Recited at the Harvard Commemoration, July 21, 1865."
10. The Canadian writer and poet Charles George Douglas Roberts (1860–1943), a member of the group known as Confederation poets, had recently published *Orion, and Other Poems* (1880).
11. Charles Pelham Mulvaney (1835–85), Irish-born Canadian historian and poet.
12. Louis Honoré Fréchette (1839–1908), French Canadian poet, writer, and politician.

13. The English poet William Wordsworth (1770–1850) helped to launch the British Romantic movement with the 1798 publication of *Lyrical Ballads* (which includes one of the poems Wilde dismisses, "The Idiot Boy").

14. Wilde refers to Wordsworth's sonnets "England, 1802" and "The World Is Too Much with Us."

15. John Alexander Macdonald (1815–91), a Scottish-born Canadian politician, was the first prime minister of Canada, holding that office for nineteen years. Susan Agnes Macdonald (née Bernard) (1836–1920), the second wife of Macdonald, was granted the title baroness Macdonald of Earnscliffe after her husband's death.

16. "Vita Nuova," or "new life," titled after Dante Alighieri's medieval autobiographical text *La Vita Nuova* (ca. 1292–94), on courtly love.

---

48. "OSCAR WILDE THOROUGHLY EXHAUSTED," *NEW YORK TRIBUNE*, 27 NOVEMBER 1882, 3

Oscar Wilde is living in furnished rooms at present in West Eleventh Street. He has not delivered any lectures recently, and although he may occasionally appear upon the platform again in this country, he does not contemplate giving any further serious attention to the lecture business for the benefit and aesthetic enlightenment of Americans. Since his return from the professional tour of the watering-places in the summer, he has been living the life of a man about town. Through the kind offices of "Sam" Ward[1] and other friends, he obtained a visitor's card to the Manhattan Club,[2] and has been for some time a frequent caller there. He still goes into society, although it is not exactly the same social circle as that which took him up on his arrival here. He dines at well-known restaurants about 7 o'clock every evening, and is a prominent figure at the theaters of first nights. He comes out into the lobby between the acts, like a very commonplace young man, lights a very small cigarette, and, throwing himself into the attitude which a prominent photographer on the payment of a satisfactory sum of money was allowed to reproduce for the benefit of the people at large, he furnishes a novel and altogether harmless diversion to the lobby loungers. After the play, and probably an incidental aesthetic agony over some "dreadful" combination of colors in the scenery, he indulges in a little supper and an accompanying cogitation over a few critical paragraphs intended for publication. In fact, it will be seen that Mr. Wilde has been leading a very speedy existence; and he now declares that "he is thoroughly exhausted, you know, and—ah—suffering from severe nervous prostration." He believes that he has four doctors.

In the meantime many persons have expressed a fear that Mr. Wilde intended staying here. An English paper printed a report that he intended marrying an American heiress. There have been rumors of his starting a society journal in New York. The story has been circulated that his name had been posted for election at the Manhattan Club, and it has been widely asserted that he intended producing his play, "Vera, the Nihilist," in a very short time. It seemed, indeed, that the life of the poet would for a long while be bound up with the life of the metropolis.

A *Tribune* reporter who called at the house in West Eleventh Street was shown into Mr. Wilde's sitting room. It is a commonplace room, with the paper portions of three Japanese parasols blown against one of the walls to denote a presence not in harmony with the remainder of the surroundings. Mr. Wilde presently sauntered in. There was a look of utter weariness on his long, smooth face. He threw back his hair in a manner that was both painful and poetic, and sank slowly, gracefully, but with an appearance of unutterable fatigue, into an armchair.

"Have you made any arrangements to produce your play?"

"Why do you ask," said Mr. Wilde, opening his eyes.

"The public might like to know."

"Oh."

Mr. Wilde closed his eyes and yielded himself up to thought.

"To persons of no reputation," he presently began "small paragraphs are doubtless an advantage. But, really, I do not care for them."

"But the production of your play might be a matter of a big paragraph."

"Oh!"

Mr. Wilde closed his eyes again.

"Well, I have made no arrangements as yet."

"Are you going to stay in this country?"

"No; I am going to Australia as soon as I get thoroughly rested. I am tired out, now, really."

Mr. Wilde here passed his hand across his brow, and his eyes again denoted that life for him was full of fatigue and disappointment.

"I am waiting to go to Australia because I cannot find anyone to go with. I shall probably stay here until January."

"And how about Japan?"

"Japan will keep. I shall doubtless go there before I am through."

1. Samuel Ward (1814–84), affectionately known as "Uncle Sam," was an influential American lobbyist, statesman, author, and epicurean.
2. The Manhattan Club was located in a mansion owned by Leonard Walter Jerome on the corner of Twenty-sixth Street and Madison Avenue.

WILDE'S LECTURE

FROM *IMPRESSIONS OF AMERICA*, ED. STUART
MASON (SUNDERLAND, U.K.: KEYSTONE, 1906)

I fear I cannot picture America as altogether an Elysium; perhaps from the ordinary standpoint, I know but little about the country. I cannot give its latitude or longitude; I cannot compute the value of its dry goods,[1] and I have no very close acquaintance with its politics. These are matters which may not interest you, and they certainly are not interesting to me.

The first thing that struck me on landing in America was that, if the Americans are not the most well-dressed people in the world, they are the most comfortably dressed. Men are seen there with the dreadful chimney-pot hat, but there are very few hatless men; men wear the shocking swallow-tail coat, but few are to be seen with no coat at all. There is an air of comfort in the appearance of the people; which is a marked contrast to that seen in this country, where, too often, people are seen in close contact with rags.

The next thing particularly noticeable is that everybody seems in a hurry to catch a train. This is a state of things which is not favourable to poetry or romance. Had Romeo and Juliet been in a constant state of anxiety about trains, or had their minds been agitated by the question of return-tickets, Shakespeare could not have given us those lovely balcony scenes, which are so full of poetry and pathos.

America is the noisiest country that ever existed. One is waked up in the morning, not by the singing of the nightingale, but by the steam whistle. It is not surprising that the sound practical sense of the American does not reduce this intolerable noise. All Art depends upon exquisite and delicate sensibility, and such continual turmoil must ultimately be destructive of the musical faculty.

There is not so much beauty to be found in American cities, as in Oxford, Cambridge, Salisbury or Winchester; where are lovely relics of a beautiful age; but still there is a good deal of beauty to be seen in them now and then, but only where the American has not attempted to create it. Where the Americans have attempted to produce beauty, they have signally failed. A remarkable characteristic of the Americans is the manner, in which they have applied science to modern life.

This is apparent in the most cursory stroll through New York. In England an inventor is regarded almost as a crazy man, and in too many instances invention ends in disappointment and poverty. In America an inventor is honoured; help is forthcoming, and the exercise of ingenuity, the application of science to the work of man, is there the shortest road to wealth. There is no country in the world, where machinery is so lovely as in America.

I have always wished to believe that the line of strength and the line of beauty are one. That wish was realised when I contemplated American machinery. It was not until I had seen the waterworks at Chicago that I realised the wonders of machinery; the rise and fall of the steel rods, the symmetrical motion of the great wheels is the most beautifully rhythmic thing I have ever seen. One is impressed in America, but not favourably impressed, by the inordinate size of everything. The country seems to try to bully one into a belief in its power by its impressive bigness.

I was disappointed with Niagara; most people must be disappointed with Niagara. Every American bride is taken there and the sight of the stupendous waterfall must be one of the earliest, if not the keenest, disappointments in American married life. One sees it under bad conditions, very far away, the point of view not showing the splendour of the water. To appreciate it really one has to see it from underneath the fall, and to do that it is necessary to be dressed in a yellow oil-skin, which is as ugly as a mackintosh—and I hope none of you ever wears one. It is a consolation to know, however, that such an artist as Madame Bernhardt has not only worn that yellow, ugly dress, but has been photographed in it.

Perhaps the most beautiful part of America is the West; to reach which, however, involves a journey by rail of six days, racing along tied to an ugly tin-kettle of a steam engine. I found but poor consolation for this journey in the fact that the boys, who infest the cars and sell everything one can eat or should not eat, were selling editions of my poems, vilely printed on a kind of grey blotting paper, for the low price of ten cents. Calling these boys on one side, I told them that, though poets like to be popular, they desire to be paid; and selling editions of my poems without giving me a profit is dealing a blow at literature, which must have a disastrous effect on poetical aspirants. The invariable reply that they made was that they themselves made a profit out of the transaction, and that was all they cared about.

It is a popular superstition that in America a visitor is invariably addressed as "Stranger." I was never once addressed as "Stranger." When I went to Texas, I was called "Captain"; when I got to the centre of the country, I was addressed as "Colonel"; and on arriving at the borders of Mexico, as "General." On the whole, however, "Sir," the old English method of addressing people, is the most common.

It is, perhaps, worthwhile to note that what many people call Americanisms are really old English expressions which have lingered in our colonies, while they have been lost in our own country. Many people imagine that the term "I guess," which is so common in America, is purely an American expression, but it was used by John Locke in his work on "The Understanding"; just as we now use "I think."

It is in the colonies, and not in the mother country, that the old life of the country really exists. If one wants to realise what English Puritanism is—not at its worst (when it is very bad), but at its best, and then it is not very good—I do not think one can find much of it in England but much can be found about Boston and Massachusetts. We have got rid of it. America still preserves it, to be, I hope, a short-lived curiosity.

San Francisco is a really beautiful city. China Town, peopled by Chinese labourers, is the most artistic town I have ever come across. The people—strange, melancholy Orientals, whom many people would call common—and they are certainly very poor, have determined that they will have nothing about them that is not beautiful. In the Chinese restaurant, where these navvies meet to have supper in the evening, I found them drinking tea out of china cups, as delicate as the petals of a rose-leaf, whereas at the gaudy hotels I was supplied with a delf cup[2] an inch and a half thick. When the Chinese bill was presented, it was made out on rice paper, the account being done in Indian ink as fantastically as if an artist had been etching little birds on a fan.

Salt Lake City contains only two buildings of note, the chief being the Tabernacle, which is in the shape of a soup-kettle. It is decorated by the only native artist, and he has treated religious subjects in the naive spirit of the early Florentine painters, representing people of our own day in the dress of the period side by side with people of Biblical history, who are clothed in some romantic costume.

The building next in importance is called the Amelia Palace in honour of one of Brigham Young's wives. When he died, the present president of the Mormons stood up in the Tabernacle and said that it had been revealed to him that he was to have the Amelia Palace, and that on this subject there were to be no more revelations of any kind!

From Salt Lake City one travels over the great plains of Colorado and up the Rocky Mountains, on the top of which is Leadville, the richest city in the world. It has also got the reputation of being the roughest, and every man carries a revolver. I was told that, if I went there, they would be sure to shoot me or my traveling manager. I wrote and told them that nothing that they could do to my traveling manager would intimidate me.[3] They are miners—men working in metals, so I lectured to them on the Ethics of Art. I read them passages from the autobiography of Benvenuto Cellini[4] and they seemed much delighted. I was reproved by my hearers for not having brought him with me. I explained that he had been dead for some little time, which elicited the enquiry, "Who shot him?" They afterwards took me to a dancing saloon, where I saw the only rational method of art criticism I have ever come across. Over the piano was printed a notice:

PLEASE DO NOT SHOOT THE PIANIST.
HE IS DOING HIS BEST.

The mortality among pianists in that place is marvellous. Then they asked me to supper, and having accepted, I had to descend a mine in a rickety bucket in which it was impossible to be graceful. Having got into the heart of the mountain I had supper, the first course being whisky, the second whisky, and the third whisky.

I went to the Theatre to lecture and I was informed that just before I went there two men had been seized for committing a murder, and in that theatre they had been brought on to the stage at eight o'clock in the evening, and then and there tried and executed before a crowded audience. But I found these miners very charming and not at all rough.

Among the more elderly inhabitants of the South I found a melancholy tendency to date every event of importance by the late war. "How beautiful the moon is to-night," I once remarked to a gentleman who was standing next to me. "Yes," was his reply, "but you should have seen it before the war."

So infinitesimal did I find the knowledge of Art, west of the Rocky Mountains, that an art patron—one who in his day had been a miner—actually sued the railroad company for damages because the plaster cast of Venus of Milo which he had imported from Paris had been delivered minus the arms. And, what is more surprising still, he gained his case and the damages.

Pennsylvania, with its rocky gorges and woodland scenery, reminded me of Switzerland. The prairie reminded me of a piece of blotting-paper.

The Spanish and French have left behind them memorials in the beauty of their names. All the cities that have beautiful names derive them from the Spanish or the French. The English people give intensely ugly names to places. One place had such an ugly name that I refused to lecture there. It was called Griggsville. Supposing I had founded a school of Art there—fancy "Early Griggsville." Imagine a School of Art teaching "Griggsville Renaissance."

As for slang I did not hear much of it, though a young lady who had changed her clothes after an afternoon dance did say that "after the heel kick she shifted her day goods."

American youths are pale and precocious, or sallow and supercilious, but American girls are pretty and charming—little oases of pretty unreasonableness in a vast desert of practical common-sense.

Every American girl is entitled to have twelve young men devoted to her. They remain her slaves and she rules them with charming nonchalance.

The men are entirely given to business; they have, as they say, their brains in front of their heads. They are also exceedingly receptive of new ideas. Their education is practical. We base the education of children entirely on books, but we must give a child a mind before we can instruct the mind. Children have a natural antipathy to books—handicraft should be the basis of education. Boys and girls should be taught to use their hands to make something, and they would be less apt to destroy and be mischievous.

In going to America one learns that poverty is not a necessary accompaniment to civilisation. There at any rate is a country that has no trappings, no pageants, and no gorgeous ceremonies. I saw only two processions—one was the Fire Brigade preceded by the Police, the other was the Police preceded by the Fire Brigade.

Every man when he gets to the age of twenty-one is allowed a vote and thereby immediately acquires his political education. The Americans are the best politically educated people in the world. It is well worth one's while to go to a country which can teach us the beauty of the word *freedom* and the value of the thing *liberty*.

1. In chapter 3 of *The Picture of Dorian Gray*, Lord Henry Wotton is asked the perplexing question "What *are* American dry goods?" He replies, "American novels" and proposes that when bad Americans die "they go to America" (43, 44).

2. Here "delf" refers to a kind of glazed earthenware made at Delf, or Delft, in Holland.

3. Actually, Wilde wrote ahead to Denver, not Leadville. See "Mr. Wilde's Presentation," *Denver Times*, 12 April 1882, 4:

    > I have been told that Denver is a bad place, and that some mischievous young men will make it hot for me. If this be true, then will I bid farewell to my vow of peace. I am resolved to no longer tamely submit to being made a target for rude youngsters to shy things at. Having shown America what gentleness is, I am now determined to discard forbearance, and defend myself, shall circumstances so demand it of me. I am practicing with my new revolver by shooting at sparrows on telegraph wires from the car window. My aim is as lethal as lightning.
    >   O. Wilde

4. Benvenuto Cellini (1500–1571) was a celebrated Florentine Renaissance sculptor, goldsmith, author, and soldier.

BIBLIOGRAPHY OF ALL KNOWN
INTERVIEWS WITH OSCAR WILDE

Interviews included in this edition are marked with an asterisk.

*1. "Oscar Wilde's Arrival," *New York World,* 3 January 1882, 1.

2. "Ten Minutes with a Poet," *New York Times,* 3 January 1882, 5.

3. "Oscar Wilde in New York," *New York Sun,* 3 January 1882, 1.

*4. "Oscar Wilde," *New York Evening Post,* 4 January 1882, 4.

5. "Oscar Wilde," *New York Herald,* 4 January 1882.

*6. "Our New York Letter," *Philadelphia Inquirer,* 4 January 1882, 7.

7. "Oscar Wilde / Why He Comes to America," *Chicago Tribune,* 4 January 1882, 5.

8. "Oscar Wilde," *San Francisco Bulletin,* 4 January 1882, 1.

9. "Of Gangling Gait," *Atlanta Constitution,* 5 January 1882, 1.

10. "Oscar Wilde," *New York World,* 6 January 1882, 5.

*11. "The Theories of a Poet," *New York Tribune,* 8 January 1882, 7.

*12. "The Science of the Beautiful," *New York World,* 8 January 1882, 2.

13. "Art's Apostle," *Boston Herald,* 15 January 1882, 8.

*14. "A Talk with Wilde," *Philadelphia Press,* 17 January 1882, 2.

*15. "The Aesthetic Bard," *Philadelphia Inquirer,* 17 January 1882, 2.

16. "Oscar Wilde and Whitman," *Philadelphia Press,* 19 January 1882, 8.

*17. "What Oscar Has to Say," *Baltimore American,* 20 January 1882, 4.

18. "Oscar Wilde on Greek Drama," *Philadelphia Inquirer,* 20 January 1882, 8.

*19. "Wilde and Forbes," *New York Herald,* 21 January 1882, 3.

20. "Oscar's Side of It," *Baltimore American,* 21 January 1882, 4.

21. "Art's Apostle," *Washington Evening Star,* 21 January 1882, 3.

22. "New York Gossip," *Boston Herald,* 22 January 1882, 4.

23. "Mr. Wilde's Stay in Baltimore," *Baltimore American,* 26 January 1882, 4.

*24. "An Interview with the Poet," *Albany Argus,* 28 January 1882, 8.

*25. "Oscar Wilde," *Boston Herald,* 29 January 1882, 7.

*26. "The Aesthetic Apostle," *Boston Globe,* 29 January 1882, 5.

27. "The Aesthete," *Brooklyn Eagle,* 4 February 1882, 2.

28. "Oscar Wilde in Brooklyn," *New York Sun,* 4 February 1882, 1.

*29. Lilian Whiting, "They Will Show Him," *Chicago Inter-Ocean,* 10 February 1882, 2.

*30. "A Man of Culture Rare," *Rochester Democrat and Chronicle,* 8 February 1882, 4.

*31. "Wilde Sees the Falls," *Buffalo Express,* ca. 9 February 1882; repr. *Wheeling Register,* 27 February 1882, 3.

*32. "The Apostle of Art," *Chicago Inter-Ocean,* 11 February 1882, 4.

33. "Weary Wilde," *Chicago Times,* 11 February 1882, 6.

*34. "Truly Aesthetic," *Chicago Inter-Ocean,* 13 February 1882, 2.

35. "Oscar Wilde," *Chicago Tribune,* 15 February 1882, 3.

*36. "Wilde," *Cleveland Leader,* 20 February 1882, 6.

*37. "With Mr. Oscar Wilde," *Cincinnati Gazette,* 21 February 1882, 10.

*38. "Oscar Wilde," *Cincinnati Enquirer,* 21 February 1882, 4.

*39. "Utterly Utter," *St. Louis Post-Dispatch,* 25 February 1882, 4.

*40. "Speranza's Gifted Son," *St. Louis Globe-Democrat,* 26 February 1882, 3.

*41. "Oscar as He Is," *St. Louis Republican,* 26 February 1882, 13.

42. "A Home Ruler / Oscar Wilde Has Some Well-Settled Opinions on the Irish Question," *St. Louis Globe-Democrat,* 27 February 1882, 6; repr. *Chicago Tribune,* 2 March 1882, 5.

43. "Oscar Wilde," *Chicago Journal,* 28 February 1882, 1.

*44. "Oscar Wilde," *Chicago Tribune,* 1 March 1882, 7.

*45. "Philosophical Oscar," *Chicago Times,* 1 March 1882, 7.

46. "Oscar Back Again," *Chicago Inter-Ocean,* 1 March 1882, 8.

47. "Oscar Wilde," *Dubuque Herald,* 3 March 1882, 4.

*48. "David and Oscar," *Chicago Tribune,* 5 March 1882, 5.

49. "Oscar Wilde in the West," *New York Herald,* 6 March 1882, 4.

50. "Oscar Wilde," *Indianapolis Saturday Review,* 11 March 1882, 7.

51. "The Apostle of Aestheticism," *St. Paul and Minneapolis Pioneer Press,* 16 March 1882, 6.

52. "Oscar Wilde," *Minneapolis Tribune,* 16 March 1882, 6.

53. "An Aesthete in Undress," *Sioux City Daily Journal,* 21 March 1882, 3.

*54. "Oscar Wilde in Omaha," *Omaha Weekly Herald,* 24 March 1882, 2.

55. "Words with Wilde," *Ogden Daily Herald,* 25 March 1882, 3.

*56. "Oscar Wilde: An Interview with the Apostle of Aestheticism," *San Francisco Examiner,* 27 March 1882, 2.

*57. "Oscar Wilde's Views," *San Francisco Morning Call,* 27 March 1882, 4.

*58. "Lo! The Aesthete," *San Francisco Chronicle,* 27 March 1882, 3.

*59. "Oscar Arrives," *Sacramento Record-Union,* 27 March 1882, 3.

60. "Oscar Wilde," *San Jose Herald,* 4 April 1882, 3.

*61. Mary Watson, "Oscar Wilde at Home," *San Francisco Examiner,* 9 April 1882, 1.

*62. "Oscar Wilde," *Salt Lake Herald,* 12 April 1882.

*63. "Oscar Wilde," *Denver Rocky Mountain News,* 13 April 1882, 8.

*64. "Art and Aesthetics," *Denver Tribune,* 13 April 1882, 8.

65. "Oscar Interviewed," *Denver Republican,* 13 April 1882, 4.

66. "Oscar Dear," *Leadville Daily Herald,* 14 April 1882, 4.

67. "Quite Too Too," *Kansas City Star,* 17 April 1882, 1.

68. "The Only Oscar," *Kansas City Times,* 18 April 1882, 5.

*69. "What Mr. Wilde Says about Himself," *Manchester Examiner and Times;* repr. *New York Tribune,* 11 June 1882, 9; *Chicago Tribune,* 17 June 1882, 3.

70. "Ah, Oscar / Beauty's Great Exponent," *Topeka Capital,* 21 April 1882, 8; repr. in Mikhail 1979:79–80.

71. "The World Wonder Wilde," *Des Moines Iowa Daily Register,* 27 April 1882, 2.

72. "Oscar Wilde," *Dayton Journal,* 3 May 1882, 4.

*73. "Aesthetic / An Interesting Interview with Oscar Wilde," *Dayton Daily Democrat,* 3 May 1882, 4.

*74. "Oscar Wilde's Return," *New York World,* 6 May 1882, 1.

75. "Oscar Wilde / His Surprise and His Views," *Chicago Tribune,* 7 May 1882, 3.

*76. "Oscar Wilde in Montreal," *Montreal Witness,* 15 May 1882, 8.

*77. "Oscar Wilde: The Arch-Aesthete on Aestheticism," *Montreal Star,* 15 May 1882, 3.

78. "An Aesthetic Discussion," *Kingston British Whig,* 16 May 1882, 1.

79. "Jottings from Ottawa," *Montreal Daily Star,* 16 May 1882, 2.

80. "Oscar Wilde," *Ottawa Daily Citizen,* 17 May 1882, 1.

81. "Oscar Wilde Interviewed," *Kingston Daily News,* 23 May 1882, 2.

*82. "Oscar Wilde," *Toronto Globe,* 25 May 1882, 3.

83. "Aestheticism's Apostle," *Toronto Evening News,* 25 May 1882, 4; repr. Mikhail 1979:86–87.

*84. "The Aesthete at the Art Exhibition," *Toronto Globe,* 26 May 1882, 6.

85. "Oscar Wilde / A Visit to the Apostle of Modern Art," *New Orleans Picayune,* afternoon edition, 16 June 1882, 1, and repr. 17 June 1882, 3; repr. in Mikhail 1979:89–90.

86. H. Rider-Taylor, "The Aesthetic Apostle," *San Antonio Light,* 21 June 1882; repr. Mikhail 1979:90–91.

*87. "Oscar Wilde Talks of Texas," *New Orleans Picayune,* 25 June 1882, 11.

88. "Oscar Wilde," *Columbus (Ga.) Enquirer-Sun,* 30 June 1882, 4.

*89. "Oscar Wilde: Arrival of the Great Aesthete," *Atlanta Constitution,* 5 July 1882, 8.

90. "Oscar Wilde on Cloaks," *Atlanta Constitution,* 6 July 1882, 7.

*91. "Oscar Dear, Oscar Dear!" *Charleston News and Courier,* 8 July 1882, 4.

*92. "Loveliness and Politeness," *New York Sun,* 20 August 1882, 5.

93. *Saint John Daily Sun,* 5 October 1882, 3.

*94. "The Apostle of Beauty in Nova Scotia," *Halifax Morning Herald,* 10 October 1882, 2.

95. "Oscar Wilde Explains," *Moncton Daily Transcript,* 18 October 1882, 2.

96. "Mrs. Langtry on the Hudson," *New York Herald,* 30 October 1882, 5.

*97. "Oscar Wilde Thoroughly Exhausted," *New York Tribune,* 27 November 1882, 3.

98. "Bunko / Oscar Wilde Reputed to Have Lost $1,100," *Chicago Tribune,* 25 December 1882, 2.

99. "Mr. Oscar Wilde and the Unutterable Wheel," *Pall Mall Gazette,* 7 May 1883, 11; repr. "Oscar Wilde on Wheels and Things," *New York Times,* 24 May 1883, 5, and *Boston Globe,* 4 June 1883, 5.

100. "Oscar Wilde Returns," *New York World,* 12 August 1883, 5.

101. "The Poet of the Intense," *Brooklyn Eagle,* 12 August 1883, 1.

102. Maurice Sisley, "La *Salomé* de M. Oscar Wilde," *Le Gaulois* (Paris), 29 June 1892, 1; excerpted in "The Rage of Bunthorne," *New York Times,* 18 July 1892, 2.

103. "The Censure and *Salomé,*" *Pall Mall Budget,* 30 June 1892, 947.

104. Percival W. H. Almy, "New Views of Mr. Oscar Wilde," *Theatre* 23 (Mar. 1894): 119–27.

105. F. E. McKay, "A Clever Dramatist's Eccentric Views," *Kate Field's Washington,* 4 April 1894, 220–21; excerpted in "Eccentric Oscar Wilde," *Ogden Standard Examiner,* 9 May 1894, 4; full article repr. *The Wildean* 32 (Jan. 2008): 3–5.

106. Gilbert Burgess, "*An Ideal Husband* at the Haymarket Theatre: A Talk with Mr. Oscar Wilde," *The Sketch,* 9 January 1895, 495.

107. "Mr. Oscar Wilde on Mr. Oscar Wilde," *St. James's Gazette,* 18 January 1895, 4–5.

· WORKS CONSULTED ·

Blanchard, Mary Warner. "Oscar Wilde in America, 1882: Aestheticism, Women, and Modernism." In *Oscar Wilde: The Man, His Writings, and His World,* edited by Robert N. Keane, 35–52. New York: AMS, 2003.

———. *Oscar Wilde's America: Counterculture in the Gilded Age.* New Haven, Conn.: Yale University Press, 1998.

Danson, Lawrence. *Wilde's Intentions.* New York: Oxford University Press, 1997.

Ellis, Mary Louise. "Improbable Visitor: Oscar Wilde in Alabama, 1882." *Alabama Review* 39 (July 1986): 243–60.

Ellmann, Richard. *Oscar Wilde.* New York: Knopf, 1988.

Finkel, Alicia. "A Tale of Lilies, Sunflowers, and Knee-Breeches: Oscar Wilde's Wardrobe for His American Tour." *Dress* 15 (1989): 4–15.

Gatton, John Spalding. "The Sunflower Saint: Oscar Wilde in Louisville." *Filson Club History Quarterly* 52, no. 1 (1978): 5–25.

Herron, Robert. "Have Lily, Will Travel: Oscar Wilde in Cincinnati." *Bulletin of the Historical and Philosophical Society of Ohio* 25 (1957): 215–33.

Hoeltje, Hubert H. "The Apostle of the Sunflower in the State of Tall Corn." *Palimpsest* 18 (1937): 186–211.

"Intermission: The Wilde West: Oscar Wilde in Texas." *Texas Theatre Journal* 3 (Jan. 2007): 83–84.

Lewis, Lloyd, and Henry Justin Smith. *Oscar Wilde Discovers America.* New York: Harcourt, Brace, 1936.

Matz, Jesse. "Wilde Americana." In *Functions of Victorian Culture at the Present Time,* edited by Christine L. Krueger, 65–78. Athens: Ohio University Press, 2002.

Mikhail, E. H., ed. *Oscar Wilde: Interviews and Recollections.* London and New York: Macmillan, 1979.

Mirzoeff, Nicholas. "Disorientalism: Minority and Visuality in Imperial London." *Drama Review* 50 (Summer 2006): 52–69.

Morse, W. F. "American Lectures." In *The Works of Oscar Wilde,* vol. 15, *His Life with a Critical Estimate of His Writings,* 73–137. New York and Boston: Brainard, 1909.

Neville, John Davenport. "Oscar Wilde: An Apostle of Aestheticism in the Old Dominion." *Virginia Cavalcade* 28 (1978): 62–69.

O'Brien, Kevin H. F. "An Edition of Oscar Wilde's American Lectures." Ph.D. diss., University of Notre Dame, 1973.

———. "'The House Beautiful': A Reconstruction of Oscar Wilde's American Lecture." *Victorian Studies* 17 (1974): 395–418.

———. *Oscar Wilde in Canada: An Apostle for the Arts.* Toronto: Personal Library, 1982.

Pepper, Robert D. "San Jose Greets Oscar Wilde: April Third, 1882." *San Jose Studies* 8 (Spring 1982): 7–32.

Rogers, William W. "Oscar Wilde Lectures in New Orleans and Across the South in 1882." *Southern Studies* 11 (Fall–Winter 2004): 31–65.

———. "Oscar Wilde, the South, Georgia, and 'Wild Oscar.'" *Southern Studies* 9 (Spring 1998): 1–12.

Saint-Amour, Paul K. "Oscar Wilde: Orality, Literary Property, and Crimes of Writing." *Nineteenth-Century Literature* 55 (June 2000): 59–91.

Snider, Rose. "Oscar Wilde's Progress Down East." *New England Quarterly* 13 (Mar. 1940): 7–23.

Wilde, Oscar. *The Artist as Critic: Critical Writings of Oscar Wilde.* Edited by Richard Ellmann. Chicago: University of Chicago Press, 1969.

———. *The Complete Letters of Oscar Wilde.* Edited by Merlin Holland and Rupert Hart-Davis. New York: Henry Holt, 2000.

———. *The Picture of Dorian Gray.* New York: Penguin Classics, 1985.

INDEX

MATTHEW HOFER is an assistant professor of English at the University of New Mexico.

GARY SCHARNHORST is Distinguished Professor of English at the University of New Mexico and the author of *Bret Harte: Opening the American Literary West* and other works.

The University of Illinois Press
is a founding member of the
Association of American University Presses.

University of Illinois Press
1325 South Oak Street
Champaign, IL 61820-6903
www.press.uillinois.edu